W9-BHJ-463

The Educator's Handbook for Inclusive School Practices

The Educator's Handbook for Inclusive School Practices

by

Julie Causton, Ph.D.
Syracuse University
Syracuse, New York

and

Chelsea P. Tracy-Bronson, M.A.
Stockton University
Galloway, New Jersey

·P·A·U·L·H·
BROOKES
PUBLISHING Co.®

Baltimore • London • Sydney

Paul H. Brookes Publishing Co.
Post Office Box 10624
Baltimore, Maryland 21285-0624

www.brookespublishing.com

Copyright © 2015 by Paul H. Brookes Publishing Co., Inc.
All rights reserved.

"Paul H. Brookes Publishing Co." is a registered trademark
of Paul H. Brookes Publishing Co., Inc.

Typeset by Scribe Inc., Philadelphia, Pennsylvania.
Manufactured in the United States of America by
Sheridan Books, Inc., Chelsea, Michigan.

Purchasers of *The Educator's Handbook for Inclusive School Practices* are granted permission to download, print, and/or photocopy the forms for educational purposes. None of the forms may be reproduced to generate revenue for any program or individual. *Unauthorized use beyond this privilege is prosecutable under federal law.* You will see the copyright protection notice at the bottom of each photocopiable form.

Individuals described in this book are composites or real people whose situations are masked and are based on the authors' experiences. In some instances, names and identifying details have been changed to protect confidentiality. Actual names and details are used by permission.

Cover image is © istockphoto/lenta.
Clip art in Chapter 6 is © istockphoto.com.

The cartoons that appear at the beginning of each chapter are reprinted by permission from Giangreco, M.F. (2007). *Absurdities and realities of special education: The complete digital set* [CD]. Thousand Oaks, CA: Corwin Press.

Portions of this book were previously published in the following: *The Paraprofessional's Handbook for Effective Support in Inclusive Classrooms* by Julie Causton-Theoharis. Copyright © 2009 Paul H. Brookes Publishing Co., Inc. All rights reserved. *The Principal's Handbook for Leading Inclusive Schools* by Julie Causton and George Theoharis. Copyright © 2014 Paul H. Brookes Publishing Co., Inc. All rights reserved. *The Occupational Therapist's Handbook for Inclusive School Practices* by Julie Causton and Chelsea P. Tracy-Bronson. Copyright © 2014 Paul H. Brookes Publishing Co., Inc. All rights reserved. *The Speech-Language Therapist's Handbook for Inclusive School Practices* by Julie Causton and Chelsea P. Tracy-Bronson. Copyright © 2014 Paul H. Brookes Publishing Co., Inc. All rights reserved.

Library of Congress Cataloging-in-Publication Data

The Library of Congress has cataloged the print edition as follows:

Causton, Julie.
    The educator's handbook for inclusive school practices / by Julie Causton, Ph.D. Syracuse University and Chelsea P. Tracy-Bronson, M.A., Stockton University.
      pages   cm
    Includes bibliographical references and index.
    ISBN 978-1-59857-925-3 (pbk.)—ISBN-10: 1-59857-925-8 (pbk.)—ISBN 978-1-68125-015-1 (epub ebook)—ISBN 978-1-68125-016-8 (pdf ebook)
    1. Inclusive education—United States. 2. Mainstreaming in education—United States. 3. Special education teachers—United States—Handbooks, manuals, etc. 4. Teachers—United States—Handbooks, manuals, etc. I. Tracy-Bronson, Chelsea P. II. Title.

    LC1201.C374 2015
    371.9'046—dc23
                                          2015006211

British Library Cataloguing in Publication data are available from the British Library.

2019   2018   2017   2016   2015

10   9   8   7   6   5   4   3   2   1

Contents

About the Forms

Purchasers of this book may download, print, and/or photocopy the blank forms for educational use. These materials are included with the print book and are also available at **www.brookespublishing.com/causton-inclusion/materials** for both print and e-book buyers.

About the Authors

Julie Causton, Ph.D., is an expert in creating and maintaining inclusive schools. She is Professor in the Inclusive Special Education Program, Department of Teaching and Leadership, Syracuse University. She teaches courses on inclusion, differentiation, special education law, and collaboration. Her published works have appeared in such journals as *Behavioral Disorders, Equity & Excellence in Education, Exceptional Children, International Journal of Inclusive Education, Journal of Research in Childhood Education, Studies in Art Education,* and *TEACHING Exceptional*  *Children.* Julie also works with families, schools, and districts directly to help to create truly inclusive schools. She co-directs a summer leadership institute for school administrators focusing on issues of equity and inclusion as well as a school reform project called Schools of Promise. Her doctorate in special education is from the University of Wisconsin–Madison.

Chelsea P. Tracy-Bronson, M.A., is an advocate for individuals with disabilities and former elementary educator who has focused her career on bringing inclusive opportunities to all. She is a graduate of Teachers College at Columbia University and is a special education doctoral candidate at Syracuse University. She works with districts and schools to redesign services to create inclusive special education and related service provision. She is Assistant Professor in the Special Education graduate program at Stockton University in Galloway, New Jersey, where she  teaches courses on inclusive special education. Her research and professional interests include curriculum design that allows access for all, leadership for inclusive school practices, differentiating instruction, educational technology, supporting students with significant disabilities in inclusive classrooms, and inclusive-related service provision.

Foreword

Since I began working in the field of inclusive education, I met three students and their families who would forever change the way I think about human potential and diversity. I want to tell these students' stories as part of this foreword for three main reasons. First, it is important to look back historically to see what lessons were being learned 30 years ago and to notice that these lessons are still being learned in some places. Second, a bedrock principle of inclusive education is that we must honor the lived-experience of individuals with disabilities. They and their families are the most passionate proponents about why inclusion is so important—they have "skin in the game"—and can often share strategies that can help make it successful. And third, I hope that these stories inspire you to read and put into practice the strategies that Julie Causton and Chelsea P. Tracy-Bronson share in this book. You don't have to spend hours searching the Internet for practical advice on inclusive education or thousands of dollars attending conferences and workshops; this book (and the others that preceded it) is an essential part of every educator's, administrator's, paraprofessional's, and related service professional's library.

JOCELYN

Jocelyn Curtin was a fourth-grader who was included in a general education classroom in her local elementary school. Jocelyn was a bright, compassionate, and engaging student whose ability to make friends would serve her well throughout her whole life. Her team contacted me to help them figure out how Jocelyn could be a more active participant in the general education curriculum in the general education classroom. Jocelyn has Rett syndrome and at that time was only able to communicate through her facial expressions and eye movements. I could also sense that her team was struggling with several other more fundamental questions: Why should a student with such significant disabilities be in general education? What would she get out of it because the academic content was so much above her apparent level of understanding? After observing in the classroom for a day, I met with Jocelyn's team and gave them an impassioned presentation about how Jocelyn's inclusion would help her develop meaningful relationships with students without disabilities. I also gave them several ideas for her participation, such as "When the rest of the class is studying about the

Aztecs, Incas, and Mayans, Jocelyn can work with her paraprofessional to make a pyramid out of sugar cubes." Brilliant, I thought! Jocelyn would be doing something related to the unit of study and working on her counting and fine motor skills at the same time! At that time I had no idea she was capable of much more and could have worked with a cooperative group to research these civilizations' contributions to modern engineering or given a poster board presentation about Mayan culture.

Despite her lack of an effective communication system, Jocelyn thrived in her inclusive classes. She also made many lifelong friends, did some modeling, volunteered at the local community theater, and was among the very first students with significant disabilities in the United States who participated in a high school graduation ceremony. A documentary film about her middle school years, *Voices of Friendship* (Martin, Tashie, & Nisbet, 1996), gained an international following. For several years during her 20s, Jocelyn and I co-taught a class at the University of New Hampshire on the foundations of inclusive education. I laugh every time I recall the course evaluations from our students. Basically, they boiled down to this: "We learned some things from Cheryl about research and teaching strategies, but Jocelyn's contributions changed the way we think about people with disabilities and inclusive education." When she was well into her 20s, Jocelyn eventually got a communication device that revealed that she knew much more than we gave her credit for in those early years; we should have expected and supported her to learn about the history and culture of Central American native societies, not just build a sugar cube pyramid. Today Jocelyn is in her early 30s, owns her own home, is still involved in community theater, and has a wide circle of friends and loved ones.

What I Used to Think and What I Now Know

Before meeting Jocelyn, I used to think that students with significant disabilities needed a special curriculum based on functional skills taught in a separate class or community setting. Now I know that students can learn really important functional skills (e.g., remembering a friend's birthday rather than setting the table) throughout the school day by being fully a part of their school communities (Shapiro-Barnard et al., 1996). I used to think that students with significant disabilities would never have real friends, that they needed to be "with their own kind." Now I know that all students can have real friends when we address the attitudinal and systemic barriers that keep students with and without disabilities apart. Finally, I used to think that general education teachers did not have the skills to teach students with significant disabilities. Now I know that when a student with significant disabilities is included in a general education class, all members of that student's team offer their expertise and the general education teacher is not expected to do it by him- or herself. High-quality general education teachers have much to offer students with significant disabilities because effective instruction for students with disabilities is more similar than dissimilar to instruction for students without disabilities. Inclusive education is about a radical mindset shift: a belief that all learners are competent and have value, an eagerness to support social connections and friendships, and a commitment to creatively problem-solve barriers.

ANDREW

I first met Andrew Dixon through his mom Beth, who participated in the New Hampshire Leadership Series "Partners in Policymaking" designed to empower parents to advocate for their children's inclusive education. Andrew has been given a variety of labels throughout his life—cerebral palsy, attention-deficit/hyperactivity disorder, autism, and Angelman syndrome—but I came to know Andrew as friendly, curious, energetic, doggedly persistent, and most at home in and by the water at his family's summer camp. By the end of the leadership series, Beth had revived her vision of a quality life for Andrew, learned about inclusive best practices, and become skilled at advocacy and community organizing. She invited me to an individualized education program meeting to plan Andrew's transition from a segregated preschool to a fully inclusive kindergarten. Oh, how I remember the feeling of panic that overcame me when I walked into the meeting and saw 21 professionals gathered around the table with stacks of reports and evaluations at the ready. I'm not sure I had much to contribute at that meeting, but Beth's quiet determination carried the day and the team agreed to enroll Andrew in a regular kindergarten classroom. Like Jocelyn, Andrew thrived in his inclusive classrooms, was an active member of his high school's Key Club, graduated with his class shortly after his 18th birthday, and took a few college courses. Today Andrew lives in his own home with roommates who receive free rent in exchange for providing him with supports, and he manages his own document shredding business operated from a mobile van that travels to businesses in the central New Hampshire area.

What I Used to Think and What I Now Know

Before meeting Andrew I thought that students with significant communication and movement difficulties needed intensive one-to-one therapy in order to remediate deficits and optimize abilities. Now I know that students with disabilities do not have to attain some prerequisite skill or become "normal" in order to be included; they have a right to embrace their disability identity (Giangreco, 1996; Hehir, 2005). Instead of focusing only on remediation of students' challenges, speech, occupational, and physical therapists can promote students' full participation in an inclusive classroom and other natural school activities and focus on academic and functional outcomes those students will need to be career and college ready in inclusive communities when they leave high school.

JEFF

I met Jeff Williamson and his mom Janet in the late 1980s, when Janet was struggling to get the local high school to include Jeff in general education classes. Jeff experiences cerebral palsy, uses a wheelchair to get around, and communicates through supported typing. He has a wry sense of humor, is a real "people person," and enjoys traveling around the United States and abroad. From preschool through middle school, Jeff was educated in an all–special education building within a public school district. In middle school, Jeff began to communicate through his behavior a profound unhappiness about his educational program and his frustration with not having a way to communicate. These behaviors became the high school's primary rationale for not including him in general education classes. Because that high school had never had students with more complex support needs in its building, much less in general education classes, the school was also concerned that Jeff would be teased or bullied. However, once Jeff was included in general education classes and extracurricular activities, a strong peer circle of support was created, the people around him presumed his competence and supported his right to communicate, and he became almost a different person. The real Jeff emerged—funny, sarcastic, inquisitive, and loving. Like Jocelyn and Andrew, Jeff lives in his own home today with a cadre of support providers, whom he interviews and supervises. He has a variety of jobs in the community and uses his money to finance his passion for traveling.

What I Used to Think and What I Now Know

Before I met Jeff I thought that some students' behavior was just too disruptive for a general education classroom. Now I know that when students' needs for belonging, sensory supports, and a means of communication are met, their behavior in a general education class is usually better than in a self-contained class. I used to think that inclusion was appropriate in elementary school but that by the time that students reached high school, they should be learning in a community setting. Now I know that students with disabilities should progress through the grades alongside their peers without disabilities and have access to the general education curriculum through the 12th grade. They should have community learning experiences through after-school and summer jobs, volunteer and community service, and co-op learning opportunities, alongside their classmates without disabilities. After participating in graduation ceremonies around the age of 18, students with significant disabilities can focus on postsecondary education, career development, and community living until they are 21 or age out of school.

I used to think that students with significant disabilities would be teased and bullied by their classmates because of their differences. Now I know that teasing and bullying are symptoms of a larger problem with school culture and climate. There is no evidence that students with disabilities who are included in general education are subjected to more teasing and bullying than those in self-contained classrooms. In fact, learning alongside classmates with wide differences in culture, language, and disability has been shown to promote more positive attitudes toward diversity in general.

SUMMARY

When I finished reading Julie and Chelsea's book, I realized that the lessons I have learned from students, their families and friends, and inclusive educators are exactly the same as those shared by Julie and Chelsea. In this book, these lessons have been translated into practical educational strategies that have broad applicability no matter where you live, the size of your school, your budget, or the unique characteristics of your students. I am confident that this book will help you become a more committed, self-assured, collaborative, and creative inclusive educator, and I wish you well on your journey.

Cheryl M. Jorgensen, Ph.D.
Inclusive Education Consultant
South Acworth, New Hampshire
Affiliate Faculty, Institute on Disability, University of New Hampshire
Durham, New Hampshire

REFERENCES

Giangreco, M. (1996). "The stairs don't go anywhere!" A self-advocate's reflections on specialized services and their impact on people with disabilities. *Physical Disabilities: Education and Related Service, 14*(2), 1–12.

Habib, D. (Producer). (2009). *Including Samuel.* Durham, NH: Institute on Disability, University of New Hampshire.

Hehir, T. (2005). *New directions in special education: Eliminating ableism in policy and practice.* Cambridge, MA: Harvard Education Press.

Martin, J., Tashie, C., & Nisbet, J. (Producers). (1996). *Voices of friendship.* Durham, NH: Institute on Disability, University of New Hampshire.

Shapiro-Barnard, S., Tashie, C., Martin, J., Malloy, J., Schuh, M., Piet, J., & Lichtenstein, S. (1996). *Petroglyphs: The writing on the wall.* Durham, NH: Institute on Disability, University of New Hampshire.

Preface

"A community that excludes even one of its members is no community at all."

—Dan Wilkins

CREATIVE INCLUSIVE EDUCATORS ARE THE KEY

We walked into a second-grade classroom in New York and found a little boy named Mark with Down syndrome on the carpet near the easel, screaming. He was kicking anyone who came near him and was clearly upset. The rest of the students in the classroom were lining up for music and paid fairly little attention; they seemed to be accepting of Mark and the situation. One student tried to get Mark off the floor. He knelt down next to him, extended his hand, and said, "Come . . . walk to music with me." But by this time, Mark was too upset. This sequence of events dramatically concluded when Mark kicked the easel and it came crashing down, surprising everyone in the room—especially Mark.

We had been asked to join Mark's team to support them with transitions to and from class (i.e., as the class made the transition to and from art, music, lunch, technology, and library). We worked with the team for about 2 months, providing ideas and suggestions for the teachers, therapists, and paraprofessionals to implement. These suggestions included a picture schedule, a partner for transitions, a comfort item, a timer, and visual prompts. However, despite our best efforts, the transition issues continued. Sometimes Mark appeared upset, sometimes he would laugh as he rolled around on the carpet, but either way he refused to get up despite many interventions and strategies. It was clear to the entire team that transitions were causing him serious anxiety. After 2 months, and several collaborative meetings, an educator on the team suggested, "What if we gave Mark the keys?" She explained further, "Seriously, what if every time we leave the classroom we ask Mark to help us to lock up the classroom. Then, when it is time to return, we can ask him to hurry so that he can unlock the classroom door." The team decided to try this new strategy.

When we observed Mark 4 months later during a transition from art to the classroom, the students were lining up in the art room. Mark rinsed his paintbrush. Mark's friend Marissa asked him, "Mark, do you have the keys?" He replied, "Yup," and actually jogged to join the line in the art room. As the class walked through the hallway, Mark continued to hustle to keep up with his classmates. He stood tall, smiling, and looking quite proud as he unlocked the door to the classroom. One of his other classmates casually said, "Thanks, Mark," as he entered the room. Mark hung the key on the hook and briskly walked to the carpet to sit for the upcoming read-aloud.

What a difference! What a great idea! Notice what the educators asked themselves: "How can we most effectively educate Mark? How can we be sure that he is a valued member of our community? What creative ideas can we find to help him maintain dignity and support his behavior effectively?" Notice the questions they did not ask: "What type of a behavior program can we institute? Does Mark even belong here? Where else could he be educated? Who else could work with him?" Creative inclusive educators ask the right questions and are the key difference between the success or failure of inclusive education. The success of inclusive education relies on general and special educators. How well students are included depends on the willingness, creativity, perseverance, continual reflection, incremental changes, collaborative efforts, and skill of educators.

ON INCLUSION

Not a day goes by when we do not think about inclusion. When we both think of the amazing students we have had the privilege of teaching, we are reminded of what *teachers* they were to us. They have taught us that everyone has a right to belong, to have friends, to have engaging curricula, and to have powerful instruction. Everyone has a right to be treated with dignity and with gentle, respectful support and to experience that learning is intimately connected with feeling like part of the classroom. Every student deserves to receive support in a warm and welcoming place. The more this happens, the more we have created the environment for substantial learning. It is not, therefore, just about creating a sense of belonging for belonging's sake; that sense of connection and welcome paves the way for academic and social growth. Therefore, this book is designed as a guide for general and special educators and other educational team members as they work to include students with disabilities in gentle and respectful ways.

HOW THIS BOOK IS ORGANIZED

The first three chapters provide the context for the rest of the book: Chapter 1 focuses on the role of the educator, Chapter 2 provides background about inclusive education, and Chapter 3 provides information about special education. These first chapters provide the foundation necessary to more effectively interpret the rest of the book. Chapter 4 is designed to help educators rethink students. In Chapter 4, we ask educators to look at students through the lens of strengths and abilities—to reconsider some of the negative descriptors—for the sake of being able to reach and teach all students more effectively. Chapters 5–8 are strategy-specific chapters that focus on collaboration, academic supports, behavioral supports, and social supports. These strategy-specific chapters provide ideas that are immediately applicable in schools. Chapter 9 focuses on how to most effectively utilize and supervise paraprofessionals. The last chapter is all about self-care and problem solving. The job of teaching students in our school systems who pose the greatest challenges and require the most complex problem solving is not an easy one. Chapter 10 is meant to give helpful ideas for how educators can care for themselves in order to provide the best possible education for students.

WHO WILL FIND THIS BOOK USEFUL?

As more and more schools move toward inclusive education, educators are the most critical factors to success because they are on the front lines—designing lessons and cultivating the classroom community, making daily decisions that support or deny access to curricula and peers. The roles of both general and special educator are changing, and this book represents cutting-edge inclusive service provision. This book serves to disrupt traditional and outdated special education service provision. This work promotes the inclusion of students with disabilities by moving away from a remove-and-remediate philosophy. Although this book will primarily serve educators who want to learn more about supporting students in inclusive classrooms, it is critical that this book is read by the administrators, related service providers, and parents who are team players in supporting students in inclusive school communities.

Practicing and preservice teachers: This book is written specifically for practicing educators teaching or those hoping to teach in inclusive classrooms in K–12 settings. However, it is also perfect for students in teacher preparation programs at colleges and universities; thus, we explain details that will be beneficial for individuals new to the field (i.e., individualized education programs, federal disability labels, and portions of the law).

General and special educators: This book is written for you, the educator. We intentionally aimed to create this resource to be empowering to both general education teachers and special education teachers. Whether you are a general education teacher in an elementary school, a middle school math teacher, or a high school biology teacher, this book is designed for you, the general education teacher in a K–12 setting. This book is also written for special educators who have a different role in inclusive education. It is written for special educators who currently have positions in various educational placement settings, including resource rooms, self-contained classrooms, schools that educate students with disabilities, and those who provide inclusive special education service delivery. Because this book identifies approaches, strategies, and suggestions for teaching all students in inclusive classrooms, it is greatly beneficial for co-teaching teams to read and discuss the content together. We encourage teams to do this in a professional development or book club format to get the most out of discussions.

Parents of students with disabilities: Parents can benefit from this book by understanding the best practices for inclusive educational services. For them, this book can be a resource to secure the appropriate training and support for the teachers working with their child.

Professional development personnel: This book offers cutting-edge approaches and resources for providing education to students with disabilities and is perfect for any professional development opportunity or team training.

The Educator's Handbook for Inclusive School Practices is a companion guide to the following books:

- *The Paraprofessional's Handbook for Effective Support in Inclusive Classrooms* (Paul H. Brookes Publishing Co., 2009)
- *The Principal's Handbook for Leading Inclusive Schools* (Paul H. Brookes Publishing Co., 2014)
- *The Occupational Therapist's Handbook for Inclusive School Practices* (Paul H. Brookes Publishing Co., 2014)
- *The Speech-Language Pathologist's Handbook for Inclusive School Practices* (Paul H. Brookes Publishing Co., 2014)

These books are designed to be used in combination and as companions to one another. You can certainly read this book on its own. It is full of strategies and ideas that will improve your practice immediately. But we think it is also useful to gather a group of key educational professionals to read these books together so that school teams can gain shared knowledge and learn more about each professional perspective and role. This book is purposefully organized in the same way as the other texts, using the same headings and much of the same information, shared from a very different perspective and point of view. We currently see these books used together as teams work collaboratively to support all students in inclusive settings.

Acknowledgments

JULIE'S ACKNOWLEDGMENTS

This book is about education—meaningful, thoughtful, humanistic education—that allows people to reach their full potential, become their best selves, and do their best work. This work is a call for a different paradigm in schools—where quality inclusive education is available for all to create a community essential for learning. This book helps us to answer the question of school inclusion with a resounding yes, and the details of that inclusive education can be carried out creatively and joyfully.

Indeed, this book and my own academic career would not have been possible without all sorts of joyful education—in elementary schools, in middle and high schools, in college classrooms, on academic panels, in school district in-services, at individualized education program meetings, and during due process hearings. Therefore, I feel it is necessary to thank the sizable community of students, teachers, scholars, family, and friends who have supported me and educated me in both visible and invisible ways as we have written this book. This journey is driven by a vision of substantive and meaningful inclusion for all children. I want to thank the many individuals who have helped me see the importance of the journey, imagine the route, and stay the course.

To my students: I have worked with many students over the years, and each taught me something new. I would especially like to thank those who have forced me to think in new ways: Chelsea, Joryann, Ricki, Josh, Moua, Brett, Shawnee, Adam, Trevor, Stephanie, Grace, and Gabe.

To my teaching partner: Kathie Crandall, my friend, you taught me that laughter is truly the best indicator of learning.

To my teachers: Lou Brown, your belief in inclusion has inspired me throughout my entire academic career, and Alice Udvari-Solner, you have sustained me with your intellectual vision, creativity, and commitment to *all* children. Your work has touched every aspect of this book, and it is impossible to say where your influence ends. I also thank Kimber Malmgren and Colleen Capper, whose mentorship has made my career in education possible.

To my friends and colleagues: Thank you George Theoharis, Chelsea P. Tracy-Bronson, Kate MacLeod, Pat Radel, Mary Radel, Paula Kluth, Michael Giangreco, Micah Fialka-Feldman, Jamie Burke, Doug Biklen, Christi Kasa, Beth Ferri, Thomas Bull, Corrie Burdick, Meghan Cosier, Christy Ashby, Beth Meyer, Tara Affolter, and Steve Hoffman.

To Paul H. Brookes Publishing Co.: I thank Sharon Larkin, Rebecca Lazo, Kevin Chalk, Steve Plocher, and all of the Brookes staff for your helpful suggestions and creative vision.

To Chelsea P. Tracy-Bronson: Thank you for being such a talented, excellent co-author and friend. It is always a pleasure!

To Kate MacLeod: I thank Kate for reading and editing several versions of this book and for bringing her special light to this work.

To Stephanie Perotti: You make me laugh every day and bring an enthusiasm and an energy to my life that is unparalleled. Thank you!

To my family: I thank Ella Theoharis and Sam Theoharis. You fill me with joy, your creativity inspires me, and you remind me of the importance of this work every single day. I thank Gail Andre, Jeff Causton, and Kristine Causton for being excited about the importance of my work.

CHELSEA'S ACKNOWLEDGMENTS

I have the deepest gratitude for the individuals in my personal, teaching, and academic spheres who have shared this journey with me. The work in this book grows out of the experiences I have had throughout my career that have spanned the many aspects of schooling and are sprinkled throughout the chapters.

To my students: I wish to acknowledge my first students who helped me conceptualize inclusive education. Quin taught me that the best teachers are compassionate and deeply embedded into the lives of their students. Michael convinced me that facilitating social interdependence is the gift that does not stop giving. I am also especially grateful to James, Tyler, Neleah, Camryn, Shantell, Maylee, Aaliyah, Emma, Amber, Hunter, Adam, Ella, and Mikayla, who taught me to think and teach in different ways, create exciting learning experiences, and to be passionate about teaching. This work started with all of you, my students, who taught me that passionate inclusive educators can truly change lives and make a difference.

To my colleagues: Katie is the epitome of a collaborative, dedicated inclusive teacher. Moe, an occupational therapist extraordinaire, enthusiastically showed me her magic tricks. Beth, Maria, and Lauren, whom I worked alongside during my initial teaching experiences, thank you for facilitating my passion to ensure access to meaningful curriculum for all learners. Lisa, my teaching partner, showed me how to dance the dance. Jenn taught me that life is washable and the best learning is messy. Thanks to Carolyn, the Tigger of the school, and to Diane, Kelly, Erin, and Amy, who all taught me their tricks of the art of teaching. Thanks to the many educators who have shared their instructional craft with me, including Patty, Melanie, Robin, Cris, Amiee, Jim, Dan, Andrew, Shaun, and Matt, demonstrating the promise of inclusive education.

To Kate MacLeod: A tremendous thank you for editing numerous versions of this book and for adding bursts of creativity!

To my teachers: Several mentors have shaped my thinking about inclusive education and designing accessible curriculum. Julie Causton, your work was infused into every lesson in my classrooms in both New York City and Upstate New York. Your vision has been the inspiring force behind so much of what I have accomplished and, more important, the ways I make an impact in the field of inclusive education. I am blessed that such a mentor has transformed into my co-author and collaborative colleague—let alone a true friend! Thomas Hatch's work in school change shaped my teaching and helped me create a vision for the future. George Theoharis always demonstrated that a compassionate disposition is the key ingredient for any teaching recipe. Your work in leading inclusive schools has strongly influenced and made a lasting impact on the direction of my scholarly contributions. It was Karen Zumwalt's teaching, vision, and guidance that pushed me to be an academic scholar. Christy Ashby, who stressed the importance of access and communication for students with significant disabilities, empowered me to create relationships with individuals who are nonverbal. Your mentorship and feedback has been remarkable throughout my journey. A special thank you is extended to many excellent Syracuse University and Teachers College, Columbia University, professors.

To my colleagues: A special thank you goes to the top-notch mentorship of Kimberly Lebak, Shelly Meyers, Mary Lou Galantino, and Bill Reynolds. I wish to also thank Claudine Keenan, Pamela Vaughan, Priti Haria, Meg White, Susan Cydis, Lois Spitzer, Darrell Cleveland, Norma Boakes, John Quinn, Ron Caro, Joe Marchetti, Ron Tinsley, Amy Ackerman, Jung Lee, and George Sharp.

To my friends and family: Aaryn, Katie, Elise, Brionna, Shelby, Brian, Fred, Vicky, Ian, Vicky, Eric, and Constance remind me of the importance of family and friendship. Heith and Holly are two of the most fun, loving, and caring souls in my life whose support I cherish. Inga, you are a best friend who balances me daily; your strength and success continue to inspire me. Lillyanna, welcome to our family. For my parents, thank you for making my dreams become reality, proving that anything is possible, and being teachers who encouraged your children to strive toward their personal best rather than settle for mediocrity! J.R., our love is a friendship set on fire. Thank you for bringing the flames, happiness, and sense of adventure that anchor our life!

To all of our amazing students who have touched our lives and to Ella and Sam, the greatest teachers

1

The General and Special Educator

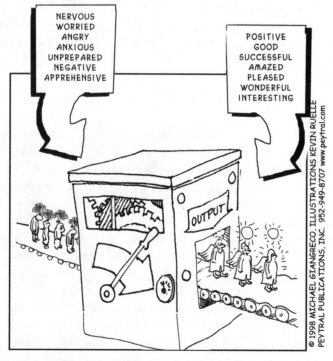

THE AMAZING INCLUSIVE EDUCATION
TEACHER TRANSFORMATION MACHINE

"Marsha and I worked in separate rooms last year. She was down the hall where she worked with special education students. I taught fourth grade. We really only saw each other at faculty meetings, though sometimes we would run into each other in the copy room. But now we spend nearly half of every school day teaching together. And we plan together a lot! There are so many benefits to co-teaching . . . mostly for our students with special needs, but really to all the students. . . . I know Marsha has definitely made me a better teacher, and I would like to think I have taught her a thing or two."

—Lisa (general education teacher)

Like Lisa and Marsha, many general and special education teachers now find themselves co-teaching, collaborating, and working closely together as schools embrace an inclusive service provision model in order to better educate all students, especially students with disabilities. This co-construction of curriculum planning and implementation of instruction leads to enhanced inclusive educational, social, and recreational opportunities. Many believe that this co-teaching arrangement is mutually beneficial and that the inclusive educational model is better for all students.

Our goal for this book is to help you, the general or special educator, to negotiate these new roles and to offer tools and strategies. This will contribute to your transformation into an incredible inclusive educator. This book is intended to build your teaching toolbox in order to purposefully include students. We start with how we came to know the previously mentioned teachers, Marsha and Lisa, and a student named Matthew.

THE LAST ROOM ON THE LEFT

As we signed into the school's main office and received visitor stickers, we asked where we could find Room 33. We were headed there to observe a fourth-grade student named Matthew. The woman seated at the desk took a deep breath. She said, "Okay, you have to walk down the first hallway on your left, all the way to the end. Then, take a right and walk down to the very end of that hallway. You will pass a few classrooms and the custodial closet. It will be there, 33, the last room on your left."

We nodded and walked down several hallways, past the custodial closet, and into Marsha's room before meeting Matthew. He was slumped way down on a beanbag chair in a classroom for students with autism. A clipboard rested on his lap. It appeared he was supposed to be doing a math worksheet using TouchMath. TouchMath is a system of numbers with dots on them intended to help students visualize the value of each number. It is a strategy to represent the abstract concepts of numbers in concrete form (Bullock, 1992). It was apparent that the room was well cared for, as its supplies were neat, tidy, and organized. Colorful, decorative posters with themes of "working hard" and "trying your best" lined the perimeter. All of the students were engaged in different activities. Three adults were present, each attending to students staggered throughout.

One student listened with headphones. Another had her face pressed close to the air conditioning vent, seeming to enjoy the breeze. Two students played a math fact game on the computer. One boy, who appeared younger than the rest, sat in a corner, crying and shouting the word *stuck* repeatedly. He was quite loud. There was a large visual timer ticking next to him. "Only 4 more minutes, Jacob," a paraprofessional reminded the boy in a friendly voice as she pointed to his timer.

As we navigated through the room, approaching Matthew, we greeted him and sat on the floor next to his beanbag. He was supposed to be adding two-digit numbers. Instead, his pencil lead became dull and deteriorated as he continuously wrote light lines across the top of his paper.

"What are you doing, Matthew?"

"Jacob sad," he responded quietly.

We nodded and attempted to help him with his TouchMath, but he continued to focus on Jacob, the small boy crying in the corner.

"Jacob sad," Matthew said again.

We reassured Matthew that Jacob was okay and tried to refocus him. He seemed unable to focus long enough to complete his math. Marsha, the special education teacher, noticed us and walked over. "Matthew," she said, "can you say 'Hi'?"

"Say 'Hi,'" she repeated as she smiled, but Matthew remained silent. "Say it. Look at me." She cupped his chin in her hand, attempting to get Matthew to look at her. "Can you say it?"

Matthew pushed Marsha's hand from his face and mumbled "Hi." He got up, ran to the window, and began to bang his head with his hand.

THE FIRST ROOM ON THE RIGHT

Four months later, we observed Matthew in an inclusive fourth-grade classroom. This was now his full-time educational placement. He sat at a table group with other fourth-grade students. They chatted to each other about the problem they were solving. Matthew participated in the conversation by typing on his iPad. We watched as a peer seated to Matthew's right read something that Matthew had just typed.

The general education teacher, Lisa, gained the class's attention and posed a question. Matthew busied himself, typing something. The paraprofessional, who was circulating the room, raised her hand to indicate that Matthew had typed a response. When Lisa nodded, the paraprofessional walked over to his table to read his answer from the iPad aloud. "It depends if the integer is negative."

Lisa smiled. "It does depend if the integer is negative, Matthew. That will determine if the answer is a positive or a negative."

Matthew looked pleased and continued to participate throughout most of the math lesson. He answered three other questions correctly, which either the paraprofessional or one of his peers shared out loud. Matthew had become a confident, engaged, social learner who successfully participated in a general education classroom. The Matthew we met in Room 33 was not the same Matthew in this inclusive fourth-grade class. His engagement with peers, teachers, and the academic curriculum had changed dramatically. What had happened between the first and second observation? Why was Matthew so different during each observation? What were the elements that transformed Matthew as a learner?

A number of factors went into supporting Matthew and his transition to general education. We had been brought in by Matthew's family to consult; they were involved in a due process hearing to get Matthew included in general education. Training was provided directly to Marsha and Lisa on how to provide social, academic, communication, and behavioral support. We discussed how to create successful adaptations and accommodations and utilize various methods of communication. All of the staff working with Matthew received training about how to include Matthew and how to support his communication. Combined, the implementation of these training elements resulted in the drastic changes we saw in Matthew's participation and engagement during the school day.

Although Matthew is remarkable and his teachers are very skilled, this is not a particularly unusual story. Repeatedly, we find that when students move from segregated settings to inclusive contexts, and when teachers learn to support students in inclusive ways, fundamental changes occur. As we have witnessed schools transforming to implement inclusive special education provision, we have learned substantial lessons from the educators who are the critical foundations for this book, along with research supporting the implementation of these lessons learned. In the subsequent sections of this chapter, we outline the lessons we have learned as an introduction to the major themes and content of this book.

RECOGNIZE THAT EDUCATORS HAVE BEEN WRONG

It is hard for us to admit, as special educators ourselves, but the field of education has been wrong about segregating students. In this case, the school district was completely wrong about Matthew. Administrators and teachers thought they understood his cognitive levels, his label, and his IQ scores. The idea was that the self-contained classroom would develop his skills. The thinking and educational placements for students were based on readiness and developmental models. Matthew was given work at "his level." However, when he learned to communicate and his teachers learned to support him more effectively, a shift occurred. It became clear that the district was wrong about what he could accomplish. In fact, it was wrong about, well, essentially everything when it came to educating Matthew. When given appropriate grade-level work with purposeful adaptations and supports, Matthew began to soar academically. Evidence of his competence became apparent. He was able to do grade-level work with the appropriate communication supports.

Students are much more capable than educators previously thought, when provided with opportunities and proper supports. Chapters 2 and 3 explore the topic of inclusive special education and the importance of presuming competence, fostering belonging, and recognizing the indicators of inclusive classrooms.

Shifting Our Thinking

Incremental realization that Matthew was a highly intelligent student was an essential shift for everyone: Marsha, Lisa, classmates, the paraprofessional, therapists, and even his family. It took a lot of mental work to change how the team thought of Matthew, his potential, and the best contexts and strategies to educate him. By shifting our thinking, we began to see him as a learner with multiple strengths, intelligences, and capabilities. Chapter 4 provides new ideas about shifting the ways educators think and talk about students, as these beliefs ultimately affect the approach to educating them. However, let us be clear: Demonstration of high levels of intelligence is not a prerequisite for including a student with a disability within general education classrooms.

Collaborative Teachers Have Increased Creativity

As Marsha and Lisa took on new roles in the inclusive classroom, they created an exciting, engaging classroom for the entire class. This happened through their collective problem solving and collaboration. In the inclusive classroom, educational professionals join forces, and each offers unique skills that benefit all of the students. Chapter 5 explores working on a collaborative inclusive team, negotiating roles and responsibilities, and strategies for collaborative instruction.

Design Purposeful Academic Learning Experiences

When Matthew is in an inclusive classroom, the planning and differentiation of curriculum and lessons is different. There, the content is co-planned and often co-taught by a general and a special education teacher. Related service providers implement inclusive service provision and contribute their expertise to the development and generalization of therapy skills across the school day. Inclusive educators need to be familiar with the concepts of universal design for instruction, differentiation, and creating inclusive lessons so that all learners can be successful. Chapter 6 focuses on those important topics to enable you to design purposeful academic learning experiences for all students.

Engage in Humanistic Behavioral Supports

We have seen great shifts in behavior as students move from segregated settings to inclusive educational contexts. Challenging behaviors tend to decrease in inclusive classrooms, as students are surrounded by peers who are positive behavioral models. This was the case for Matthew. His frustration, head banging behavior, and other negative behavior decreased. However, he still required extensive behavioral supports; the inclusive educators implemented positive behavior support (PBS), focused on his sense of belonging, developed a strong relationship with him, and provided him with what he needed. Chapter 7 presents the concept of humanistic behavioral supports and provides many new strategies and ideas about how to successfully support student behavior.

Facilitate Genuine Social Relationships

Separate special education classrooms create separate lives. When students are removed from general education environments, they live academic and social lives separate from those of their community of peers. In Matthew's case, when he was in the special education classroom, he never had a play date with a student who did not also have a disability. After moving to a general education classroom, his social calendar became quite full. Matthew is not planning a segregated life for himself after completion of high school; the best way to learn to live in an inclusive society is in an inclusive classroom. Chapter 8 describes many strategies for providing social supports and facilitating close-knit connections to classmates.

Develop Purposeful Support Systems

It is commonplace to see students with disabilities with a paraprofessional seated directly next to them. This is not the most effective way to support students. We closely examined the type of supports that Matthew received, and one of the major changes that he requested was more independence. Chapter 9 focuses on being thoughtful about support and how to effectively utilize and guide paraprofessionals who may be supporting students in inclusive classrooms.

Implementation of Inclusive Education Is a Challenge

It takes creativity, problem solving, and hard work to successfully provide inclusive education. There must be a willingness to try, fail, and try again to make inclusive education effective. More important, this work toward cultivating inclusive educational opportunities for students is critical. It literally changes the lives of students with disabilities. It makes a difference. The classroom for students with autism, located down the hall and next to the custodial closet, is brimming with potential. It is full of students like Matthew who deeply deserve and desire friendship, connection, and belonging, as well as access to rich academic content. Such students cannot wait. Chapter 10, the last chapter of this book, is dedicated to ways for maintaining momentum as you do the challenging and important work of creating more inclusive classrooms and schools. The practical strategies offered there will help sustain core beliefs as you continue to make a difference in the lives of the students you teach.

Be a Change Agent

Students like Matthew cannot wait. This book asks you, the reader, to think critically about the current practices that may be present in your school. Be open to change. Hone your advocacy skills as you become an agent of change. Expand your level of influence to make a real and lasting impact in your classrooms and schools. In this book, we challenge you to make a difference. We commend you for taking on this challenge.

In order to provide a context for this important work, the remainder of this chapter describes the evolving role of the inclusive educator. We outline a brief history of inclusive education before discussing the roles of general educators and special educators. Some commonly asked questions are answered in the concluding section of this chapter and in every chapter in the book.

EVOLUTION OF INCLUSIVE SPECIAL EDUCATION AND THE ROLE OF EDUCATORS

The history of inclusive education has had an evolutionary impact on the role of educators. It has only been since the passage of the Education for All Handicapped Children Act of 1975 (PL 94-142) that students with disabilities have had a legally protected right to attend public school. Historically, students with disabilities were educated mainly in the home, in segregated school buildings, or in separate institutions. As a result, general education teachers rarely worked with students who had disability labels. Special education teachers mainly worked in segregated schools and settings.

In the 1970s and 1980s, a strong, parent-driven push initiated education of children with disabilities in general education settings alongside students without disabilities. At this time, the regular education initiative began (Will, 1986), and parents began to learn about the idea of mainstreaming. Students with so-called mild disabilities were often mainstreamed but were still viewed as visitors and lacked full membership in general education classrooms. Sole responsibility continued to rest on the special educators.

By the 1990s, a wider array of students with more significant disabilities was included in classrooms across all grade levels in schools. The roles of teachers shifted accordingly, as students with disabilities began participating in general education classrooms. Since 2000, inclusive education has become more established in the educational community. The Elementary and Secondary Education Act, now called the No Child Left Behind Act (NCLB) of 2001 (PL 107-110), initially set accountability and educational standards for all children, including students with disabilities. The federal legislation that had a particular impact on students with disabilities was the Individuals with Disabilities Education Improvement Act (IDEA) of 2004 (PL 108-446), which established outcome expectations for students with disabilities receiving special education and related services. In the Findings section of IDEA 2004, Congress acknowledged that the purpose was to "ensure that all children with disabilities have available . . . a free appropriate public education that emphasizes special education and related services designed to meet their unique needs" (20 U.S.C. § 1400 [c]) and that they have "access to the general education curriculum in the regular classroom, to the maximum extent possible" (IDEA 2004, 20 U.S.C. § 601 [c][5][A]).

In inclusive classrooms, general and special education teachers share responsibility for all students. Inclusive educators create a learning environment that adequately meets the needs of all learners. Educators have learned that students with disabilities are just as capable of learning as their general education counterparts. Consequently, the goals many students now have in their individualized education programs (IEPs) more closely resemble those of their same-age peers.

"I consider myself the specialist when it comes to learning strategies and pedagogical techniques, and I see Lisa as the content specialist. What we have learned is that in order for students to be successful, we have had to share this knowledge and expertise."

—Marsha (special education teacher)

SOME IMPORTANT DEFINITIONS

The following subsections provide introductions to some of the important concepts discussed in this book.

Social Model of Disability

In the example of Matthew, when his performance and his ability in the two classrooms are compared, two completely different students become evident. The social model of disability suggests that disability is created or comes to light within certain environments. In other words, people can experience disability due to the environment, attitudes, or lack of support. This model suggests that the classroom, others' expectations, and available supports and resources actually construct or cause disability. Therefore, educators can support students by removing barriers, changing expectations, and supporting students differently. The object of remediation becomes the classroom environments and supports. Compare those ideas to the more common yet outdated model, the medical model of disability, which suggests that disability resides in the student and the student needs to be remediated or fixed. Throughout this book, we focus on the social model of disability and remind educators of their agency to help students reach their full potential.

Inclusive Classrooms

Inclusive classrooms are educational environments in which students with and without disabilities are educated together. The needs, supports, and related services of all learners are addressed in inclusive, heterogeneous environments. Other current terms are *general education classroom, third-grade classroom, world history classroom,* or *typical classroom.* A more outdated term for an inclusive classroom is a *mainstreamed classroom.* Mainstreaming came into popularity in the 1970s, when students with disabilities who had previously been segregated from public schooling (e.g., were not sent to school at all or were housed in institutions) were moved into the general education (public school) setting. *Mainstreaming* referred mostly to the physical placement of students in general education and often did not focus on comprehensive services and accommodations to help remove barriers to learning. In the 1990s, however, the practice of inclusion began to replace mainstreaming. Students were no longer merely provided with a desk in the general education classroom but were thoughtfully and comprehensively provided any and all special education services required to support their learning. This means that in an inclusive classroom, related services or therapy interventions and supports can be delivered in the classroom. More information about inclusive education can be found in Chapter 2.

Therapy Rooms

A therapy room is a place in which students are generally supposed to spend a short amount of time working on a specific skill, performance, or routine before returning to the least restrictive environment (LRE; e.g., general education classroom, lunch room, hallway). In inclusive schools, therapists often provide much of their related service provision (e.g., occupational therapy, speech-language pathology, physical therapy) within the natural context of the student's school day and work in collaboration with educators.

Resource Rooms

A resource room is a place in which students are generally supposed to spend a short amount of time working on a specific skill or subject before returning to the general education classroom. The instruction in these classrooms is typically delivered in a small group, with one teacher teaching a small group of students or with one teacher working directly with one student.

Self-Contained Classrooms

A self-contained classroom is designed for instructing only students who have disabilities. The original purpose of this kind of classroom was to group students who had similar learning needs. These kinds of classrooms have become very controversial because not only do students in self-contained classrooms interact on a very limited basis, if at all, with students who do not have disabilities, but also they do not make greater educational gains than students with disabilities who are included in general education classes (Banjeri & Daily, 1995; Causton-Theoharis & Theoharis, 2008; Causton-Theoharis, Theoharis, Bull, & Cosier, 2011; Vaughn, Moody, & Schumm, 1998; Waldron & McLeskey, 1998). Most inclusive-oriented schools are not utilizing self-contained classrooms.

Self-Contained or Alternative School

A self-contained school or alternative school is a place where students with similar learning, behavior, or social needs are provided instruction for the duration of the school day. These school buildings are highly controversial because students in self-contained buildings spend their entire day without contact with peers who do not have disabilities. Most inclusive-oriented districts are not utilizing self-contained school buildings.

Community-Based Instruction

Some special education teachers work in community-based settings. The idea behind community-based instruction is that some students require instruction to prepare them for life in the community by working on job skills and independent living skills that facilitate the transition from school to work. Therefore, some students receive their instruction at job sites, recreational facilities, grocery stores, or other community locations.

USING THIS BOOK

The transformational educational experience that Matthew had reveals that it makes a difference when students have a sense of belonging, access to intellectually stimulating academic learning experiences, purposefully designed instruction, and natural adult and peer support. These elements are the keys to success for cultivating an inclusive learning environment designed for learners' needs in mind.

Approach this book with a reflective mindset. Think about the structure and organization of special education in your school. Be critical as you aim to develop and implement inclusive educational practices. Engage in problem solving with collaborative teams. Kunc (1992) reminded us that belonging and access are the initial step:

> What our structures of society and schools does is places me in a separate classroom and says no you are not good enough yet to be with those other kids. And once you learn to walk better, talk better, become more like the other kids, then you'll get to belong. Of course . . . you can't learn those things because you never get to belong in the first place. And then your lack of progress is used as justification for further segregation. (p. 4)

This book is meant to provide essential knowledge and guidance for K–12 general and special education teachers. Specifically, this book focuses on 1) what it means to be a general or special educator in an inclusive school setting, 2) essential information about inclusive education, 3) some important special education basics, 4) new ways to think and talk about students, 5) how to work within a collaborative team, 6) tools and strategies for providing academic supports, 7) how to provide effective behavioral supports, 8) how to provide social supports, 9) how to support the work of paraprofessionals, and 10) how to take care of yourself while doing this important work.

COMMONLY ASKED QUESTIONS ABOUT INCLUSIVE EDUCATION

Q.   What is wrong with pull-out services?

A.   Pull-out service provision has deleterious effects on a student's self-esteem and ability to learn, and it disrupts a sense of belonging. Students with disabilities have the right to learn and socialize alongside their grade-level peers. Most important, however, the purpose of these services is to support students in navigating their school day and gaining independence. The school day contains naturally occurring contexts for the skills, routines, activities, or performance tasks that have typically been worked on in isolation; these contexts are the LRE (IDEA 2004) for students to learn and practice. Many educators are transforming their practice, keeping in mind that special education services are portable, meaning they can be delivered directly in these naturally occurring contexts.

Q.   Can my school choose to adopt or reject inclusive educational structures?

A.   A public school cannot "decide" whether it wants to create inclusive structures. Schools are mandated by IDEA 2004 to educate all students with disabilities in the LRE. This means students with disabilities, to the maximum extent possible, have the right to be educated in the general education classroom, alongside their peers without disabilities, in the school they would attend if they did not have a disability (IDEA 2004). Students cannot be removed from a general education setting simply because the school is not prepared to meet the child's needs or does not think it wants to "do" inclusion.

Q.   Does every student with a disability need a paraprofessional to succeed in an inclusive class?

A.   Inclusion in the general education classroom does not necessarily mean the student will need an adult assigned to support him or her. The general and special education teachers are expected to work together to adapt instruction, learning experiences, and the environment in order to provide access and support for the student. This support can often be provided best by peers or related service personnel in the general education classroom. However, if paraprofessional support is needed, it is important to know that this, too, is individualized for each student and can be provided for all or part of the student's day (e.g., only in English class or in physical education class).

Q.   Is inclusion easier at the elementary level?

A.   No. High school and middle school inclusion is not more difficult. Some scholars even find inclusion in the older grades to be easier. Schedules are more flexible, students can have more choice in the types of classes taken, and educators are often content specialists with a deep understanding of how to teach and differentiate their specific content areas. Also, it is known that utilizing natural peer supports is beneficial, and because students are more mature in secondary schools, excellent peer-to-peer relationships can form.

Q.   Can a general educator or a special educator lead and run small groups in an inclusive class?

A.   Yes. Both general and special educators can lead whole-class and small-group lessons within an inclusive classroom. The key is that all instruction is co-planned through collaboration.

Q.   Is the special educator ultimately responsible for teaching the students who receive special education services?

A.   In inclusive education, students are not separated by ability or disability. All students are taught in a heterogeneous classroom where the general education teacher and the special education teacher work together to create an engaging, exciting, and joyful classroom where all students learn from both teachers. Both the general and special education teachers have shared responsibility and accountability in the education of students with disabilities.

Q.   Who is ultimately responsible for managing the IEP goals?

A.   The special education teacher, general education teacher, and related service providers assigned to the student are all responsible. That is, the team of educators and therapists is jointly vested in ensuring that students with disabilities meet their IEP goals.

Q.   What if the academic gap between the student and her or his peers is "too large"?

A.   A student's placement in school is based on individual needs, not achievement or cognitive levels as compared to grade-level peers. The role of special education is to provide the academic supports to help each student gain access to the general education content. Many students across the country who work at different levels from their peers are actively engaged in age-appropriate general education content within inclusive classrooms. For example, if a student is not yet writing, he or she can utilize technology to assist in getting ideas across. We aim to provide you with many more examples of adaptations, modifications, and accommodations that will help you to support all levels of learners in inclusive classrooms.

Q.   What does it take to create and maintain an inclusive classroom?

A.   It takes creativity, collaboration, student advocacy, agency, resourcefulness, a heart for this work, and a set of skills related specifically to inclusion. Inclusive educators engage in critical reflection and develop an expectation of ongoing problem solving in order to create conducive learning environments for all students. Our aim throughout this book is to provide you with the tools for accomplishing these goals.

CONCLUSION

In this chapter, we introduced you to Matthew and surveyed some of the critical foundations of inclusive education, discussed the roles and responsibilities of educators today, and provided answers to some commonly asked questions. As you can see, inclusive education requires that educators take on new roles and responsibilities in order to meet the needs of all students collaboratively. The next chapter is designed to provide background on inclusive education.

2

Inclusive Education

THE EVOLUTION OF SWIMMING LESSONS:
SURPRISINGLY SIMILAR TO THE EVOLUTION
OF INCLUDING STUDENTS WITH
DISABILITIES IN GENERAL EDUCATION.

"I started teaching in a self-contained classroom for students with intellectual disabilities years ago. Since then, our school has moved toward inclusion. This special education service delivery model is better for students' sense of belonging, academic outcomes, and social skills. In order to make the shift, we all had to learn new teaching strategies and become more thoughtful and proactive in curriculum design and collaboration became essential. Now, I still am a special educator in my school, but that means that I work with multiple teachers and all the students within those classrooms."

—Kim (special education teacher)

"The oppressive silencing of even one voice through any form of segregation eliminates that set of experiences from our collective conversation and diminishes the culture of community."

—Christopher Kliewer (1998, p. 5)

"Educators have a choice. We can either continue to blame the lack of progress in segregated classrooms on the severity of the disability, or we can have the courage and integrity to seriously question whether there is, in fact, a more effective way to prepare students with disabilities to enter the community after graduation."

—Norman Kunc (1992, p. 27)

"Educators have the power to create an environment of equity and tolerance, but sometimes it takes courage. I see it as my responsibility to be a role model and, if necessary, an activist for educational practices that foster understanding, acceptance, and inclusion of everyone whom we are trusted to educate."

—Kathleen (Vermont Teacher of the Year, as quoted in Remick, 2006)

In this chapter, we identify the concepts necessary to understanding inclusive education, such as belonging, the history of inclusive education, major legal concepts, the definition of inclusive education, indicators of inclusive education, IEPs, and commonly asked questions.

BELONGING

"To be rooted is perhaps the most important and least recognized need of the human soul."

—Simone Weil (2001)

One central reason that students with disabilities are being included in general education settings is that every child, with or without disabilities, has the right to belong. All human beings desire friendships, relationships, and academic challenge. Students with disabilities are no different.

Think for a moment about yourself. Think of a time you believed that you truly belonged somewhere. Was it a group, a club, a sports team, or a work environment? Now think about your behavior in that setting. How did you behave? How did you feel? If someone glanced over, how did you act? Most people are more willing to take risks, to contribute, to share, and to learn in such environments. With a strong sense of connectedness to a group of people, you are likely more talkative, more engaged, and more willing to be yourself. The same is true for students.

Now, on the contrary, think of a time that you believed you did *not* belong or felt ostracized from a group. How did you behave? How did you feel? In those situations, many people respond by being withdrawn and quiet, shutting themselves off from the group. A person also might respond by leaving the situation or getting angry. The same is true for students in school. It is essential to feel connected to a group or part of the school community. Not only is this important for self-worth, but it is also important for learning.

When working with a group of teachers, therapists, and paraprofessionals, we asked the preceding questions. Their responses are shown in Table 2.1.

Examine the responses shown in the table. How do they relate to students in your school? Have you seen students in school who feel sick, angry, withdrawn, or hurt? Have you seen students who behave in ways that let you know they do not believe that they belong? On the other hand, have you noticed students who are engaged, acting like themselves, and freely taking risks? As teachers, we have observed students who regularly felt connected and those who did not. Students who feel connected are more likely to take educational risks, be engaged and motivated, and consequentially, learn. Helping students feel that they belong is one of the most important jobs of the educational team.

If a system of special education excludes people and places children in rooms, hallways, or schools that are separate from the general educational population, it is likely that these children will not behave as well or learn as well. School administrators, therapists, and teachers all over the country are rethinking the practice of isolating students with disabilities in one room or pulling students out for services (Causton-Theoharis & Theoharis, 2008; McLeskey & Waldron, 2006). Isolating students in this way causes them to feel different from everyone else and not part of the larger school community. This type of segregation has real consequences for students' self-esteem and ability to learn (Peterson & Hittie, 2002). The educational placement

Table 2.1. Feelings associated with inclusion and exclusion

When I was included	When I was excluded
I felt comfortable	I felt upset
I felt loved	I was angry
I felt cared for	I was withdrawn
I took risks	I was quiet
I felt smart	I was self-conscious
I was confident	I was hurt
I was myself	I cried
I laughed often	I felt sick
I was creative	I did not participate
I was open to learning	I tried to leave the group

of students with disabilities matters, as does the quality of curriculum design and pedagogy that provides students with access to the general education curriculum with the appropriate supplemental aids and services. Inclusive education was built on the foundation that all people have the basic human right to belong.

"I like regular ed because my friends are there and they don't teach stuff that you already know."

—Jesse (a student with attention-deficit/ hyperactivity disorder [ADHD] and Asperger syndrome, age 13)

THE HISTORY OF INCLUSIVE EDUCATION

You might have attended a school in which students with disabilities were educated down the hall, in a separate wing, or in a separate school building. You also might have attended a school in which you sat beside students with disabilities. Your own schooling experience has likely shaped your personal thoughts about inclusive education.

Before 1975, students with disabilities did not have the legal right to attend school. As a result, many students with more significant disabilities were educated in separate schools (paid for by their parents) or institutions; some were not educated at all. In 1975, Congress passed the Education for All Handicapped Children Act (PL 94-142), which has since been reauthorized, most recently as IDEA (2004, PL 108-446). This law, which guarantees all students with disabilities the right to a public education, has proved a major step forward for people with disabilities and their families. This law ensures that all students with disabilities have access to free appropriate public education (FAPE) in the LRE. Each of these terms is defined in the next subsections.

Free Appropriate Public Education

In order to explain what is meant by FAPE, consider each term separately:

Free: All students with disabilities have the right to attend school, and the supports and services necessary to their education will be paid for at public expense.

Appropriate: All students with disabilities must be provided the assistive technology, aids, and services that allow them to participate in academic and nonacademic activities through an IEP.

Public education: Special education and related services are guaranteed in a public school setting.

Least Restrictive Environment

The terminology that is used to support inclusion in the law is *LRE*. This concept is explicitly cited in IDEA 2004, which stipulates that all students with disabilities have the legal right to be placed in the LRE.

LRE means that, to the maximum extent appropriate, a school district must educate any student with a disability in the regular classroom with appropriate aids and supports, referred to as *supplementary aids and services,* along with the student's peers without disabilities, in the school he or she would attend if the student did not have a disability (IDEA 2004).

Under LRE, the general education classroom is preferred and is the first place to be considered for placing a student with a disability before more restrictive options are considered. In other words, services should first be provided in the general education classroom.

What Are Supplementary Aids and Services?

The law intends that students not only benefit from special education but also gain access to supplementary aids and services. These include any "aids, services, and other supports that are provided in general education classes, other education-related settings, and in extracurricular and nonacademic settings, to enable children with disabilities to be educated with nondisabled children to the maximum extent appropriate" (34 C.F.R. § 300.42). The purpose is to provide the necessary supports that will allow students with disabilities to be full participants and learners with students without disabilities and enable their access to the general education context and curriculum. Supplementary aids and services that educators have successfully used include modifications and accommodations to the general education class curriculum (e.g., preferential seating, use of a computer, taped lectures, reduced seat time, tiered content, altering how a learning product is created, change in teaching process delivery), assistance of a teacher with special education training, special education training for the regular teacher, use of computer-assisted devices, provision of notetakers, and changes to materials. See Figure 2.1 for a long reproducible list of supplementary aids and services.

Educators must utilize all of the possible supplementary aids and services before determining that a student should leave the general education classroom. Inclusion is not mentioned in the law, but it is implied, and people use LRE and the multitude of supplementary aids and services to support the idea of inclusion and provision of special education and related services within general education contexts.

DEFINING INCLUSIVE EDUCATION

There are many ways to define *inclusion,* but our favorite definitions of inclusive education follow.

Kunc defined *inclusive education* as

> The valuing of diversity within the human community. When inclusive education is fully embraced, we abandon the idea that children have to become "normal" in order to contribute to the world. . . . We begin to look beyond typical ways of becoming valued members of the community, and in doing so, begin to realize the achievable goal of providing all children with an authentic sense of belonging. (1992, p. 20)

Checklist of Sample Supplemental Supports, Aids, and Services

Directions: When considering the need for personalized supports, aids, or services for a student, use this checklist to help identify which supports will be the least intrusive, only as special as necessary, and the most natural to the context of the classroom.

Environmental
☐ Preferential seating
☐ Planned seating
    ☐ Bus
    ☐ Classroom
    ☐ Lunchroom
    ☐ Auditorium
    ☐ Other
☐ Alter physical room arrangement. (Specify:_____)
☐ Use study carrels or quiet areas.
☐ Define area concretely (e.g., carpet squares, tape on floor, rug area).
☐ Reduce/minimize distractions.
    ☐ Visual
    ☐ Spatial
    ☐ Auditory
    ☐ Movement
☐ Teach positive rules for use of space.

Pacing of Instruction
☐ Extend time requirements.
☐ Vary activity often.
☐ Allow breaks.
☐ Omit assignments requiring copying in timed situations.
☐ Send additional copy of the text home for summer preview.
☐ Provide home set of materials for preview or review.

Presentation of Subject Matter
☐ Teach to the student's learning style/strength intelligences.
    ☐ Verbal/Linguistic
    ☐ Logical/Mathematical
    ☐ Visual/Spatial
    ☐ Naturalist
    ☐ Bodily/Kinesthetic
    ☐ Musical
    ☐ Interpersonal
    ☐ Intrapersonal
☐ Use active, experiential learning.
☐ Use specialized curriculum.
☐ Record class lectures and discussions to replay later.

Figure 2.1. Checklist of Sample Supplemental Supports, Aids, and Services.

(continued)

From Villa, R.A., Thousand, J.S., & Nevin, A.I. (2013). *A guide to co-teaching: New lessons and strategies to facilitate student learning* (3rd ed., pp. 198–201). Thousand Oaks, CA: Corwin Press; adapted by permission of SAGE Publications.

In *The Educator's Handbook for Inclusive School Practices*
by Julie Causton & Chelsea P. Tracy-Bronson (2015, Paul H. Brookes Publishing Co., Inc.)

Figure 2.1. *(continued)*

(page 2 of 4)

❏ Use American Sign Language and/or total communication.
❏ Provide prewritten notes, an outline, or an organizer (e.g., mind map).
❏ Provide a copy of classmate's notes (e.g., use NCR paper, photocopy).
❏ Use functional and meaningful application of academic skills.
❏ Present demonstrations and models.
❏ Use manipulatives and real objects in mathematics.
❏ Highlight critical information or main ideas.
❏ Preteach vocabulary.
❏ Make and use vocabulary files or provide vocabulary lists.
❏ Reduce the language level of the reading assignment.
❏ Use facilitated communication.
❏ Use visual organizers/sequences.
❏ Use paired reading/writing.
❏ Reduce seat time in class or activities.
❏ Use diaries or learning logs.
❏ Reword/rephrase instructions and questions.
❏ Preview and review major concepts in primary language.

Materials

❏ Limit amount of material on page.
❏ Record texts and other class materials.
❏ Use study guides and advanced organizers.
❏ Use supplementary materials.
❏ Provide note-taking assistance.
❏ Copy class notes.
❏ Scan tests and class notes into computer.
❏ Use large print.
❏ Use braille material.
❏ Use communication book or board.
❏ Provide assistive technology and software (e.g., Intelli-Talk).

Specialized Equipment or Procedure

❏ Wheelchair
❏ Standing Board
❏ Computer
❏ Electronic typewriter
❏ Modified keyboard
❏ Switches
❏ Catheterization
❏ Braces
❏ Customized mealtime utensils, plates, cups, and other materials

☐ Walker
☐ Positioning
☐ Computer software
☐ Video
☐ Voice synthesizer
☐ Augmentative communication device
☐ Suctioning
☐ Restroom equipment

(continued)

From Villa, R.A., Thousand, J.S., & Nevin, A.I. (2013). *A guide to co-teaching: New lessons and strategies to facilitate student learning* (3rd ed., pp. 198–201). Thousand Oaks, CA: Corwin Press; adapted by permission of SAGE Publications.

In *The Educator's Handbook for Inclusive School Practices*
by Julie Causton & Chelsea P. Tracy-Bronson (2015, Paul H. Brookes Publishing Co., Inc.)

Figure 2.1. *(continued)* (page 3 of 4)

Assignment Modification

☐ Give directions in small, distinct steps (written/picture/verbal).
☐ Use written backup for oral directions.
☐ Use pictures as supplement to oral directions.
　　☐ Lower difficulty level.
　　☐ Raise difficulty level.
　　☐ Shorten assignments.
☐ Reduce paper-and-pencil tasks.
☐ Read or record directions to the student(s).
☐ Give extra cues or prompts.
☐ Allow student to record or type assignments.
☐ Adapt worksheets and packets.
☐ Use compensatory procedures by providing alternate assignments, when demands of class conflict with student capabilities.
☐ Ignore spelling errors/sloppy work.
☐ Ignore penmanship.

Self-Management/Follow-Through

☐ Provide pictorial or written daily or weekly schedule.
☐ Provide student calendars.
☐ Check often for understanding/review.
☐ Request parent reinforcement.
☐ Have student repeat directions.
☐ Teach study skills.
☐ Use binders to organize material.
☐ Design/write/use long-term assignments time lines.
☐ Review and practice real situations.
☐ Plan for generalization by teaching skill in several environments.

Testing Adaptations

☐ Provide oral instructions and/or read test questions.
☐ Use pictorial instructions/questions.
☐ Read test to student.
☐ Preview language of test questions.
☐ Ask questions that have applications in real settings.
☐ Administer test individually.
　　☐ Use short answer.
　　☐ Use multiple choice.
　　☐ Shorten length.
　　☐ Extend time frame.
　　☐ Use open-note/open-book tests.
☐ Modify format to reduce visual complexity or confusion.

(continued

From Villa, R.A., Thousand, J.S., & Nevin, A.I. (2013). *A guide to co-teaching: New lessons and strategies to facilitate student learning* (3rd ed., pp. 198–201). Thousand Oaks, CA: Corwin Press; adapted by permission of SAGE Publications.

In *The Educator's Handbook for Inclusive School Practices*
by Julie Causton & Chelsea P. Tracy-Bronson (2015, Paul H. Brookes Publishing Co., Inc.)

Figure 2.1. *(continued)* (page 4 of 4)

Social Interaction Support
❏ Use natural peer supports and multiple, rotating peers.
❏ Use peer advocacy.
❏ Use cooperative learning group.
❏ Institute peer tutoring.
❏ Structure opportunities for social interaction (e.g., Circle of Friends).
❏ Focus on social process rather than end product.
❏ Structure shared experiences in school and extracurricular activities.
❏ Teach friendship, sharing, and negotiation skills to classmates.
❏ Teach social communication skills.
    ☐ Greetings
    ☐ Conversation
    ☐ Turn taking
    ☐ Sharing
    ☐ Negotiation
    ☐ Other

Level of Staff Support (Consider *after* considering previous categories)
❏ Consultation
❏ Stop-in support
❏ Team teaching (parallel, supportive, complementary, or co-teaching)
❏ Daily in-class staff support
❏ Total staff support (staff are in close proximity)
❏ One-to-one assistance
❏ Specialized personnel support (if indicated, identify time needed)

Support	Time Needed
❏ Instructional support assistant	_____
❏ Health care assistant	_____
❏ Behavior assistant	_____
❏ Signing assistant	_____
❏ Nursing	_____
❏ Occupational therapy	_____
❏ Physical therapy	_____
❏ Speech-language pathologist	_____
❏ Augmentative communication specialist	_____
❏ Transportation	_____
❏ Counseling	_____
❏ Adaptive physical education	_____
❏ Transition planning	_____
❏ Orientation/mobility	_____
❏ Career counseling	_____

From Villa, R.A., Thousand, J.S., & Nevin, A.I. (2013). *A guide to co-teaching: New lessons and strategies to facilitate student learning* (3rd ed., pp. 198–201). Thousand Oaks, CA: Corwin Press; adapted by permission of SAGE Publications.

In *The Educator's Handbook for Inclusive School Practices*
by Julie Causton & Chelsea P. Tracy-Bronson (2015, Paul H. Brookes Publishing Co., Inc.)

Udvari-Solner used another definition of inclusion:

Inclusive schooling propels a critique of contemporary school culture and thus, encourages practitio-
ners to reinvent what can be and should be to realize more humane, just and democratic learning communities. Inequities in treatment and educational opportunity are brought to the forefront, thereby
fostering attention to human rights, respect for difference and value of diversity. (1997, p. 142)

WHAT DOES INCLUSION LOOK LIKE?
INDICATORS OF INCLUSIVE CLASSROOMS

Some indicators of inclusive schooling environments include natural proportions, co-
planning, team teaching, community building, differentiation, access, heterogeneous
seating, and engaging instruction.

Natural Proportions

In any one classroom, the number of students with disabilities should reflect the natural population of students with disabilities in the school. For example, if students with
disabilities comprise 12% of the overall school population, then no more than 12%
of students in any one of its classrooms should have a disability. In an inclusive classroom, half the class will not be made up of students with disabilities. Having a greater
number of students with disabilities clustered in one setting increases the density of
need, making the class more like a special education setting.

Co-planning

General and special educators must establish a common planning time weekly to
brainstorm and design upcoming curriculum units and lessons. In addition, communication systems are implemented so that educators can discuss lesson specifics as
well as student needs and issues that arise. Co-planning also occurs with related service
providers so that therapy skills are seamlessly integrated throughout the day.

Co-teaching

Inclusive classrooms often have two teachers (one general and one special education
teacher) with equitable responsibilities for educating all the students. These teachers work together in flexible and coordinated ways. No group of students is the sole
responsibility of one educator. Educators often co-teach or teach small heterogeneous
groups in the general education classroom. Not all inclusive classrooms have two
teachers present. Sometimes the general education teacher carries out modifications
and adaptations that have been designed by a special educator. Sometimes the co-
teaching that takes place is between a general education teacher and a paraprofessional. Co-teaching is also referred to as *team teaching* or *collaborative teaching*.

Community Building and Culture

In inclusive classrooms, educators continually use community building to ensure
that students feel connected to one another and to their teachers. A common theme

in community building is that different people learn in different ways. Community building approaches vary, but in an inclusive classroom the day or the class period may start out with a morning meeting at which students share something with the class or an important life event. You might see organized community building in which students learn about each other in systematic ways. For example, the students might be doing a community-building exercise called "Homework in a Bag"; in this exercise, each student brings one item that represents him- or herself and shares the item with a small group of other students. Diversity, difference, and disability are embraced, as community building is used to ensure students feel connected and a part of a close-knit community.

Differentiation

In an inclusive classroom, it is clear that learners of various academic, social, and behavioral levels and needs share one learning environment. Differentiation of instruction is a strategy inclusive educators use to respond to various learning needs (Tomlinson, 2000; Tomlinson & Kalbfleisch, 1998; Tomlinson & Strickland, 2005). The content, process, or product is differentiated. Students might work on similar goals, but they do so in different ways, allowing for multiple entry points into the learning goals and objectives. For example, all students might be working on math problems, with some using manipulatives, some drawing out their answers, some checking their problems on calculators, and some using wipe-off markers and whiteboards. One hallmark of inclusive education is that both general and special educators are crucial in planning and implementation of meaningful differentiation that enhances academic skills.

Students Do Not Leave to Learn

In inclusive schools, all students are full-time members of general education classrooms. An inclusive classroom does not have a virtual revolving door of students leaving for specialized instruction in a specific skill or subject area. Special education services, content area interventions, and related services occur right within the context of the general education classroom. Lesson materials might be differentiated, modified, or adapted for a student to be successful. As an alternative to a student going to a small therapy room to make use of sensory materials, the occupational therapist sets up a sensory diet toolbox that can be used during English class or during math instruction. A student might work on tripod grip during writers' workshop, a naturally occurring time to hold pencils. One of the key features of inclusive schooling is that students are not removed from the classroom for remediation. Instead, services and supports are brought directly to them.

Grouping and Seating Are Heterogeneous

In inclusive classrooms, educators must thoughtfully consider seating and grouping. Students with disabilities should be physically spread out in the classroom. In other words, students with disabilities should not be clustered or seated together. The location of lockers of students with disabilities should also be naturally distributed. When engaging in small group instruction, teachers should be sure to group students heterogeneously, not by ability, as often as possible.

Engaging Instruction

Inclusive classroom instruction is rich and accommodating for all students. Lessons do not entail a lot of large-group lectures in which the teachers talk and the students passively sit and listen. Learning is engaging and exciting in inclusive classrooms. Teachers plan instruction with the range of learning styles in mind. In inclusive classrooms, students experience active learning; they often are up and out of their seats and are frequently engaged in partner work and group work. The content is planned to meet the needs of students who need to move around, to work with others, and to physically touch and interact with the content. Learning experiences are designed to incorporate multiple sensory modalities. In other words, good, solid teaching techniques are necessary in an inclusive classroom.

WHY SHOULD SPECIAL EDUCATION AND RELATED SERVICES BE PROVIDED WITHIN INCLUSIVE CLASSROOMS?

The first reason for providing special education and related services within the physical context of the general education classroom is that the law supports it (IDEA 2004; NCLB 2001). A second reason is that national professional organizations, such as the American Speech-Language-Hearing Association (ASHA) and the American Occupational Therapy Association (AOTA), and federally funded centers, such as the School-wide Integrated Framework for Transformation (SWIFT), clearly support inclusive services and collaborative service delivery. Third, students tend to perform much better academically when they are educated alongside their peers and not removed from the general education classroom (Theoharis, Causton, & Tracy-Bronson, 2015). In part, this is because when they are pulled out, they miss significant portions of the classroom content. Last, it is likely that the students being pulled out are the least likely to be able to handle multiple transitions each day. Providing inclusive special education and related services not only allows educational professionals to follow the spirit of the law and the intention of national organizations, but also provides the best educational setting for students to maximize their academic and social potential.

HOW DOES INCLUSIVE EDUCATION FIT WITH RESPONSE TO INTERVENTION?

Many schools and districts across the country have adopted the response to intervention (RTI) three-tiered prevention model, usually represented as a triangle: The base of the triangle is good curriculum and instruction, then some students are given prescribed intervention, and fewer students receive additional and even more focused intervention. Seen within the context of RTI, or the similarly structured three-tiered framework for PBS, authentic inclusive education is a way to significantly expand the base of the triangle to allow many students who typically struggle in that base to be more successful. It is important to recognize that the schools that embrace inclusive education are seeing positive results for students who typically receive interventions in more restrictive settings.

Whereas some schools are looking for the prescriptive intervention to be delivered to a targeted group of students, inclusive education can offer a way to provide more seamless and integrated support. Schools that embrace inclusion are improving the way they meet all students' needs within the context of the general education setting through differentiation, thereby giving students access to a rich social environment and the academic core curriculum with built-in supports.

WHAT DO I NEED TO KNOW ABOUT THE INDIVIDUALIZED EDUCATION PROGRAM?

Every student who receives special education services must have an IEP. A student who has an IEP has already been tested and observed, and a team has determined that the student has a disability. An IEP is a legal plan written by a team that documents the learning priorities for the school year (Huefner, 2000). This team includes the parent, the student (when appropriate), a general education teacher, the special education teacher, a representative of the school district, and other professionals whose expertise is needed (e.g., psychologist, speech-language pathologist, occupational therapist, physical therapist). When writing this document, the team comes together annually to determine and document the student's unique needs and goals regarding his or her participation in the general school curriculum for the upcoming school year. According to the U.S. Department of Education (2004), every IEP must legally include the following information:

- *Present levels of performance*—this states how a student is performing across all subject areas
- *Measurable goals and objectives*—this indicates the annual goals for a student across subject areas
- *Special education and related services*—this is the type, level, and amount of service that will be provided by special education staff
- *The extent of participation with children without disabilities*—the IEP must note how much time a student spends with general education peers
- *A statement of how the child's progress will be measured*—the team needs to describe how often and how a student's progress will be measured
- *Modifications*—the student's modifications or adaptations must be listed
- *Participation in statewide tests*—the IEP indicates whether the student will participate in statewide tests and, if so, what modifications will be provided

- *Locations of services to be provided*—this explains the amount of time students will receive services and the location (e.g., general education classroom)
- *Statement of transition services*—each student who is at least 16 years of age must have a statement of preparation for adult life

The role of general and special educators in the IEP process is vitally important to help construct the present level of performance related to academic, sensory, social, and behavior management goals. Educators will support the IEP team in writing goals relevant to those areas of need. In addition, educators must collaborate with the IEP team to decide the number of minutes required of each special education and related service to support the child in meeting the goals, as well as to decide the location of service delivery. An outdated way of thinking about this process is for educators to arrive at the IEP meeting with their goals written and information completed, rather than constructing these with other members of the IEP team. Examples of academic, social, behavior, and therapy goals for elementary students are shown in Table 2.2.

Table 2.2.   Examples of individualized education program goals for second-graders educated in inclusive contexts

Skill	Inclusive goal example
Writing	Given raised-line paper, a slant board, and pencil grip, James will write three complete sentences as part of a nonfiction procedural text so they are legible to a peer in the classroom.
Grip strength	At recess, while playing jump rope, Neleah will maintain the hand positioning and hand grip necessary to hold on for 15 consecutive twirls.
Cutting	Given visual supports for vocabulary, adaptive scissors, a role within a cooperative group, and a project task, Adison will cut and affix appropriate images, content-specific items, and vocabulary words on a poster.
Math	Given peer support, a See 'N' Solve Visual Calculator, and manipulatives, Paige will solve addition story problems using number combinations to 10.
Sensory	Given a weighted vest or weighted animal, a disc cushion, fidgets, and a rocker board, Aiden will respond to literal and inferential comprehension questions after a classroom read-aloud that is no longer than 10 minutes with 90% accuracy
Phonological sound production	Given a repeated chant during morning meeting that uses the /s/ sound, a visual model of the "s," and a classroom of peers modeling the sound, Brycin will articulate the /s/ sound audibly in three out of five repeated trials.
Voice intonation	Given a community builder that requires students to ask questions, Enzo will ask questions to a peer with appropriate intonation (pitch rise and respiration at the conclusion of each question) on four out of five trials.
Turn taking	During small-group science lab discussion using a talking object (e.g., a koosh ball), Imari will delay speaking until he is handed the koosh ball to share on eight out of eight repeated opportunities.
Jaw position and muscle memory for speech production	Given a large piece of gum (e.g., Hubba Bubba sized) during large-group lecture time, Joslyn will chew the gum for 15-minute increments on both right and left sides to increase jaw strength and symmetrical stability for speech production.

When creating IEP goals, it is important that the educational team include annual goals that are aligned with grade-level academic standards. In Table 2.3, examples of academic, social, behavior, and therapy goals are aligned with the ninth-grade Common Core State Standards for a high school student, and in Table 2.4, IEP goals are aligned with the sixth-grade Common Core standards for a middle school student.

A SHIFT IN OWNERSHIP: FROM "MY" TO "OUR"

Educators in inclusive schools shift from thinking about students as "my students" and "your students" to "our students." This shift in language is emblematic of a larger notion that all students are the responsibility of all of the educators on a team. This notion even translates to teaching spaces and curriculum responsibilities. For example, one team avoids the terms *my* or *mine* or *I* when talking about students and

Table 2.3. Examples of individualized education program goals for a ninth-grade student educated in inclusive contexts

Subject area	Inclusive goal example
Reading: Literature	Given digital audio of grade-level texts, a graphic organizer, and peer prompting, Caleb will use textual evidence to identify the narrative elements of the story (e.g., theme or central idea, characters, plot) with 80% accuracy over three consecutive probes.
Reading: Informational text	Given digital audio of grade-level texts, a graphic organizer, and peer prompting, Caleb will use textual evidence to determine the central idea, draw one inference, and provide an objective summary of the text with 80% accuracy.
Reading: Foundational skills	Given appropriate text based on Caleb's readability level, he will use combined knowledge of all letter–sound correspondences, syllabication patterns, and morphology to read with 90% accuracy.
Writing	Given access to assistive technology, Inspiration Software, peer support, extended time, and developmental spelling, Caleb will make an argument or claim, include supporting evidence, and provide a concluding statement that supports the argument presented with 80% accuracy.
Math	Given manipulatives, assistive technology, and math tools that aid in computation, Caleb will complete grade-level math curriculum problems with 80% accuracy over three consecutive probes.
Behavior	Given a whispered verbal prompt or visual prompt, Caleb will raise his hand during a structured lesson prior to commenting/calling out.
Speech and language	Given auditory stimuli in a language activity, Caleb will offer a reasonable response to inference questions, "how" questions, "when" questions, and "why" questions with 80% accuracy across three consecutive therapy sessions. Given adult support, Caleb will engage in reciprocal conversation about common core content with a grade-level peer with 80% accuracy by verbally participating in a minimum of five exchanges.

Table 2.4. Examples of individualized education program goals for a sixth-grade student educated in inclusive contexts

Subject area	Inclusive goal example
Literacy in history/social studies	Given access to an adapted text, assistive technology (iPad and Big Red Switch), peer support, and extended time, Christina will identify the key steps in a text's description of a process related to history/social studies with 80% accuracy.
Reading: Literature	Given access to an adapted version of the text with Mayer-Johnson symbols, assistive technology, and peer support, Christina will describe how a character feels/responds as the plot of the text moves toward a resolution with 80% accuracy.
Writing	Given a list of relevant topic ideas, a peer to brainstorm with, and an assistive technology writing device, Christina will write an explanatory text that introduces a topic and includes three broader categories, two details in each of the categories, headings, and graphics with 75% accuracy.
Math	Given a visual calculator, a scribe, a peer, and needed formulas, Christina will find the areas of right triangles and other triangles with 90% accuracy.
Behavior	Given a list of possible break ideas and a timer, Christina will appropriately use breaks to segment work sessions with 95% accuracy.
Speech and language	Given a communication device, a communication board, and simple cue cards, Christina will initiate partnerships and free-time activity preferences with peers with 95% accuracy.

uses language that communicates to others that the educators have embraced a team approach. Therefore, the general education teacher calls it "our classroom," and she signs all notes that go home as "the third-grade team" and then lists each adult (including the educators, therapists, and paraprofessionals) underneath. All professionals' names are listed on the classroom door, and each of the professionals has a space in the room for belongings and materials. It is important to note that, when done well, the students are typically not aware of the specific roles of each educator. The students see all of the adults as educators in the room.

Inclusive education guides us in the creation of school environments in which *all* students feel welcome, socially fulfilled, and academically challenged. In inclusive schools, diversity, not uniformity, is celebrated and valued.

COMMONLY ASKED QUESTIONS ABOUT INCLUSIVE EDUCATION

Q. Is inclusive education really best for a particular student?

A. This question is common to teachers. Research has consistently shown that the inclusive environment is better educationally and socially for students with disabilities. The challenge is to figure out how to make the general education environment suitable to the student's needs. This requires problem solving, collaborating, and designing differentiated supports that seamlessly integrate curriculum with the student's needs.

Q. What do I communicate to families about inclusive services?

A. For some, inclusive service provision will be a new concept. Educational professionals may have been extolling the virtues of pull-out special education, resource room settings, separate school building placements, and individual related services to them for years. How can educators communicate the virtues of inclusive schooling? See Table 2.5 for ideas of what to tell families about inclusive services.

Q. How do I meet the number of minutes for special education services on the IEPs unless I pull students out?

A. Services can be carried out in many ways. The law suggests that services are portable and should be brought to the student. Therefore, your time could be spent pushing into the general education classroom, running a center, or even recommending ideas to the other educators about how to carry out specific skills while they teach. Your time could be spent modifying or adapting the material so the student can be successful in the general education classroom and throughout the school day. Planning or specially designing the instruction or the materials so that goals can be met seamlessly throughout the day is more effective than pulling a student out.

Table 2.5. Communicating with families about inclusive services

Question	Possible response
Where will the services take place?	The services are now brought to the student instead of having the student leave the classroom to receive services.
Will that be embarrassing for my child?	Services are not delivered at the back table in an inclusive classroom for all other students to see. Instead, each student's educational goals are infused into the school day in a natural way.
Why will the services be delivered inclusively?	Educators are finding that students who have uninterrupted access to the general education classroom perform better overall. Federal laws have prioritized inclusive service delivery over pull-out services, as students tend to perform better when all of the special education and related services are worked into the school day. Many students find leaving for specialized services to be stigmatizing and they feel an impact socially and emotionally. Skills taught in intervention rooms or therapy settings often do not generalize to natural contexts; therefore, teaching them in a natural context the first time helps students to be able to apply the new skills.
So does that mean my child is receiving less service?	Special educators and related service providers will be working with the general education teacher to help to infuse all of the needed skills in the classroom, so it is likely that your child will be receiving even more services and support for goals in the individualized education program.

Q. I am a special education teacher and have so many students on my caseload. How can I provide services to them all inclusively?

A. One thing that has become clear in the law is that staff convenience is not a justification to pull students. Therefore, you might determine which students need direct support, which students can receive consult services, and for which students you will stop by to monitor progress. Then, arrange your schedule to match those needs. Instead of thinking about your caseload as static and unchanging (e.g., 11:30–11:45 a.m., Chloe receives supplemental phonemic awareness instruction in the special education room), think of appropriate times to provide such services and generally problem-solve across a student's day.

Q. Is inclusion really the law?

A. IDEA 2004 does not use the term *inclusion*. Nonetheless, the law stipulates that all students must be placed in the LRE. The first consideration must be the general education setting, and schools must prove that they have attempted to teach all children in the general education setting with appropriate supplementary aids and services before considering placement in more restrictive settings.

CONCLUSION

Schools today are becoming increasingly inclusive. Therefore, educators working in inclusive settings need to understand the rationale for inclusive schooling, the history of inclusive schooling, major concepts in inclusive schooling, indicators of inclusion, and the concept of the IEP as a framework to most fully support students in inclusive settings. You will not be expected to do this alone; you will be part of an educational team. The next chapter focuses on specific elements of special education that both general and special educators will need to know in order to teach inclusively.

3

Special Education

WHAT DO YOU CHOOSE TO SEE?
WEEDS OR WILDFLOWERS?

"I prefer to think of my disability as a type of diversity rather than deviance or deficiency: my disability is just one characteristic or attribute among many that make me who I am. People do not need to prove their worthiness. Obviously, what we are talking about here is a human rights issue. We need to establish the unconditional and inherent worthiness of people regardless of what combinations of diverse characteristics they present."

—Norman Kunc (Giangreco, 1996b/2004)

"I got my degree as a special education teacher in a program that focused on students with learning disabilities. I now have a cross-categorical license, and often find myself feeling a bit unprepared to support students with different disability labels."

—Susan (special education teacher)

"I have been teaching for 17 years in this district. Then this new mandate came down that we needed to be teaching special education students in our classrooms. I was initially very surprised, shocked, and in general dismay. I had no special training, and now I was responsible for students with disabilities—you know . . . students with autism, with Asperger's syndrome, with Down syndrome for all or part of the school day. I had a lot of learning to do."

—Tina (general education teacher)

"There is more than one way to walk, talk, paint, read and write."

—Thomas Hehir (2002, p. 17).

"Special education should not mean a different curriculum, but rather the vehicle by which students with disabilities access the curriculum and the means by which the unique needs that arise out of the child's disability are addressed."

—Thomas Hehir (2002, pp. 23–24)

What is *special education?* In this chapter, we answer that question, along with the following ones: Who receives special education? What does *disability* mean? Why should people be cautious of educational labels? What does special education terminology mean? What are the different categories of disabilities? At the end of this chapter, we also answer other commonly asked questions.

This chapter identifies the important concepts and ideas that are essential for anyone in the field of education to understand, especially general and special educators. By knowing this information, educators can understand the larger educational systems of which they are an essential part. As inclusive education has become part of the landscape of education, it is critical for all in the field to understand basic special education knowledge.

WHAT IS SPECIAL EDUCATION?

Simply put, *special education* is individualized instruction designed to meet the unique needs of certain students. This type of customized instruction may require a student to have accommodations or modifications to his or her class work. *Accommodations* are adaptations to the curriculum that *do not* fundamentally alter or lower standards (e.g., test location, student response method). *Modifications* are changes to the curriculum that *do* alter the expectations (e.g., changes to the course content, timing, or test presentation). As mandated by IDEA 2004, any student who receives special education services may receive specialized materials (e.g., books on tape), related services (e.g., speech and language services), equipment (e.g., a communication system), or different teaching strategies (e.g., visual notes). For example, a student who is deaf may require the services of a sign language interpreter in order to follow along in the classroom. A student who has autism may require specialized materials such as a visual schedule to prepare for the changing routines in the school day. A student with a learning disability may require additional reading instruction or extended time for completing written assignments.

Special education is a part of general education. It is a system of supports to help students learn the general education curriculum. The legal definition of *special education* under federal law is "specially designed instruction, at no cost to the child's parents, to meet the needs of a student with a disability" (IDEA 2004, 20 U.S.C. § 1401 [25]). This definition recognizes that some students have difficulty learning, behaving, or physically engaging in general education and, because of such disabilities, need individualized supports to help them to build their skills and abilities to reach their full potential in school. These additional services do not cost the students' parents any money and are funded by the local and federal governments.

WHAT ARE RELATED SERVICES?

Sometimes, the supports a student with a disability needs can be fully addressed by a special educator, other teaching personnel, and teaching assistants or paraprofessionals. However, sometimes additional supports are required for a student to benefit from special education services. These additional supports are called *related services* in special education law. IDEA 2004 defines the term related services as follows:

> Transportation, and such developmental, corrective, and other supportive services (including speech-language pathology and audiology services, interpreting services, psychological services, physical and occupational therapy, recreation, including therapeutic recreation, social work services, school nurse services) designed to enable a child with a disability to receive a free appropriate public education as described in the individualized education program of the child, counseling services, including rehabilitation counseling, orientation and mobility services, and medical services . . . as may be required to assist a child with a disability to benefit from special education, and includes the early identification and assessment of disabling conditions in children. (20 U.S.C. § 1401 [602][26][A])

All related services are also provided at no cost to the students' parents. In other words, all of these services are related services that are available to allow students to benefit from special education.

SPECIAL EDUCATION IS A *SERVICE*, NOT A PLACE

In the past, when the term *special education* was used, a special place or class came to mind. People thought of a room, a school, or another separate place to which students with disabilities went to receive special education services. This notion, however, is outdated. Special education and related services are no longer limited to a specific location. It has been established that all students—including students with autism, intellectual disabilities, multiple disabilities, and emotional or behavioral disabilities—learn best in classroom settings and can benefit from instruction side by side with general education peers (Causton-Theoharis & Theoharis, 2008; Peterson & Hittie, 2002). It is important to remember that special education and related services are portable services (e.g., help with reading, math, or fine motor skills) that can easily be brought directly to individual students within general education contexts, instead of bringing students to the services.

Special education occurs in general education classrooms all over the United States and the rest of the world. When students with disabilities are educated primarily in general education settings, this is called *inclusive education*. In inclusive classrooms, general and special education teachers, related service providers, and paraprofessionals should ensure that students with disabilities are part of the general education curriculum, instruction, and social scene as much as possible within the LRE.

WHO RECEIVES SPECIAL EDUCATION?

Every year, under IDEA 2004, more than 6.5 million students in the United States between the ages of 3 and 21 receive special education services (U.S. Department of Education, 2015). In other words, roughly 11% of all school-age students qualify for special education services because they have disabilities that have adverse educational impact.

Under IDEA 2004, the definition of a student with a disability is "one who has certain disabilities and who, because of the impairment, needs special education and related services" (PL 108-446, 20 U.S.C. § 1401 [3]). Each student qualifies for special education because he or she has at least one type of disability. Each of the different types of disability is defined and described later in this chapter.

When one examines the population of students who receive special education, several disturbing trends appear within the areas of gender, socioeconomic status, and race. First, even though the numbers of males and females in the general school population are equal, the population receiving special education is roughly two-thirds male (U.S. Department of Education, 2007). Second, the poverty rate is proportionately much higher among students who qualify for special education than in the entire school population (U.S. Department of Education, 2007). Last, a disproportionate number of certain racial or ethnic groups are served in special education. For example, because African American students make up 14% of the general school population, one might assume that only 14% of students who qualify for special education would be African American (Turnbull, Turnbull, Shank, & Smith, 2004). In fact, African American students represent 44.9% of the total number of students labeled as having learning disabilities (U.S. Department of Education, 2007). Further, African American students are three times more likely than Caucasian students to receive special education and related services. Educators should be cognizant of these national demographic trends and actively work against the continuation of a biased cycle of labeling students for special education services. For example, extra care should be given when determining if a student qualifies for special education from one of these demographic groups.

HOW DOES A STUDENT GET A LABEL? THE REFERRAL PROCESS

If a student does not come to school with an educational label, it is important to understand how a student receives a label. What follows in this section is a description of the special education referral process.

1. *Student is suspected of having a disability and needing services.* Any school professional or parent can ask that a student be evaluated to see if he or she is eligible for services. However, parent consent is required before the student may be evaluated. Evaluation needs to be completed within 60 days of parent consent.

2. *Eligibility is decided.* The evaluation process would likely involve providing data from RTI to the team of professionals. Then, the team of professionals would evaluate the student in all of the areas related to the suspected disability; for example, hearing tests would be given to students suspected of a hearing impairment. The various evaluations are conducted by a multidisciplinary team, including the school psychologist, special educators, general educators, related service providers, and medical personnel, if appropriate. Families also provide important observations regarding the student's academic, behavioral, social, and communication needs. Then all qualified professionals and the parents look closely at the evaluation results along with the definitions of disability.

   a. *If a student is found eligible for services,* this means the student qualifies for special education services and is identified as having a disability. The process then moves on to the next step.

   b. *If a student is not found eligible for services,* this means the student does not qualify for special education services. He or she is not identified as being a student with a disability. However, educators continue to educate the student and provide support as needed.

3. *IEP meeting is scheduled.* Within 30 calendar days, an IEP must be written. Therefore, the team must convene to schedule a meeting that is mutually agreeable to parents and educators. As the educator, you should inform parents that they may invite people to the meeting who have knowledge or special expertise about the student.

4. *IEP is written during the meeting.* The team of educational professionals, parents, and student come together to collaboratively write the IEP.

5. *Services are provided.* The district has a legal obligation to carry out the services as written in the IEP. This includes the accommodations, modifications, and supplemental supports and services that must be provided to the student.

6. *Progress is measured and reported to parents.* The student's progress toward annual goals is measured and reported to parents. This can happen with report cards.

7. *IEP is reviewed.* Every year, the student's IEP is reviewed and new goals are written.
8. *Student is reevaluated.* At least every 3 years, the student must be reevaluated to see if he or she still qualifies as a student with a disability. However, the parent and the school can agree that such an evaluation is not necessary and can be waived.

WHAT IS AN INDIVIDUALIZED EDUCATION PROGRAM?

Every student with a federally recognized category of disability has the right to an IEP. It includes information about the student and the educational program that is designed to meet specific needs. At the minimum, an IEP must include the following:

- A statement of the student's current educational performance in multiple subject areas
- A statement on annual goals and measurable objectives
- A section on measuring progress toward goals and objectives, also describing how that information will be reported to families
- A statement of the specific special education, specially designed instruction, and related services to be provided
- Any needed accommodations or supplemental aids and supports
- A statement of the extent to which the student will participate in general education. This is to ensure that students are educated in the LRE to the greatest extent possible. Thus, their participation in the general education program with students without disabilities must be noted. Also, the team must consider the student's participation in state and district assessments. Any testing accommodations and modifications are also noted.
- The dates when services will begin, as well as the duration and frequency
- Beginning at age 16 or younger, a transition plan, which must include the needed transition services based on individual student needs, needed activities in instruction, community experiences, daily living skills, and vocational skills. If these areas are not needed, a statement must be provided about the basis for that decision.

Both general and special educators can lead IEP meetings. Most often, they are led by special educators, and general educators participate. Figure 3.1 presents useful tips to ensure all team members have input and ensure all who are part of the process actually feel like part of the process. It is not simply about compliance with IEP procedures: it is about how to keep the student at the heart of the work and how to create a meaningful IEP in a collaborative manner.

WHAT ARE THE DISTINGUISHING FEATURES BETWEEN A 504 PLAN AND AN INDIVIDUALIZED EDUCATION PROGRAM?

Some students who do not qualify for an IEP may qualify for a 504 plan. It is imperative that inclusive educators know the difference between these two support plans. You likely will be responsible for implementing both to meet the educational needs of your students. Table 3.1 outlines the differences between the two.

A Month Before the Individualized Education Program (IEP) Meeting

Have a conversation with the parents. Let them know who is likely to be at the meeting. Tell them about the typical format of the meeting. Remind parents that they can bring anyone they wish to the meeting. Determine where the meeting will be held and be sure the family is comfortable with that location. Also, let families know that they are welcome to share a statement or photos of the student to kick off the meeting. Some teachers send a questionnaire home for parents to assist them in formulating ideas to discuss at the meeting. Sample questions might be as follows:

- What are your child's strengths, gifts, and talents?
- What are your dreams and goals for your child?
- What are your concerns or worries?
- What is really working this year in terms of your child's schooling experience?
- What would you like to see changed or fixed?
- When you look at last year's goals, what changes would you like to see?

Two Weeks Before the IEP Meeting

Weeks before the meeting, invite all members (including family) to informally jot down what they wish to see on the new IEP. Gather the responses from the questionnaire.

One Week Before the IEP Meeting

Write up all ideas in draft form. Send the draft out to everyone (including families) for feedback. Be sure that, if any reports will be shared, families have at least 1 week to read them before the meeting (no one should be expected to read or process this kind of information while seated at a meeting). This way, the meeting can focus only on discussing progress and implementing changes that parents would like to make.

The Day of the IEP Meeting

Think About the Vibe

Think about what it may feel like to be parents walking into a room of educational professionals. Ask yourself the following questions: How can we make the room and meeting space more welcoming? How can we bring a positive vibe to the atmosphere? Consider the subsequent ideas. Meet the parents at the office and walk with them to the room. Provide snacks for everyone. If young students are present, have several activities ready so students can keep their hands busy while participating. Consider seating, lighting, and general comfort. Be sure to greet everyone and provide name tags for any team members that the family has not yet met.

Start with the Family or the Student

Have the family begin by sharing anything they wish. Some families start with a video of their student demonstrating all that the student can do. Others start with a statement of hopes and dreams. Others start with a funny story. The purpose of this is to ensure the meeting starts with the focus on positive aspects of the student, highlighting right away that the family loves and cares deeply about the student. Again, purposefully begin with a positive vibe.

As an alternative, have the student kick off the meeting, talking about his or her progress. For some students, creating a PowerPoint presentation might be a more comfortable way to share. We suggest inviting students to their own IEP meetings at a very young age—it is the best way to teach students to be their own advocates. Then, if they are invited, be sure to listen to their ideas and suggestions.

Proceed Through the Meeting

Discuss an agenda for the meeting and, by doing so, prioritize the student's needs to ensure that the focus of the meeting is on the student's goals. Make sure that all team members are in agreement with the goals. Always have something to write with—chalkboard, whiteboard, chart paper, or a SMART Board—to record goals, ideas, and concerns for the entire team.

Share assessments and data across subject areas and always share positive information *first*. Explain any unfamiliar assessment results, terminology, or recommendations. Check in with all present.

(continued)

Figure 3.1. How inclusive educators lead the individualized education program process.

Figure 3.1. *(continued)*

Ask questions like "How does that sound?", "Does anyone have an issue with that goal?", and "Does this make sense to everyone?"

Take a Break

Remember that anyone can request a break at any time.

After the IEP Meeting

Send a simple note to the student and the parents. Thank them for coming! Let them know that you will be sending a finalized version of the IEP soon (be clear on the date) and open the door for communication. Remind them that if they have any further questions or concerns, they should let you know.

Tips to Remember

1. Partner with parents! Parents are coequal members on the team and should be treated as such.
2. Do not expect anyone to process a lot of information at the meeting; do not share evaluation reports, assessment data, and drafts for the very first time at the meeting.
3. General and special educators are also coequal partners in the process. Although the general education teacher might not lead the meeting, he or she is coequally responsible for the content of the IEP and for carrying it out.
4. Think like a parent! Think about how it might feel to walk into a room of professionals to talk about one of the most important things in your life: your child. Be thoughtful about your communication.

WHAT DOES *DISABILITY* MEAN?

Disability categories are used to "classify and think about the problems developing children may encounter" (Contract Consultants, IAC, 1997, p. 8, as cited in Kluth, 2010, p. 3). Understanding a student's label is only the beginning point in learning about a child. As the quote by Kunc at the beginning of this chapter poignantly reminds us, disability is one type of diversity, "one characteristic or attribute among many that make me who I am" (Giangreco 1996b/2004). A disability label reveals nothing about the student's individual gifts, talents, and strengths. A disability is one of many parts of a student. A disability does not describe who a person is; it describes only one aspect of the person.

To illustrate this point, take a moment to write down five descriptors about yourself. What did you include? Julie might include descriptors about who she is in relation to others, or her profession, or personality traits. The list might include *mother, professor, lover of nature, daughter,* and *outgoing*. Chelsea would include the following: *compassionate, spunky, educator, professor, driven,* and *athlete*. Note that our lists did not include any deficits. We do not use negative descriptors as major identifiers of who we are generally. For example, we do not first think about the fact that, as individuals, we do not balance our checkbooks very well. The same is true for any individual with a disability. That person's area of disability is one (possibly very small) part of who he or she is. As educators, we need to examine our own beliefs and understandings about disabilities. Do we see disability first? Do we think only of deficits? Or do we think of each student's human potential, strengths, and talents?

Table 3.1. Distinguishing features between a 504 plan and an individualized education program

A 504 plan	An individualized education program
Governed under Section 504 of the Rehabilitation Act of 1973. Included within civil rights law to protect and allow full participation of people with disabilities in organizations and schools that receive federal funds.	Governed under the Individuals with Disabilities Education Act (IDEA) of 2004, federal education legislation that guarantees a free and appropriate education for students who are identified with one of the federal disability categories.
To protect a person with a disability from discrimination across his or her life in multiple contexts (e.g., employment, public buildings, education, transportation). A person with a disability is defined as a person who has a physical or mental impairment that limits one or more major life activities (speaking, walking, seeing, learning, working, hearing, or breathing) and has a record of that impairment.	For a student ages 3 to 21 with an identified educational disability, within IDEA disability categories, whose disability adversely affects the student's educational performance or ability to benefit from general education.
Evaluation data is collected from a variety of sources. Professionals can make decisions without parent consent, but parents must be notified.	Evaluated by a multidisciplinary team of educational professionals. Informed and written parent consent needed.
Does not require specialized instruction but instead requires accommodations or educational services to eliminate any barriers to full participation.	Requires specialized instruction and individual accommodations and educational services that allow students access to and benefits from the general curriculum.
No additional federal funding. State and local jurisdictions have responsibility. IDEA federal funds may not be used to support Section 504 services.	State and local educational agencies receive federal funding to support special education and related services.
Does not include a provision to allow independent evaluations at the district's expense.	Parents can request an independent educational evaluation, at the school district's expense, that meets the district's criteria if the parents disagree with the evaluation conducted by the district.
Districts are required to have a grievance procedure for parents who disagree with the least restrictive environment (LRE) placement, identification, evaluation, or implementation of the individualized education program (IEP). A due process hearing is not necessary prior to the U.S. Department Office of Civil Rights being involved. Enforcement is provided by the Office of Civil Rights.	Due process hearings allow parents who disagree with the LRE placement, identification, evaluation, or implementation of the IEP rights. A stay-put provision ensures the current IEP and educational placement continues to be implemented until all disagreements are resolved through the hearing. Enforcement is provided by the U.S. Department of Education, Office of Special Education.
Reporting of student's progress is not required.	Progress reporting is required.

Social Construction of Disability

It is important to recognize that people create disability categories, and that those categories shift and change over time. Medical professionals, teachers, and researchers—along with the federal government—have created these categories, and they are not static; they do change and have changed. An extreme example of how disability is constructed is that, at one point in time, to qualify as having an intellectual disability (ID, or *mental retardation,* as it was initially called in federal legislation), a person needed to have an IQ of 80 or below. In 1973, the federal government lowered the cutoff IQ score to 70 points or below. So, in essence, with the single stroke of a pen, hundreds of thousands of people were "cured" (Blatt, 1987).

Once created, these categories are reinforced. In other words, people see what they look for. Once a student is assigned a label, educators begin seeing through a different lens—the lens of disability. We have seen this process at work numerous times. For example, during a research project conducted in a third-grade classroom, all of the students were busy working and talking as they finished their art projects. The room was bustling and busy. Suddenly, the art teacher shouted, "Jamie, that is the last time!" The teacher walked to the chalkboard and wrote Jamie's name down. Nearly all of the students were talking, yet Jamie, who happens to have a label of emotional disturbance (ED), was noticed for being too talkative or out of line. In reality, Jamie's behavior looked no different from that of many of the other students.

Disability categories are created, and then teams of people determine who qualifies and who does not. Have you ever worked with someone who had a label but you really did not think he or she had a disability? Have you ever seen a student who did not qualify for special education even though you thought he or she might? Disability labels are not hard-and-fast rules that describe people; they are indicators of patterns of difficulty for individuals and are determined by the perceptions of other people. Notably, as educators, we are often the people providing our perceptions of whether or not a student should qualify for having a disability label.

Labels: Proceed with Caution

A disability label may have both positive and negative effects on an individual. On the one hand, many believe labels to be helpful for defining a common language for parents and professionals. This common language allows students access to certain supports and services that they need. In a way, a label is the necessary first step toward certain educational supports and services.

On the other hand, there are real problems with the labeling or categorizing of individuals. Kliewer and Biklen stated that labeling students can be a "demeaning process frequently contributing to stigmatization and leading to social and educational isolation" (1996, p. 83). The use of and overreliance on disability labels poses many problems. Disability labels can lead to stereotyping by causing teachers to see certain students in one, and only one, way. Labeling tends to highlight the differences among people. For example, when a student is assigned a label, teachers, therapists, and paraprofessionals begin to notice the differences between that student and his or her peers. Labels can lead to poor self-esteem as students begin to see themselves differently because of such labels. Also, labels convey the impression of permanence, even though, in some cases, students are only "disabled" when they are in school. Unfortunately, labels give professionals a real sense of security. They allow professionals to believe that "disability categories are static, meaningful, and well understood when in fact they are none of these things" (Kluth, 2010, p. 7).

Throughout this book, we use the language that is most common to the current educational system. We are well aware, however, of the real problems and, at times, dangers of thinking about difference in these ways. Some people use the term *dis/ability* (with a slash) to indicate that all students should focus on their individual abilities. Although we prefer the word *dis/ability*, we are purposefully using the language most common to general and special education so that readers can easily connect this information to other professional knowledge.

The Alphabet Soup of Educational Terminology

Alphabet soup is a metaphor that represents how the use of acronyms in the field of inclusive special education sometimes sounds to parents and those outside the field. The following is an alphabetical listing of many educational terms often referred to by acronyms.

Quiz yourself. Cover up the right side of this list. How many of these acronyms do you know? How many have you heard or used? Which ones should be explained to parents and others when used in IEP meetings?

- AAC: augmentative and alternative communication
- ABA: applied behavior analysis
- ADA: Americans with Disabilities Act
- ADD/ADHD: attention deficit disorder and/or attention-deficit/hyperactivity disorder
- AOTA: American Occupational Therapy Association
- ASD: autism spectrum disorder
- AT: assistive technology
- AYP: adequate yearly progress
- BIP: behavior intervention plan
- CART: communication access realtime translation
- CBI: community-based instruction
- CBM: curriculum-based measurement
- COTA: certified occupational therapy assistant
- CST: child study team
- DS: Down syndrome
- EBD: emotional behavioral disturbance (or disorder)
- ED: emotional disturbance
- ELL: English language learner
- ESL: English as a second language
- ESY: extended school year
- FAPE: free appropriate public education
- FBA: functional behavioral assessment
- FERPA: Family Educational Rights and Privacy Act
- FVA: functional vision assessment
- HI: hearing impaired

- ID: intellectual disability
- IDEA: Individuals with Disabilities Education Improvement Act
- IEP: individualized education program
- IFSP: individualized family service plan
- LD: learning disability
- LRE: least restrictive environment
- MAPS: Making Action Plans
- MTSS: multi-tiered systems of support
- NCLB: No Child Left Behind Act
- ODD: oppositional defiance disorder
- OI: orthopedic impairment
- OHI: other health impairment
- OT: occupational therapist
- PBIS: positive behavioral interventions and supports
- PBS: positive behavior support
- PECS: Picture Exchange Communication System
- PLP: present level of performance
- PT: physical therapist
- RTI: response to intervention
- SDI: specially designed instruction
- SI: sensory integration
- SLD: specific learning disability
- SLP: speech-language pathologist
- TBI: traumatic brain injury
- UDL: universal design for learning
- VI: visual impairment

FEDERALLY RECOGNIZED CATEGORIES OF DISABILITY

How many different categories of disability are you aware of? There are 13 federal categories of disability. Every student who receives special education services has received a formal label representing one of the 13 categories. As educators, you may have learned this information in your preservice training programs, but these categories shift and change over time. Remember that educators should exercise real caution in using these categories of disability or these labels as descriptors for students, but because it is important for educators to understand how students qualify for services, we explain and define the categories of disability in the following subsections.

The 13 current federal categories of disability include the following: 1) autism, 2) deafblindness, 3) deafness, 4) ED, 5) hearing impairment, 6) ID (formerly called *mental retardation*), 7) multiple disabilities, 8) OI, 9) OHI, 10) SLDs, 11) speech and language impairments, 12) TBI, and 13) VI, including blindness. In the following subsections, we include the IDEA 2004 definition for each; however, the most useful way to understand each disability is to listen carefully to the people who have been labeled with the disability in order to understand the disability more fully. Therefore, after each of the definitions, we include voices of people who have been labeled with each of the particular disabilities. These voices are not meant to be complete examples; one person cannot possibly represent the entire population of students who have the same disability. Note the differences between the legal definitions and the definitions that the individuals themselves use. It is interesting that the legal definitions focus on what students cannot do or the difficulties they have, whereas the student voices focus more on the gifts and abilities of each individual.

Autism

Autism is defined by law as a developmental disability that significantly affects verbal and nonverbal communication and social interaction and adversely affects educational performance; autism is generally evident before age 3. Characteristics often associated with autism include engaging in repetitive activities and stereotyped movements, resistance to change in daily routines or the environment, and unusual responses to sensory experiences (IDEA 2004, 34 C.F.R. § 300.8 [c][1][i]).

A person who has autism and lives with it every day offered a quite different definition of the disability:

> Some aspects of autism may be good or bad depending only on how they are perceived. For example, hyperfocusing is a problem if you're hyperfocusing on your feet and miss the traffic light change. On the other hand, hyperfocusing is a great skill for working on intensive projects. This trait is particularly well suited to freelancers and computer work. I would never argue that autism is all good or merely a difference. I do find that my autism is disabling. However, that doesn't mean that it is all bad or that I mean I want to be someone else. (Molton, 2000)

Another individual with autism described it this way: "I believe Autism is a marvelous occurrence of nature, not a tragic example of the human mind gone wrong. In many cases, Autism can also be a kind of genius undiscovered" (O'Neill, 1999, p. 14, as cited in Kluth, 2010, p. 3). A person we encountered expressed it this way: "I strongly believe that living with autism should not be any different from living without autism. All people actually have different strengths, weaknesses, and challenges. Instead of looking at us as a group with identical needs we should be viewed as individuals who have needs in certain areas" (Rubin, 2010).

Deafblindness

Deafblindness is defined by law as "concomitant [simultaneous] hearing and visual impairments, the combination of which causes such severe communication and other developmental and educational needs that they cannot be accommodated in special education programs solely for children with deafness or children with blindness" (IDEA 2004, 34 C.F.R. § 300.8 [c][2]).

In other words, students with deafblindness have both hearing and visual impairments. The population of students with deafblindness constitutes less than 0.0001% of the overall population of students receiving special education services (U.S. Department of Education, 2011). Therefore, most educators probably will not support someone with this disability label. Many people who are deaf and blind learn to use tactile sign, a form of sign language that is felt with the hands.

Helen Keller is one of the most famous examples of a person with deafblindness. She wrote articulately about what it was like to live with this label in her autobiography entitled *The Story of My Life* (1903). One quote from Keller describes how she interacted with the world: "The best and most beautiful things in the world cannot be seen or even touched. They must be felt within the heart" (1903, p. 6).

Deafness

Deafness is legally defined as a "hearing impairment so severe that a child's educational performance is adversely affected; people with deafness have difficulty, with or without amplification, in processing linguistic information" (IDEA 2004, 34 C.F.R. § 300.8 [c][3]). Students who qualify for special education under the category of deafness typically use sign language. These individuals can gain access to the general education curriculum through the use of a sign language interpreter, through oral methods of speech reading, or by reading other people's lips and facial expressions.

A deaf college student identified as Mavis shared her experiences of living as a deaf person:

> It is true. Every weekend, I ride my high quality road racing bicycle at high speeds (sometimes as fast as 40 mph on the flats) with a bunch of men from my bicycle club. I am the only deaf person in that 500 member club. I also enjoy going to the shooting range to fire handguns and socialize. (Mavis, 2007)

Emotional Disturbance

ED is legally defined as the following:

> A condition exhibiting one or more of the following characteristics for a long period of time and to a marked degree that adversely affects a student's educational performance:
>
> a. An inability to learn that cannot be explained by intellectual, sensory, or health factors.
>
> b. An inability to build or maintain satisfactory interpersonal relationships with peers and teachers.
>
> c. Inappropriate types of behavior or feelings under normal circumstances.
>
> d. A general pervasive mood of unhappiness or depression.
>
> e. A tendency to develop physical symptoms or fears associated with personal or school problems. (IDEA 2004, 34 C.F.R. § 300.8 [c][4])

Students with labels of ED make up about 8% of the special education population (U.S. Department of Education, 2011). This category of disability relates to how students behave. For a student to qualify for this category of disability, the student's behavior should look significantly different from that of peers (Taylor, Smiley, & Richards, 2009). Kerri, who has ED, described it this way:

> I misinterpret half of what [people] say to me and translate it to mean they don't want to be my friend anymore. Why should they? I am not worth their time or love or attention. Then I get angry with them and I turn on them. Hurt them before they can hurt me. It is so stupid, and I realize it later, but only after it is too late. (Information on bipolar and other mental health disorders, n.d.)

Hearing Impairment

Being identified as having a hearing impairment means that there is "an impairment in hearing, whether permanent or fluctuating, that adversely affects a child's educational performance but that is not included under the definition of deafness" (IDEA 2004, 34 C.F.R. § 300.8 [c][5]). Students who have hearing impairments generally do not use sign language. Instead, they might use an amplification system. One individual (Sarahjane Thompson) with hearing impairment described her experience:

> The way I tend to explain [hearing impairment] is that it's not necessarily that you can't hear the words that people are using, it's that you hear sounds that resemble words, but you can't quite figure out what the sounds are. Like when a hearing person only just hears something, and asks someone to repeat themselves. Like that. Except for me it's way more frequent. So that's why I tend to use other strategies to figure out what's going on. I lip-read. . . . But lip-reading isn't perfect. A lot of the words look the same and so it's hard for me to use it exclusively to talk to someone. I tend to guess a lot. I'll catch most of a sentence and then sort of try to fill in the gaps myself. Usually it works. Sometimes it doesn't. . . . Every now and then I'll mis-hear an entire sentence and my brain will fill in the random words that sort of fit the syllables and sounds, but together those words do not make sense at all. . . . It's just so normal for me to be hearing impaired. People ask me what it's like to be [hearing impaired] and I just don't have a perfect answer for them. "What's it like to be able to hear?" There's no real comparison and so I don't really know what is different about it. Obviously hearing people can hear more and understand more sounds, but what does that mean? It can be really hard to explain. It's all about perception. (Williams, 2008)

Intellectual Disability

The ID label is legally assigned to students who have "significantly subaverage general intellectual functioning, existing concurrently with impairments in adaptive behavior and manifested during the developmental period, that adversely affects a child's educational performance" (IDEA 2004, 34 C.F.R. § 300.8 [c][6]). The term *mental retardation* is cited in IDEA 2004 but was changed in 2010 under Rosa's Law (PL 111-256) to *intellectual disability*. The definition, however, did not change. Another term commonly used is *cognitive disability*. Students with this disability constitute 8.86% of the population of students receiving special education services (U.S. Department of Education, 2011). People with ID have a wide variety of abilities. Some students have speech and can write, whereas other students do not use speech and are unable to write. Lacking the ability to write or speak, however, does not mean that the person has no ideas or no desire to communicate with others. These students, like all students, deeply desire connections with others and, when given the tools to communicate, engage with other students and with the content.

The following is a first-person account from someone labeled with cognitive disabilities:

> What I would like is for you to understand that my biggest problem is not a neurological dysfunction. It is being misunderstood by people who think my problems are due to poor parenting. My mom has really tried to teach me proper social behaviors, but it just does not click all the time. Sometimes I can't remember the social rules. (FAS Community Resource Center, 2008)

Ollie Webb explained her life with an ID:

> I was often the target of cruel jokes. It was easy to take advantage of me. People called me retarded . . . [but] I worked out there—17 years—and I made salads, sandwiches, and soup, and washed pots

and pans. You name it, I done it out there. . . . One time I came in and the boss said, "I am going to take you off of salads." I said, "Why?" He said, "Cause you can't read." I said, "It make no difference. I can make salads and sandwiches." I said, "It make no damn difference." . . . It came time to leave the sad word retarded [to history]. . . . To say that people should be known by their names [and accomplishments], not by their disabilities, I ain't different from you. I am the same as you. I got a name, and I want you to call me by my name. My name is Ollie Mae Webb. (Schalock & Braddock, 2002, pp. 55–57)

Multiple Disabilities

The term *multiple disabilities* is legally defined as concomitant impairments (e.g., ID and blindness, ID and OI), the combination of which causes such severe educational needs that the student cannot be accommodated in a special educational setting solely for one of the impairments. The term does not include deafblindness (IDEA 2004, 34 C.F.R. § 300.8 [c][7]). Roughly 2% of the population receiving special education services is considered to have multiple disabilities (U.S. Department of Education, 2011). Therefore, it is statistically unlikely that you will work with someone who has this label.

Orthopedic Impairments

OI means a severe physical impairment that adversely affects a student's educational performance. The term includes impairments caused by congenital impairments (e.g., clubfoot, absence of a body part), impairments caused by disease (e.g., poliomyelitis, bone tuberculosis), and impairments from other causes (e.g., cerebral palsy, amputations, fractures or burns that cause contractures; IDEA 2004, 34 C.F.R. § 300.8 [c][8]).

Angela Gabel, a high school student with cerebral palsy who uses a wheelchair, described herself and her experience in school as follows:

When you see me, I think the first thing you would notice is that I'm a pretty positive person. I love to listen to music, go horseback riding, and draw. . . . When I was in elementary school . . . I had friends and liked to play the same games as everyone else, but the teachers were always worried that I was too fragile and would hurt myself. (Gabel, 2006, p. 35)

Other Health Impairment

OHI is legally defined as having limited strength, vitality, or alertness to environmental stimuli, resulting in limited alertness with respect to the educational environment, that

(a) is due to chronic or acute health problems such as asthma, attention deficit disorder or attention deficit hyperactivity disorder, diabetes, epilepsy, a heart condition, hemophilia, lead poisoning, leukemia, nephritis, rheumatic fever, and sickle cell anemia; and (b) adversely affects a child's educational performance. (IDEA 2004, 34 C.F.R. § 300.8 [c][9])

This impairment includes students who have ADHD. The label *ADHD* is assigned to students who have difficulty maintaining attention, knowing when to slow down, or organizing themselves to finish tasks (American Psychiatric Association, 2013). Obviously, not everyone who has each of these disorders qualifies for special education, but if such a condition has been diagnosed by a medical professional and adversely affects a student's educational performance (and if the student needs additional supports), he or she is likely to qualify.

Jonathan Mooney, an author and public speaker with ADHD and dyslexia, explained his disability:

> I have the attention span of a gnat. When I am forced to sit in a desk . . . [my] mind wanders a little bit. I start to bounce my foot. I get called inattentive. What happens the moment I can get up? The moment I can move around? . . . How disabled am I at that moment of time? Not at all. (Mooney, 2008)

Specific Learning Disability

An *SLD* is legally defined as a disorder in one or more of the basic psychological processes involved in understanding or using spoken or written language; it may manifest itself in an imperfect ability to listen, think, speak, read, write, spell, or do mathematical calculations. The term includes such conditions as perceptual disabilities, brain injury, minimal brain dysfunction, dyslexia, dyscalculia, and developmental aphasia. The term does not include learning problems that are primarily the results of visual, hearing, or motor disabilities; of ID; of ED; or of environmental, cultural, or economic disadvantages (IDEA 2004, 34 C.F.R. § 300.8 [c][10]).

Almost half of all students categorized as having disabilities fall under this category. This is the most frequently occurring disability; thus, you are quite likely to work with students who have the label of *SLD*.

In an article about being a student with a learning disability, Caitlin Norah Callahan wrote her advice to others:

> I believe one key idea is to find one's own definition of the dual identity within oneself as a learner and as a student. The learner is the one who makes an effort to be curious, involved and motivated. Not all knowledge is taught in school. It is the student identity that gets labeled as the disabled. The "learning disability" should not be allowed to overwhelm one's desire to attain knowledge. The learner in you must prevent it. (Callahan, 1997)

Speech and Language Impairment

Speech and language impairment is legally defined as a communication disorder such as stuttering, impaired articulation, a language impairment, or a voice impairment that adversely affects a student's educational performance (IDEA 2004, 34 C.F.R. § 300.8 [c][11]).

This is the second most common disability category. Approximately 20% of students who qualify for special education are served under this category (U.S. Department of Education, 2011). Students who qualify for this disability have a wide range of impairment. Some students who receive speech and language services have difficulty with articulation or fluency (e.g., stuttering). Other students might not use speech.

The following is a story from a person who did not have speech in his early years but who later was able to communicate through the use of a communication system. This story illustrates the frustration inherent in not having a reliable method of speech:

I know what it is like to be fed potatoes all my life. After all potatoes are a good basic food for everyday, easy to fix in many different ways. I hate potatoes! But then who knew that but me? I know what it is like to be dressed in reds and blues when my favorite colors are mint greens, lemon yellows, and pinks. I mean really can you imagine [what it is like not to communicate]? Mama found me one night curled up in a ball in my bed crying, doubled over in pain. I couldn't explain to her where or how I hurt. So, after checking me over the best she could, she thought I had a bad stomachache due to constipation. Naturally, a quick cure for that was an enema. It did not help my earache at all! (Paul-Brown & Diggs, 1993, p. 8)

Traumatic Brain Injury

TBI is legally defined as an acquired injury to the brain caused by an external physical force, resulting in total or partial functional disability or psychosocial impairment, or both, that adversely affects a student's educational performance. The term applies to open or closed head injuries resulting in impairments in one or more areas, such as cognition; language; memory; attention; reasoning; abstract thinking; judgment; problem solving; sensory, perceptual, and motor abilities; psychosocial behavior; physical functions; information processing; and speech. The term does not include brain injuries that are congenital, degenerative, or induced by birth trauma (IDEA 2004, 34 C.F.R. § 300.8 [c][12]).

This type of disability differs from the others because it is acquired during the person's lifetime (e.g., car accident or blow to the head). People are not born with this condition—instead, they acquire the disability. The emotional adjustment to acquiring a disability is an issue not only for the student but also for parents or guardians and teachers, therapists, and other members of the educational team.

A teenager who endured a TBI reflected on what she saw as her new life:

The three-month coma that followed and the years of rehabilitation are only a blur to me. I slowly awoke over the next two years becoming aware of my surroundings as well as myself and my inabilities, one being that I could no longer sing as I was left with a severe speech impediment. (Parker, 2008)

Visual Impairment, Including Blindness

VI is legally defined as an impairment in vision that, even with correction, adversely affects a student's educational performance. The term includes both partial sight and blindness (IDEA 2004, 34 C.F.R. § 300.8 [c][13]).

The services received by students under this category of disability differ depending on the severity or type of VI. Some students with VI use magnifiers and larger print texts; students who have no vision receive mobility training (or training on how to walk around their environment), instruction in how to read braille, and instruction in the use of assistive technologies such as screen readers and voice technology. The following is the perspective of Sam, a 12-year-old with VI: "Would I change my vision if I could? No, it makes me who I am, I am awesome! I have more technology, and of course less vision. But, I am proud of who I am and all I have accomplished."

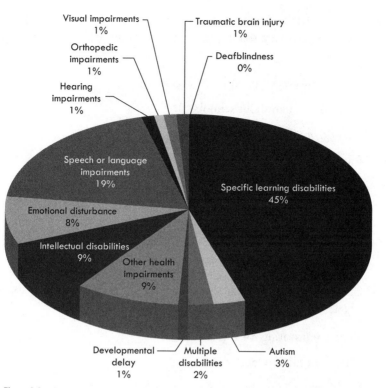

Figure 3.2. Percent distribution of students with disabilities. (*Source:* Data Accountability Center, n.d.)

Distribution of Students with Disabilities in Each Category

How many students qualify for each of the different types of disabilities? The pie graph shown in Figure 3.2 depicts the percentages of students receiving special education services from ages 6 to 21 who fall under each of the categories of disabilities. As Figure 3.2 indicates, the high-incidence (or most common) disabilities are LD, speech and language disabilities, ID, and OHI. The rest of the categories are considered low incidence (or not as common).

Now that you have read through each of the definitions of disabilities, we reiterate the importance of knowing these definitions, but keep in mind that this is only a (very small) step in fully understanding a student. Chapter 4 focuses more on how to think about students in general, with very little focus on individual disabilities.

COMMONLY ASKED QUESTIONS ABOUT SPECIAL EDUCATION

Q. I am a general education teacher, and I do not think that I have enough information about a certain student. How can I get more specific information?

A. Start by reviewing each student's IEP and talking to the student. Then, meet with his or her parents to seek their knowledge and expertise. You can also get to know the student by asking questions about his or her likes, dislikes, interests, and struggles. Here are some questions that would be helpful when getting to know a student:

- What do you want me to know about you?
- What do you like about school?
- What do you not like about school?
- What do you enjoy doing outside of school?
- Would you tell me about your friends?
- How do you prefer to be supported?
- What do you need from me?
- What do you not want me to do?

You can also ask the previous teachers about the strengths and needs of the student. Here are some good questions you could ask:

- What is motivating for this student?
- What does this student enjoy?
- Would you tell me about this student's friends?
- How can we support this student's social needs?
- What are this student's academic needs?
- How can we best support this student's academic needs?
- Does this student have challenging behavior?
- How can we best support this student's behavior?
- Does this student have sensory needs of which I need to be aware?
- Does this student have communication needs that I might need to know?
- What modifications does this student use?
- Does this student use assistive technology?
- What else do I need to know about this student?

Q. I have a student with a disability that I have not heard of before. Where can I get more training about how to effectively work with this student?

A. You should ask. Start with the head of special education in your school. The following elements could be included in an e-mail, phone call, or letter to your school administration:

- Be specific about the type of training you need. For example, you could say, "In my current position, I need to know more about working with students with fragile X syndrome."

- Ask administrators whether they know of any training that is being offered, find a conference to attend that features training about the disability, or ask whether the school could hire someone to come in to work with the school or team.

- Specifically request training on teaching strategies, accommodations and modifications, and differentiation techniques that may support that student.

- Request to brainstorm or problem-solve with the head of special education and other members of the special education team in order to find ways to meaningfully include the student in all social and academic aspects of the school day.

Q. A student in my class has diabetes but does not receive special education services. Why might this be?

A. A student who has diabetes might have an IEP and an educational label of OHI only if it "adversely affects a child's educational performance" (IDEA 2004, 34 C.F.R. § 300.8 [c][9]). If the medical issue is managed properly outside of school, does not cause weakness or fatigue, and does not affect the student's learning and performance, that student would not need an IEP. However, a Section 504 plan of the Rehabilitation Act of 1973 and under the Americans with Disabilities Act (ADA) of 1990 (PL 101-336) is for a student with a disability who requires accommodations or adaptations to participate in school activities but does not qualify for special education or related services under IDEA 2004. If a cognitive or physical disability is evident and a major life activity (e.g., seeing, hearing, walking, breathing) is affected, a student may qualify for supports and services under Section 504. If the health condition requires services that affect the student's learning, an IEP would be required.

Q. I have a student with Down syndrome in my class. Our district is moving toward inclusive services across the content areas, and I teach sixth-grade English language arts (ELA). How am I supposed to teach a middle-school class with a student who has a second-grade reading level?

A. Instead of designing curriculum units that focus on one text at a time or use selections from one textbook series, develop lessons around specific genre themes. Then, find texts at differentiated readability levels. This allows all students to discuss and learn characteristics of that genre using a variety of text types. Consult Chapter 6, Providing Academic Supports, for many other ideas.

CONCLUSION

Understanding disability is critical to understanding the larger systems of special education and related service provision. Nonetheless, the only way to truly understand certain individual students is to get to know people who have experience with those disabilities. In addition, developing an authentic relationship with the individual is the best way to understand that person's strengths, interests, talents, and needs. Reading the definitions of the 13 federal categories of disability is simply one step to understanding the students you teach.

Having covered some of the basics of special education, we commence the joyful work of helping you to learn about individual students and helping to best educate them. Chapter 4 focuses on presuming competence, getting to know students, and rethinking students with disabilities through a strength-based lens.

4

Rethinking Students

Presuming Competence

THE MOST APPROPRIATE LABEL IS
USUALLY THE ONE PEOPLE'S PARENTS
HAVE GIVEN THEM.

"In my experience as a general education teacher, I have always had students included with mild disabilities, but not until this year have I had a student who uses a communication device to engage in conversation and content. This is all new to me. My first realization was that this student is very capable. I hadn't thought of him as smart when I saw him in the hallways last year. My first step is learning just how smart he is and tapping into his intelligences."

—Lena (general education teacher)

"I often see my role as helping other teachers see the strengths of the students on my caseload. Sometimes I feel like I am selling something by asking if a student could be included. [laughing] . . . Joe is great, he likes video games and is really funny. Include him in science . . . Please?!"

—Kathie (special education teacher)

"When I approach a child, [s]he inspires in me two sentiments: tenderness for what [s]he is, and respect for what [s]he may become."

—Louis Pasteur (Institut Pasteur, n.d.)

This chapter introduces the concept of rethinking students. Rethinking a student entails getting to know the student and then reflecting on how you see, treat, educate, and support him or her. First, we discuss how to describe students to others through student strengths and multiple intelligences. Then, we describe the concept of presumption of competence and using age-appropriate and person-first language.

STUDENT DESCRIPTIONS

Shawntell Strully is a 22-year-old who lives in her own home with roommates, attends classes at Colorado State University, volunteers on campus, travels during spring break, gets around in her own car, has her own interests, likes and desires, has a boyfriend, and speaks out on issues of concern to her.

Shawntell Strully is 22 years old, is severely/profoundly mentally retarded, is hearing impaired, visually impaired, has cerebral palsy, has a seizure disorder, does not chew her food (and sometimes chokes), is not toilet trained, has no verbal communication, has no reliable communication system, and has a developmental age of 17–24 months.

(Strully & Strully, 1996, pp. 144–145)

These two radically different descriptions of Shawntell come from two different groups of people. The first description comes from her parents. The second comes from her teachers. Although not all educational professionals would describe Shawntell in these ways, this is how her team described her. It is surprising to compare these statements side by side. The stark contrast raises the question of how the same person can be described in such disparate ways.

The principal reason for these radically different descriptions is that each group of people looks for different things and approaches Shawntell from a different perspective. Shawntell's parents know her deeply. They have spent a great deal of time with her, know her intimately, and understand her as a person who has wide interests and capabilities. Their description of her cites her interests, gifts, and talents. Conversely, the description generated by Shawntell's teachers reflects a more distant understanding of her; it is a cold, clinical account that focuses exclusively on her impairments.

As an educator working with students with disabilities, you will often hear and may have even written impairment-driven descriptions of students. You may be an educator who already sees students through the lens of gifts. Either way, it is often helpful to do the mental work to understand all students through their strengths, gifts, and talents. You may read a student's IEP, and it might abound with terms such as *mental age of 2, phobic,* or *aggressive*. Reading those descriptors, you will need to realize that you are getting only one perspective on the student. Get to know the student yourself, develop an authentic relationship, and work to learn about what he or she can do. Ideally, your descriptions of a student would look much closer to the parents' perspective on Shawntell than that of the teachers. Develop a Positive Student Profile (see Figure 4.1) that provides a person-centered, strengths-based, and in-depth understanding of the individual.

"I like LEGOs. I like Minecraft. I like Star Wars. I like them to do [lessons] in a fun way, not just teach it. Partner us up more often. I like when [teachers] pick our partners and we don't pick because we get to know more people. I want teachers to learn about me!"

—Aliyah (middle school student)

"I'm not a series of deficits to be remediated."

—Jamie (Syracuse University student who has autism)

BEGIN WITH STRENGTHS

We were working with a team of educators, and we asked them to describe Micah, a student who has a disability and is educated in an inclusive setting. They shared their descriptors of Micah as engaging, stubborn, easily frustrated, a gifted singer, and having cerebral palsy. These descriptions speak to the team's *beliefs* about the student. Think of a student in your life. On a piece of paper, write down the first 10 descriptors that come to mind when you think of that student. Now, look over the list. Were your descriptors positive, negative, or a combination?

Your beliefs about a student will affect how you educate, support, and work with that student. For example, if you believe a student is lazy or defiant, you will approach him or her in a different way than you will if you believe that student is motivated or cooperative. You can alter your beliefs about students by spending some time rethinking them. Reframing your conceptions of students in more positive ways creates opportunities for student growth as well as growth in your relationship.

Consider the work of educational researcher Thomas Armstrong (2000a, 2000b) on using multiple intelligences theory in the classroom. Armstrong recommended

Positive Student Profile

Strengths, likes, intelligences

_____

Dislikes

_____

Communication

_____

Behavior

_____

Academic performance

_____

Subject-specific performance

_____

Social information

_____

Concerns

_____

Other pertinent information

_____

Figure 4.1.   Positive Student Profile.

The Educator's Handbook for Inclusive School Practices by Julie Causton and Chelsea P. Tracy-Bronson.
Copyright © 2015 by Paul H. Brookes Publishing Co., Inc. All rights reserved.

that education professionals purposefully rethink the ways they describe students. By changing their language, people will begin to change their impressions. Armstrong emphasized that all behavior is part of the human experience and that behavior is based on a multitude of influences (e.g., environment, sense of safety, personal well-being). Armstrong has proposed that, instead of considering a student learning disabled, people should see the student as *learning differently*. Table 4.1 lists further suggestions for describing students.

What would happen if all educators changed how they viewed and spoke about students? What if every student was viewed as a capable learner? One of the best ways to think about the students you support is to look through the lens of his or her strengths. Ask yourself the following questions: "What can this student do?" "What are this person's talents?" "What are this person's strengths?" "How would a parent who deeply loves this student speak about him or her?" Now, return to your list and take a moment to develop a list of strengths, gifts, and interests.

During a professional development day with general educators, special educators, therapists, and paraprofessionals, Suzie, a general educator, did just that. First, she wrote a list of descriptors. Then, after spending some time rethinking the student, she came up with a completely different list. She had originally described the student, Brian, as "lazy, smart, sneaky, a liar, cute, cunning, and mean (at times)." After talking about viewing students differently, she took out a new piece of paper. She wrote, "relaxed, intelligent, good in math, cute, needs some support with peer relationships, a great sense of humor, and a beautiful smile." We asked Suzie whether this still accurately described Brian. She said that the second list was a much more accurate description of him, and the first list was more about her frustration. More important, the second list helps Suzie think about how to educate Brian more successfully.

Table 4.1. Turning lead into gold

A child who is judged to be	Can also be considered
Learning disabled	Learning differently
Hyperactive	Kinesthetic
Impulsive	Spontaneous
ADD/ADHD[a]	A bodily kinesthetic learner
Dyslexic	A spatial learner
Aggressive	Assertive
Plodding	Thorough
Lazy	Relaxed
Immature	Late blooming
Phobic	Cautious
Scattered	Divergent
Daydreaming	Imaginative
Irritable	Sensitive
Perseverative	Persistent

From *In Their Own Way: Discovering and Encouraging Your Child's Multiple Intelligences, Revised and Updated Edition* by Thomas Armstrong, Copyright © 1987, 2000 by Thomas Armstrong. Used by permission of Tarcher, an imprint of Penguin Publishing Group, a division of Penguin Random House LLC.

[a]*Key:* ADD, attention deficit disorder; ADHD, attention deficit-hyperactivity disorder.

"I would like for future and practicing special education teachers to know that I expect, and need, for them as professionals to take genuine interest in understanding the needs of the students they are teaching and 'learning from' everyday. It isn't enough to have a good grasp on pedagogy . . . it is vitally important to see the whole child and therefore acknowledge their struggles as a person as well as a student."

—Twila (parent of a student with disabilities who is educated in an inclusive classroom)

MULTIPLE INTELLIGENCES

There is a pervasive myth in education that some people are smart and others are not. *Intelligence, functioning level, academic potential,* and *competence* are words often used to describe "smartness." In education, this belief can best be seen through the system of labeling people with disabilities. A clear example is IQ testing. Students take IQ tests, and if a student's IQ score falls below 70 and he or she has other issues with functional skills, the student receives the label of *intellectual disability.* Howard Gardner (1993) challenged the way psychologists and educators defined intelligences and offered a different way to look at intelligence. He used the term *multiple intelligences.*

Gardner viewed each of the multiple intelligences as a capacity that is inherent in the human brain and that is developed and expressed in social and cultural contexts. Instead of viewing intelligence as a fixed number on an aptitude test, Gardner argued that every person, regardless of disability label, is smart in different ways. All of the eight intelligences are described in Table 4.2. We have also added a column entitled "So teach using," which might help you to think of your students and how to best reach and teach them. If you work with a student who prefers to learn in a certain intelligence area or who is strong in a certain area, consider some of the suggested activities and teaching styles.

PRESUME COMPETENCE

In the school setting, assumptions about students can affect their education. Take Sue Rubin, for instance.

Sue, a student with autism, had no formal way of communicating until she was 13 years old. Before that time, her IEP read that she had the mental age of a 2-year-old. Mental age is often based on a person's score on an IQ test. For example, if a 14-year-old girl's score on an IQ test was the score of a "typical" or "normal" 3-year-old, she would be labeled as having the mental age of a 3-year-old. This is not a useful way to think about intelligence, as it is often not an accurate depiction of a student's skills or abilities. When Sue acquired a form of communication called *facilitated communication,* those long-held assumptions were no longer valid. People began to realize that she was very smart. She subsequently took advanced placement classes all through her high school career, and she graduated from college in 2013 (Biklen, 2005; Rubin, 2003; Rubin, 2014).

Table 4.2. A guide to teaching through multiple intelligences

Intelligence	Which means	So teach using
Verbal/linguistic intelligence	Good with words and language, written and spoken	Jokes, speeches, readings, stories, essays, the Internet, book making, biographies, writing, debates, e-mail, newsletters, poems
Logical mathematical intelligence	Preference for reasoning, numbers, and patterns	Mazes, puzzles, time lines, analogies, formulas, calculations, codes, games, probabilities, problem solving, measuring, logic games, spreadsheets
Visual spatial intelligence	Ability to visualize an object or to create mental images or pictures	Mosaics, drawings, illustrations, models, maps, videos, posters, graphics, photography, puzzles, visualization, using organizers, analogies
Bodily kinesthetic intelligence	Knowledge or wisdom of the body and movement	Role playing, skits, facial expressions, experiments, field trips, sports, games, activities, moving, cooperative groups, dancing
Musical intelligence	Ability to recognize tonal patterns, including sensitivity to rhythms or beats	Performances, songs, instruments, rhythms, compositions, melodies, raps, jingles, choral readings, humming, background music, singing, memorization songs
Interpersonal intelligence	Good with person-to-person interactions and relationships	Group projects, group tasks, dialogues, conversation, debate, games, interviews
Intrapersonal intelligence	Knowledge of an inner state of being; reflective and aware	Journals, meditation, self-assessment, recording, creative expression, goal setting, affirmation, poetry
Naturalistic intelligence	Knowledge of the outside world (e.g., plants, animals, weather patterns)	Field trips, observation, nature walks, forecasting, star gazing, fishing, exploring, categorizing, collecting, identifying, reading outside, cloud watching, using a microscope, dissecting

Sources: Armstrong (2000a, 2000b); Gardner (1993).

Because education professionals may not be able to accurately determine what a student understands, they should presume that every student is competent or capable. Donnellan used the term *least dangerous assumption* to describe this idea: "Least dangerous assumption states that in the absence of absolute evidence, it is essential to make the assumption that, if proven to be false, would be least dangerous to the individual" (1984, p. 24). In other words, it is better to presume that students are competent and that they can learn than to expect that they cannot learn.

Biklen and Burke (2006) have described this idea of presuming competence by explaining that outside observers (e.g., therapists, teachers, parents, paraprofessionals) have a choice: They can determine that a person is either competent or incompetent. The presumption of competence recognizes that no one can definitively know another person's thinking unless the other person can (accurately) reveal it. As Biklen and Burke put it, "Presuming competence refuses to limit opportunity . . . it casts the teachers, parents, and others in the role of finding ways to support the person to demonstrate his or her agency" (2006, p. 167). See Figure 4.2 for a listing of strategies for presuming competence. In addition, because students without language offer educators unique challenges, we have included Figure 4.3, which provides ideas about how to support students who do not speak verbally.

AGE-APPROPRIATE LANGUAGE

There is a tendency for people to speak down to individuals with disabilities (as if they were younger than they actually are) because of an assumption that people with disabilities are at younger developmental levels. For example, we have heard someone ask a high school student, "Do you have to use the potty?" You would not ask a high school student who did not have a disability that same question in that same way. We have also overheard someone describe a young man with Down syndrome who attends college as "a real cutie." Individuals with disabilities should be described in accordance with their actual chronological ages.

In addition to age-appropriate language, educators should also work with students in age-appropriate ways. A team of teachers were problem solving about a ninth-grade student who enjoyed *Dora the Explorer* and wanted to reference the characters throughout the English class. To address this issue, the educators ran a "lunch bunch" with other ninth-grade girls during which they discussed age-appropriate music, movies, and television. This exposure to age-appropriate popular culture helped the student to shift interest away from Dora and toward more appropriate topics.

- Examine your attitude—practice saying, "How can this work?" or "How can this child be successful?"
- Question your stereotypes—how someone looks, walks, or talks does not tell you about how he or she thinks and feels.
- Use age-appropriate talk—examine your tone of voice and topic.
- Support communication.
- Listen openly—work to shed judgments.
- Teach peers and others how to interpret potentially confusing behavior.
- Do not speak in front of someone as if he or she were not there.
- In conversation, refer to the person in a way that includes him or her in the conversation.
- Ask permission to share information with others.
- Be humble.
- If possible, always let the person explain for himself or herself and do not speak for him or her.
- Assume that every student will benefit from learning age-appropriate academic curriculum.
- Look for evidence of understanding.
- Support students to show understanding using their strengths.
- Design adaptations and accommodations to support access to academics.
- Be sure to acknowledge the presence of a person with a disability in the same way you would acknowledge others.
- "If you want to see competence, it helps if you look for it."

Figure 4.2.   Strategies for presuming competence. (From Kasa-Hendrickson, C., & Buswell, W. [2007]. *Strategies for presuming competence.* Unpublished handout; adapted by permission.)

"Not being able to speak is not the same thing as not having anything to say."

—*Rosemary Crossley*

A note on communication: All students who struggle with communication deserve to have a generative communication system in place so that they can express thoughts, feelings, ideas, critiques, and requests. This may include the use of sign language, an augmentative communication device, strategies to teach a person to type or point to communicate, and/or the use of eye gaze or blinking to indicate choices. While it is the right of all students to have a communication system, many students go without any way to share their thoughts.

The strategies below are useful in supporting a student who has an effective communication system or a student who does not have a system in place. If a student does not have a system in place, it is imperative that the team consults with a speech-language pathologist who is skilled in implementing augmentative communication systems that would meet the need of the individual child.

Keep Respect and Humanness First

- Never talk about someone as if he or she were not there. Always acknowledge the person's presence and make sure that communication in the child's presence is respectful.

- Some people may not be able to communicate that they understand what you are saying or that they are listening; assume they are listening and understand what you are talking about.

- Question your stereotypes—how someone looks, walks, or talks does not tell you about how they think and feel.

- If a student uses a wheelchair, stutters, flaps hands, or does not make eye contact, this does not mean that he or she cannot learn high-level academics, does not desire to make friends, and does not want the chance to voice independence. Work to open up opportunities.

- In conversation, refer to the person in a way that includes him or her in the conversation. For example, when Ms. Mayfield began to read the book *Splish Splash* to the class, she said, "Maya, you are going to love this book—it is all about swimming." Maya is a student who does not speak to communicate. When Ms. Mayfield shared in front of the class that Maya will enjoy this book, she taught that Maya has interests and ideas that are similar to those of her peers. In doing this, Maya did not have to respond or say anything, but her active participation and competence were made clear by her teacher's public acknowledgement.

- Ask permission to share information with others. Too often students with disabilities do not have any privacy. Be sure not to share information on using the restroom, sexuality, health, family, embarrassing situations, and/or relationships. Ask first, and err on the side of privacy always.

Embrace a Strength-Based Attitude

- Embrace an optimistic attitude. Practice saying, "How can this work?", "How can this child be successful?"

- Work with family members to identify the student's strengths and design methods to include the student in the general education classroom using those strengths.

- Teach students to identify and use their own strengths.

- When the going gets tough, write down a list of the student's strengths and strategies to help you spring into action and begin to problem-solve (see http://www.paulakluth.com/readings/inclusive-schooling/strengths-and-strategies/).

Please Act My Age: Age-Appropriate Talk and Materials

- Talk in an age-appropriate manner, using age-appropriate content. A singsong voice or a tone typically used with a young child should be reserved for babies and toddlers; be sure to check your tone of voice and the content you are talking about.

- Be sure as a teacher to acknowledge the presence of a person with a disability in the same way you would acknowledge other students.

- Let students make mistakes, get in trouble, and act out. Be sure they have the opportunity to talk and play with peers without adult interaction.

(continued)

Figure 4.3. Guidelines for supporting the active participation of nonverbal students in school. (From Kasa, C., & Causton-Theoharis, J. [n.d.]. *Strategies for success: Creating inclusive classrooms that work* [pp. 16–17]. Pittsburgh, PA: The PEAL Center; reprinted by permission. Retrieved from http://wsm.ezsitedesigner.com/share/scrapbook/47/472535/PEAL-S4Success_20pg_web_version.pdf)

Figure 4.3. *(continued)*

Learning to Talk to Someone Who Does Not Speak

- While teaching, be sure to acknowledge the nonverbal student's presence often. You should not go an entire lesson without saying, "Sean, I bet you'll like this part. I know you like to ski with your family," or "Megan, I see you smiling. I am sure you will like learning about volcanoes."
- Take every opportunity to teach peers how to talk to people who communicate differently. Talk about current events, age-appropriate interests, things you like to do, places to go, events around school; also, use their communication strategy to enable them to make lots of choices throughout the day: food to eat, materials to use, where to sit, what to read, what to play. Ask their opinion on various topics.

Use Communication Methods Efficiently and Often

- If a student uses a yes/no communication strategy, be sure to use this during a lesson. You can do this during a whole-group lesson by saying, "Do you all think that 5 times 5 equals 25?" Or do this in an individual way: "Was Harry a hero in the story?" This will allow the student to use his or her yes/no strategy and be included in the lesson. If he or she answers incorrectly, then you can say, "Oh, I don't think that is quite right. Does anyone have other ideas?"
- If the student uses an augmentative communication system, you need to be sure to have them utilize it throughout the lesson. Make sure the device is ready to go with content related to the lesson so that the student can participate.

Teach Peers to Support and Understand Confusing Behavior

- Use partners during lesson activities. Model and encourage peers to talk about topics with each other. This can be done in cooperative learning groups or with peer activities such as think, pair, and share or turn and talk (see Udvari-Solner & Kluth, 2008).
- Be sure to include the student in the academic curriculum in the classroom. Assume learning is possible and ask content-related questions.
- Teach peers and others how to interpret potentially confusing behavior and support each other.

Assume Benefit from Academic Learning and Look for Understanding

- Assume that every student will benefit from learning age-appropriate academic curriculum.
- Look for evidence of understanding. This will occur in unique instances and times.
- Support students to show understanding using their strengths.
- Design adaptations and accommodations to support access to academics.

PERSON-FIRST LANGUAGE

"If thoughts corrupt language, language can also corrupt thought."

—George Orwell (1981)

When describing, speaking, or writing respectfully about people who have disabilities, many people use a common language. It is called *person-first language*. The concept of person-first language is simple and is detailed in the following subsections.

The Same as Anyone Else

Think first about how you might introduce someone who does not have a disability. You might use the person's name, say how you know him or her, or describe what he or she does. The same is true for individuals with disabilities. Instead of saying, "Pat, who has Down syndrome," you might say, "Pat, who is in my fourth-grade class." No one should be identified solely by one aspect of who he or she is, especially if that aspect represents a difficulty or struggle. Ask yourself why you would need to mention that the person has a disability.

Words are powerful. The ways we talk about and describe people with disabilities do not just affect our beliefs and interactions with our students; they also provide models for others who hear these descriptions.

If your own child broke his arm, would you introduce him to someone new as "my broken-armed child"? If one of the students in the school had cancer, would you expect to hear a teacher state, "She is my cancerous student"? The short response is, "Of course not!" No one should feel ashamed about having a broken arm or having cancer, but regardless, a broken bone or malfunctioning cells do not define a person.

Avoid the Label

Would you like to be known for your medical history? Probably not. The same is true for people with disabilities. Yet, students with disabilities are invariably described with labels or with staffing patterns instead of person-first language. Have you ever heard phrases such as *the learning-disabled student, the autistic boy, that Downs child, the resource room kids,* or *the inclusion kids?*

It is important to understand the preferences of people with disabilities regarding how they would like others to speak about them. The guidelines listed in Table 4.3 come from two self-advocacy groups (Disability Is Natural and TASH).

"His teacher is just one of those who wants to continue learning and changing and doing stuff and is just flexible and adaptable and everything you'd want . . . she just helps Mark soar. Mark does things I don't even—you know I wouldn't even expect him to be able to do. She somehow motivates him and he feels confident enough to do it."

—Mary (parent of a student with Down syndrome)

COMMONLY ASKED QUESTIONS ABOUT RETHINKING STUDENTS

Q. What if a student prefers an age-inappropriate toy or game?

A. Often, people with disabilities have been treated as if they were younger than they are. As a result, they have been exposed to cartoons, dolls, or games to which their same-age peers have not been exposed; their peers are not likely to think these activities are interesting. One option, then, is to expose the student to more age-appropriate music and activities.

Table 4.3. Examples of person-first language

Say	Instead of	Because
People with disabilities	The disabled or handicapped	Place emphasis on the person.
People without disabilities	Normal/healthy/typical	The nonpreferred terms assume the opposite for students with disabilities (i.e., abnormal, unhealthy, atypical).
Ella, the fourth-grade student	Ella, the student with Down syndrome	Omit the label whenever possible; it is most often not relevant.
Communicates with her eyes/ device, and so forth	Is nonverbal	Focus on strengths.
Uses a wheelchair	Is confined to a wheelchair	Use possessive language to refer to assistive technologies; the nonpreferred language implies the person is "stuck."
Accessible parking spot	Handicapped parking spot	Accurate representation
Beth has autism.	Beth is autistic.	Emphasize that disability is one attribute— not a defining characteristic.
Gail has a learning disability.	Gail is learning disabled.	Emphasize that disability is one attribute— not a defining characteristic.
Jeff has a cognitive disability.	Jeff is retarded.	Emphasize that disability is one attribute— not a defining characteristic; also, *cognitive disability* is a preferred term.
Ben receives special education services.	Ben is in special education.	Special education is a service, not a place.
The student who is blind	The blind student	Place the person before the disability.
Denis writes using the computer.	Denis cannot write with a pencil.	Focus on strengths.
Needs a magnifier, laptop, or cane	Problems with vision; cannot write or walk	Focus on needs, not problems.

Source: Snow (2008).

Q. I believe all of my students are brilliant, but what do I do for a student who really is not reading at grade level yet?

A. In Chapter 6, we discuss and provide many ideas about how to support a student who is not yet reading at grade level.

Q. Are there any exceptions to person-first language?

A. Yes. People who are deaf often prefer the term *deaf* instead of *person with deafness*. A group called Deaf First suggests that deafness is a major component of identity, and this group prefers disability-first language. Some people with autism prefer to be called *autistic,* and some use insider language such as *autie* to describe themselves. It is inaccurate to say that all people with disabilities prefer one way over another. Person-first language serves as a helpful guideline because many advocacy groups consider it a respectful way to refer to people.

Q. What should I do if a colleague I work with is not using person-first language?

A. There are number of strategies you could utilize in order to shift the language that is used within the school. The first is to model person-first language. Upon hearing you use person-first statements, colleagues might alter their language to place the emphasis on the person and his or her strengths. Second, use Table 4.1 to show people you work with the examples of person-first language and have a discussion about the reasons you advocate for using person-first language.

Q. I honestly do not know how this student is smart. This student has a label of intellectual disabilities. How can I presume competence?

A. This person may not perform well on standardized tests of intelligence. However, your responsibility when working with this student is to identify the student's strengths. Keep those strengths in mind. Every person is intelligent in different ways; this will help you learn how to reach and teach this student.

CONCLUSION

Remember, disability labels are not accurate descriptors of people. Students who have disabilities are unique individuals with unlimited potential, just like everyone else (Snow, 2008). This recognition is not only about having a good attitude or believing that all students are smart; it also will allow you to provide the most effective education and work with all students in ways that promote dignity and respect. The Credo for Support poignantly reveals the importance of rethinking students (see Figure 4.4). In Chapter 5, we discuss how educational professionals will fit into a collaborative team that will work together as they presume competence to educate all students.

Throughout history people with physical and mental disabilities have been abandoned at birth, banished from society, used as court jesters, drowned and burned during The Inquisition, gassed in Nazi Germany, and still continue to be segregated, institutionalized, tortured in the name of behavior management, abused, raped, euthanized, and murdered.

Now, for the first time, people with disabilities are taking their rightful place as fully contributing citizens.

The danger is that we will respond with remediation and benevolence rather than equity and respect.

And so, we offer you

A Credo for Support

Do not see my disability as the problem.
Recognize that my disability is an attribute.

Do not see my disability as a deficit.
It is you who see me as deviant and helpless.

Do not try to fix me because I am not broken.
Support me. I can make my contribution to the community in my own way.

Do not see me as your client.
I am your fellow citizen.

See me as your neighbour.
Remember, none of us can be self-sufficient.

Do not try to modify my behavior.
Be still and listen. What you define as inappropriate may be my attempt to communicate with you
    in the only way I can.

Do not try to change me, you have no right.
Help me learn what I want to know.

Do not hide your uncertainty behind "professional" distance.
Be a person who listens and does not take my struggle away from me by trying to make it all better.

Do not use theories and strategies on me.
Be with me.
And when we struggle with each other, let that give rise to self-reflection.

Do not try to control me. I have a right to my power as a person.
What you call non-compliance or manipulation may actually be the only way I can exert some
    control over my life.

Do not teach me to be obedient, submissive and polite.
I need to feel entitled to say No if I am to protect myself.

Do not be charitable towards me.
The last thing the world needs is another Jerry Lewis.
Be my ally against those who try to exploit me for their own gratification.

Figure 4.4. A credo for support. (From Kunc, N., & Van der Klift, E. [1996]. *A credo for support*. Vancouver, Canada: The Broadreach Centre; reprinted by permission.)

Do not try to be my friend. I deserve more than that.
Get to know me, we may become friends.

Do not help me, even if it does make you feel good.
Ask me if I need your help.
Let me show you how you can best assist me.

Do not admire me.
A desire to live a full life does not warrant adoration.
Respect me, for respect presumes equity.

Listen, support, and follow.

Do not work on me.
Work with me!

5

Collaborating with Others

Working within a Team

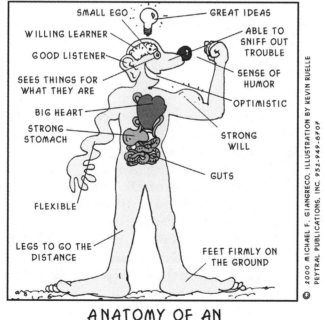

© 2000 MICHAEL F. GIANGRECO, ILLUSTRATION BY KEVIN RUELLE
PEYTRAL PUBLICATIONS, INC. 952-949-8707

SMALL EGO

GREAT IDEAS

WILLING LEARNER

ABLE TO SNIFF OUT TROUBLE

GOOD LISTENER

SEES THINGS FOR WHAT THEY ARE

SENSE OF HUMOR

OPTIMISTIC

BIG HEART

STRONG STOMACH

STRONG WILL

GUTS

FLEXIBLE

LEGS TO GO THE DISTANCE

FEET FIRMLY ON THE GROUND

ANATOMY OF AN EFFECTIVE TEAM MEMBER

*"I used to see it as my space. Now, I see the classroom as ours. My entire thought pro-
cess has changed not only about the physical classroom environment, but also my thinking about students, designing curriculum from the onset to include all learners, options
available to engage students in the learning process, and just everything . . . my ideas
have improved drastically. When we all come together to think creatively and purposefully
about students and what happens in the classroom . . . it's like magic . . . we are unlimited
in our ideas and what we make happen in the classroom!"*

—Kelly (general education teacher)

*"There was a change. All of a sudden, [the general education teacher] realized that I was
value-added. Now, in eighth-grade social studies, he did not have to teach using a lecture
format. He brought his expertise on the social studies content and Common Core State
Standards. I contributed thoughts on universal design for learning, supplemental aids and
services, and ways to facilitate authentic learning for a student who uses a communication
device so this student could have full membership within the general education classroom."*

—Diane (special education teacher)

*"We were just so lucky—[the school professionals] just seemed very vested. . . . They were
very willing. Anything I brought in to discuss they would take a look at it, and I mean that
was the attitude . . . it was openness to learn. It was just huge."*

—Sheree (parent of a student with disabilities who is educated in an inclusive classroom)

*"We've each been invited to this present moment by design. Our lives are joined together
like the tiles of a mosaic; none of us contributes the whole of the picture, but each of us is
necessary for its completion."*

—Casey and Vanceburg (1996, p. 138)

All students in a classroom community can benefit from a team of professionals working together, which includes educators, related service providers, and paraprofessionals
working together in ways that promote meaningful learning and a sense of belonging
for all students. This collaboration between professionals on educating students with disabilities is a fundamental aspect of the federal IDEA 2004 legislation (§ 614 [d][1][B];
§ 636 [a][1]; § 652 [b][1]; § 653 [b]; § 654 [a][1][C]). In an inclusive classroom, the
professionals are like tiles of a mosaic. Each person is an important contributor to
the larger picture. In today's inclusive classrooms, it is quite common for educators to
work alongside other educators, therapists, and paraprofessionals.

This chapter provides information and tools that will enable educators to engage
in effective collaboration. To achieve this, the available resources are maximized to
ensure all students' participation, content learning, and meeting of IEP goals. In some
cases, however, teachers, therapists, and paraprofessionals work in isolation during the
planning or teaching stages. This type of structure creates many common problems.
Special educators, who may have unclear roles in the classroom, can feel devalued or
perceived as glorified teaching assistants when they provide push-in special education

services that are not meaningfully planned. A similar feeling can result for related service providers. Purposeful planning is needed to make the best use of each professional's expertise and to align curriculum standards, learning strategies, and teaching strategies to meet students' IEP goals.

This chapter is designed to help you to see your role as a member of the larger educational team and to address the roles and responsibilities of each team member. We propose general ways to communicate with the whole teaching team, outline co-teaching structures, and provide strategies for handling conflict. Finally, we address commonly asked questions about collaboration.

"I ask those that teach, is it your ideal to provide what you love to teach to all who desire to learn? If so, basic steps are to presume every person able and anxious to learn, and then to strengthen the supportive systems they need to do so and to always communicate and to collaborate to vitally feel the sense of success and freedom that being a true teacher can bring."

—Jamie (Syracuse University student who has autism)

ROLES AND RESPONSIBILITIES

Roles and responsibilities of school professionals vary among schools, districts, and even states. Nonetheless, despite these variations, there are generally accepted roles and responsibilities that hold true from school to school. The next subsections provide some general guidelines for how school personnel can work effectively as a team to meet the needs of all students together.

Special Educators

A special educator is largely responsible for designing each student's IEP. Each year, a team of teachers, related service providers, the student, and the student's parents determines each student's goals and objectives, as well as the appropriate special education services. The special education teacher helps to ensure that the goals and objectives on each student's IEP are met. In collaboration with general education teachers, therapists, and other support staff, the special education teacher is responsible for helping to differentiate curricula and instruction and also for providing and recommending modifications and adaptations that would be appropriate for each student. Special education teachers are also responsible for solving problems that arise in the classroom, evaluating each student's services, and communicating student progress to the team.

General Educators

A general educator is expected to educate the students in his or her class. A general educator plans lessons, teaches those lessons, and assesses each student's skills. A general educator is responsible not only for each student with an IEP but also for all of the students who do not have disabilities. Typically, a general educator is considered the content expert for the particular grade level and subject(s) being taught.

The Family

"Be open to the beauty of parent knowledge, vision and undying motivation for their child to be included. Help parents learn to advocate without angry fighting. Assist parents in understanding the beauty of their teachers and schools and to be able to hear the viewpoint of school confines and restriction. React to problems not with no's and can't, but with creativity! It's a process and a long-term relationship."

　　—Kim (parent of a student with disabilities who is educated in an inclusive classroom)

"I can handle the truth and I'm pretty good at finding solutions to hiccups in the program! I'm the most important person on this team, if you're not honest we will never fully serve this child. Once that trust is lost it will be the hardest thing to repair."

　　—Sue (parent of a student with disabilities who is educated in an inclusive classroom)

"Explain your plans ahead of time. Keep your promises. Share your thought process and give reasons for your decisions. Be patient. Treat us like partners, not pests."

　　—Mary (parent of a student with disabilities who is educated in an inclusive classroom)

Family members are undoubtedly the most important people in a child's life. With IDEA 2004, parents or guardians became equal members of students' IEP teams. Parents or guardians are expected to be active members of their children's education teams because they know their children better than anyone else. Therapists, teachers, and paraprofessionals can help parents play active roles by communicating all that happens in the school setting and, further, by listening closely to the wishes and concerns of family members.

Physical Therapists

Physical therapy is a related service and is provided by a qualified and licensed PT. PTs address areas such as gross motor development skills, orthopedic concerns, mobility, adaptive equipment, positioning needs, physical access to the school environment, and other functional skills that may interfere with students' educational performance. A PT either works with individual students or leads small groups. PTs also consult with teachers, other therapists, and paraprofessionals. Examples of therapies include practice walking up and down stairs safely, body stretching for students who use a wheelchair, supporting access to school environments, or help performing other physical activities.

Physical Therapy Assistants

Some PTs have assistants who are responsible for carrying out therapy plans, supporting students in classrooms and the school environment, keeping track of data for the IEP goals, and supporting self-care needs. These assistants work under the direction of certified PTs.

Speech-Language Pathologists

SLPs help students with communication and with all of the skills required to communicate effectively. These skills include all issues related to language, the voice, articulation, swallowing, and fluency. Some students who work with SLPs have issues with stuttering. Others work on understanding and producing language. In schools, SLPs collaborate with teaching teams to support participation in classroom activities and effective communication.

Occupational Therapists

For a student who works with an OT, the student's disability necessitates support in daily life skills or functioning within the school. The therapist may evaluate the student's needs, provide therapy, modify classroom equipment, restructure environmental conditions, and generally help the student participate as fully as possible in school experiences and activities. A therapist may work with students individually or lead small groups. Therapists also may consult with teachers and paraprofessionals to help students meet their goals within the context of general education settings. Specific therapy strategies may include help with handwriting or computer work, fostering social play, and teaching life skills such as getting dressed or eating with utensils.

Occupational Therapy Assistants

Some OTs have assistants who are responsible for carrying out therapy plans, supporting students in classrooms and the school environment, keeping track of data for the IEP goals, and supporting self-care needs. These assistants work under the direction of certified OTs.

School Psychologists

The goal of school psychologists is to "help children and youth succeed academically, socially, behaviorally, and emotionally" (National Association of School Psychologists, n.d.). School psychologists work closely with teaching teams to build positive learning environments and to support connections between each student's home and school. Psychologists assess students and are often involved in standardized testing to determine whether a student qualifies as having a disability. Psychologists also work directly with others on teaching teams by helping to problem-solve and, at times, provide direct support services to students.

School Social Workers

Like psychologists, school social workers help provide links connecting each student's home, school, and community. The services provided by social workers are intended to help enable students and families to overcome problems that may impede learning. School social workers provide individual and group counseling, consult with teachers, and teach or encourage social skills. They collaborate with community agencies and provide service coordination for students who require many different agencies or services.

Vision Teachers

Vision teachers support students who have VI or are blind. Vision teachers typically work with classroom teachers to make modifications and adaptations to the curricula. They also help provide needed equipment (e.g., magnifiers and computer equipment) and needed materials (e.g., worksheets in braille).

Audiologists

Audiologists typically work with students who have hearing impairments, providing amplification systems and sign language interpreters for students who are deaf.

Paraprofessionals

Paraprofessionals are expected to perform many different tasks. Supporting students academically, socially, and behaviorally in the school community is essential. Paraprofessionals review and reinforce instruction under the direction of special education teachers or general education teachers. They might lead a station lesson, read aloud, or team-teach with other educators.

Students

Students themselves are crucial members of the team. It is essential to ask the student how he or she would like to be supported, what activities suit his or her learning style, how you can help make friend connections, and how the student wants you to intervene during challenging situations. You may also ask classmates and friends for their help in brainstorming creative ideas to support specific students.

HOW DO ALL THESE PEOPLE WORK TOGETHER?

"Coming together is a beginning; Keeping together is progress; Working together is success."

—Edward Everett Hale

Every school differs, but one thing is certain: All the adults on a teaching team must work together for the purpose of promoting student growth. One example of effective collaboration involves a seventh-grade team.

• • • • • • •

This team involves all of the staff members who support Adam, a student with autism, VI, and sensory needs. The core team of people supporting Adam in English class includes the general education teacher, the special education teacher, the vision teacher, the OT, and a paraprofessional. This team meets monthly to discuss Adam's support in English class. Every week, the vision teacher and the English teacher meet with the paraprofessional to create enlarged materials for upcoming units of study. In addition, the special education teacher and the English teacher plan lessons together with Adam in mind so that each lesson is designed to meet his needs. For example, they planned a unit using a book from the Harry Potter series. In addition to having the paraprofessional enlarge the text in the packet of information, the special education teacher suggested having the entire class listen to an audio version of the book instead of reading silently. The educator and OT collaboratively set up a box of sensory tools with fidgets, pencil grips, a choice of writing utensils, an AlphaSmart keyboard, and gum. The OT joins the monthly meeting to problem-solve sensory-related issues in English class. Over the course of each meeting, the team sets plans outlining the anticipated type and level of support that Adam needs during each activity.

• • • • • • •

Your team can fill out the grid in the reproducible form in Figure 5.1 to help determine the roles and responsibilities of all colleagues. Many teams have found it useful to determine who has primary, secondary, and shared responsibilities for each of the necessary tasks in inclusive classrooms. Then together, answer the questions provided in the following subsection to help the team make decisions about whether any roles should be changed or shared.

Guiding Questions for Teams to Discuss

Getting to know your teammates on a personal level is necessary for real and true collaboration to occur. Some questions that will help you as you sit down with other educators, therapists, or paraprofessionals are listed in this section. You may consider this list as some simple suggestions, or you may decide to go through each question with your team.

Work Styles

- Are you a morning or afternoon person?
- How direct are you?
- Do you like to do several things at once, or do you prefer doing one thing at a time?
- How do you prefer to give feedback to others on the team?
- What do you consider your strengths and weaknesses when working in a team situation?

Philosophy

- The goal of inclusive education should be . . .
- To me, *normalcy* means . . .
- To me, *advanced planning* means . . .

Determining Roles and Responsibilities Among Team Members

Directions: Read through the following common roles and responsibilities. Determine which team member should take on each of the roles and responsibilities:

P = Primary responsibility   **S** = Secondary responsibility

Sh = Shared responsibility   **I** = Input in the decision making

Major role or responsibility	General education teacher	Special education teacher	Related service provider	Paraprofessional
Developing student objectives				
Designing differentiated curriculum				
Creating student-specific modifications and adaptations				
Creating classroom materials				
Co-teaching curriculum				
Providing one-to-one instruction				
Teaching the whole class of students				
Leading small groups				
Monitoring student progress				
Examining student work to determine next steps				
Assessing and assigning grades				
Communicating with parents				
Consulting with related service personnel				
Participating in individualized education program meetings				

Figure 5.1.   Determining Roles and Responsibilities Among Team Members.   (continued

Adapted from Causton-Theoharis, J. (2003). *Increasing interactions between students with disabilities and their peers via paraprofessional training* (Unpublished doctoral dissertation). University of Wisconsin, Madison.

In *The Educator's Handbook for Inclusive School Practices*
by Julie Causton and Chelsea P. Tracy-Bronson (2015, Paul H. Brookes Publishing Co., Inc.)

Figure 5.1. *(continued)* (page 2 of 2)

Major role or responsibility	General education teacher	Special education teacher	Related service provider	Paraprofessional
Disciplining students				
Writing in communication notebooks				
Providing community-based programming				
Developing peer supports				
Scheduling common planning time				
Participating in regularly scheduled team planning meetings				
Facilitating meetings				
Communicating information from meetings to other team members				
Other				

When you have finished determining roles and responsibilities for each of the team members, ask yourselves the following questions:

1. Could any of these roles and responsibilities be shared or changed?

2. Does anyone feel uncomfortable with any of the roles as outlined?

3. Does anyone believe he or she needs more information or training to perform the above-mentioned responsibilities?

4. What messages are sent to students, parents, and others about the way adults work together as a team in this classroom through the division of responsibilities?

5. What changes need to be made?

Adapted from Causton-Theoharis, J. (2003). *Increasing interactions between students with disabilities and their peers via paraprofessional training* (Unpublished doctoral dissertation). University of Wisconsin, Madison.

In *The Educator's Handbook for Inclusive School Practices*
by Julie Causton and Chelsea P. Tracy-Bronson (2015, Paul H. Brookes Publishing Co., Inc.)

- All students learn best when . . .
- In general, I think the best way to deal with challenging behavior is . . .
- In general, I think it is important to increase student independence by . . .
- I think our team relationship needs to be . . .

Logistics

- How should we communicate about students' history and progress?
- How should we communicate about our roles and responsibilities?
- How and when should we communicate about lessons and modifications?
- If I do not know an answer in class, should I direct the student to you?
- Do we meet often enough? If not, how often should we meet?
- How do we communicate with the families? What is each person's role in this?
- Are there other logistical concerns?

Questions for the Family

- How would you like to communicate about your child's progress?
- If we are using a communication notebook or e-mail, how often would you like to hear from the school?
- Are there things you are especially interested in hearing about?
- How would you like to see your child supported?
- What are your hopes and dreams for your child?
- What are your child's strengths and successes?
- Is there other information that would be helpful for the team to know?

Questions for the Student

- What are your greatest strengths?
- How do you learn best?
- What are your favorite activities in school? What about outside of school?
- How should we support you during a challenging moment?
- What are areas in which you would like to improve?
- How can we support your connections with friends and classmates?
- How often would you like to check in about your progress?
- How would you like to communicate with teachers about progress (e.g., meetings, e-mails, notebook)?

After having personal discussions using these questions as a guide, teams are better able to negotiate the logistical and philosophical components of teamwork, allowing team members to feel more comfortable in knowing the roles and expectations within the classroom setting. The next section describes some co-teaching arrangements that should give further clarity to the collaborative work of educational professionals in the classroom.

CO-TEACHING ARRANGEMENTS

Co-teaching involves two or more educational professionals sharing the instructional responsibility for a group of students within a single classroom setting. Educators can include a general education teacher, a special education teacher, therapists or other specialists, bilingual teachers, content area specialists (e.g., reading specialists, math intervention teachers), and paraprofessionals who work together to deliver special education services—including designing curriculum, implementing instruction, and assessing learning—for students with disabilities within the general education context. Co-teaching structures can be utilized with anyone who has instructional roles within the school community. Table 5.1 shows some types of co-teaching you might provide in different situations, as suggested by Murawski and Dieker (2004).

The logistics and strategies involved in two adults sharing space in the classroom have been most extensively researched in terms of co-teaching. The following subsections explain various co-teaching arrangements.

Parallel Teaching

A heterogeneous class is split into two groups, providing a smaller teacher-to-student ratio. Teachers have the same objectives and divide the class and teach simultaneously. The process of learning could also be different. If one teacher is particularly skilled at visual spatial content delivery, the lesson utilizes pictures, while the other teacher emphasizes learning through hands-on learning experiences. This approach might be

Table 5.1. Ideas for purposefully including other educational professionals as co-instructors

If you are doing this	A co-instructor can be doing this
Lecturing	Providing visual notes simultaneously to allow students to see what they are listening to; creating graphic organizers that allow students to remember key words and phrases; providing sentence starters
Giving directions	Writing the directions on the board so all students have a place to look for the visual cues; providing to-do lists or individual agendas for students with reminders or cues for positioning
Providing large-group instruction	Collecting data, problem solving, improving environmental factors (e.g., lighting), or making modifications for an upcoming lesson
Giving a test	Reading the test to students who prefer to have the test read to them; before the test, making sure student is well positioned, lighting is right, and test is modified to support the student's learning strengths (e.g., enlarged font or one problem per page)
Facilitating stations or small groups	Also facilitating stations or groups
Teaching a new concept	Providing visuals or models to enhance the whole group's understanding; creating a multisensory approach to the content to increase the learning for all
Reteaching or preteaching with a small group	Monitoring the large group as the students work independently; thinking about body positioning and learning environment for all students

Source: Murawski and Dieker (2004).

used for teaching nonfiction text features using two different science topics (e.g., electricity and life cycles).

Station Teaching

A heterogeneous class is split into three groups. Teachers co-plan the stations. Two stations are educator facilitated while one station allows students to work independently, in pairs, or as a cooperative group. Students rotate to each of the stations, while each educator is the lead instructor at one station. Each teacher teaches the content to one group, then repeats the instruction for the other groups. Having co-planned and co-taught stations in the classroom allows students with disabilities to continue having access to general education curriculum and work on IEP goals while being educated in the LRE alongside peers. It is important that students are often grouped heterogeneously and rotate to each educator.

Team Teaching

Educators share leadership in the instruction and classroom activities. One teacher might read a story aloud while the other teacher contributes in a complementary manner, such as creating a corresponding concept map. One teacher might lead a social studies lesson while the other teacher might demonstrate note-taking skills. In a workshop model, one teacher might conduct the 10-minute minilesson, then both teachers would circulate and conference while students are working, and then the other teacher would lead the culminating sharing or instructional points at the end of the session. Both teachers have an interdependent role with the large-group instruction.

One Teach, One Observe

One teacher leads the lesson while the other gathers data on student performance. For example, while one teacher leads a geography lesson, the other teacher records observations in the form of anecdotal notes and a checklist on students' learning and misconceptions. Educators might collect data on students' participation during group discussions, independent work, decoding skills, and other aspects. They also could collect information on the students' skills and abilities as well as environmental supports and barriers to students' participation and independence. A teacher might observe the effectiveness of specific assistive technology implemented, note the lack of external supports or technology, observe or adjust positioning and seating arrangements, and note opportunities for movement breaks or other types of supports. It is imperative that teachers rotate these roles so that each is able to lead instruction and observe class learning experiences.

Alternative Teaching

One teacher works with most of the class while the other provides instruction for a small group. This small group could be used for preteaching core concepts in order to provide background knowledge for the upcoming lesson or unit. It could also be used to provide enrichment experiences for students who have mastered the grade-level content objectives. This approach should be used cautiously so that it does not become a remediation group in the back of the classroom. This option must be used along with the other co-teaching options and only used occasionally.

One Teach, One Assist

One teacher leads the lesson while the other provides unobtrusive, individualized instruction and assistance to specific students. This assisting teacher may answer questions, keep students on task, and provide prompt support to students who need it. That teacher could help students choose which type of writing paper or tools fits their needs. He or she also could write or draw examples on the chalkboard. Having one educator take visual notes that include diagrams, pictures, and labels while the educator is teaching is a useful strategy. Educators must switch roles and both take the lead in instruction so that one adult is not always merely assisting. Again, this option should be used sparingly and along with other co-teaching options.

COMMUNICATE THAT YOU ARE CO-TEACHERS

In addition to co-teaching structures and arrangements, educators often think about the collaborative message sent to students and families. Table 5.2 provides strategies that successful co-teachers have used to communicate their joint venture in educating all learners. Use these ideas to evaluate your co-teaching and brainstorm additional strategies to create an effective co-teaching arrangement with your colleagues.

SHARING CRITICAL INFORMATION

It is important that all people working with a student have a basic knowledge of the student's IEP. We have found that information sharing can get tricky across bigger teams. One tool that has helped teams to communicate about the student's IEP is the IEP at a Glance (Figure 5.2). This reproducible form can be filled out and shared with substitute teachers or special area teachers. It is essentially a one-page summary of the IEP with important information such as goals and objectives and other essential information listed.

The Therapy Plan at a Glance is useful for related service providers to communicate the priority skills for a supported student, as well as the useful materials and verbal prompts used to help each student practice the skill within the context of an inclusive classroom. One OT we know fills out a Therapy Plan at a Glance based on the IEP for every student she is assigned, photocopies them, and dispenses them to all educational team members, special area teachers, and substitutes who work with the student. See Figure 5.3 for an Occupational Therapy Plan at a Glance example, Figure 5.4 for a Speech and Language Therapy Plan at a Glance example, and Figure 5.5 for a Physical Therapy Plan at a Glance example.

Table 5.2. Strategies that rocking co-teachers think about

Rocking co-teachers . . .

Say it proud. They make sure both names are on the door and classroom web site.

Communicate collectively. They refer to the classroom as both of theirs and talk about their shared space and joint teaching duties with students, families, and colleagues.

Switch it up. They rotate co-teaching arrangements, and *often*. They switch on and off, leading lessons and supporting. They rotate who begins lessons. They work with all students. They do not work with the same small group of students daily. They switch groups.

Let the office know that any announcements should be addressed to both of the teachers, using both of their names. The message of joint teaching and of inclusive co-teachers is infused throughout the school.

Ensure that newsletters, letters, and notes are sent jointly, signed by both teachers.

Schedule conferences for times that both can be available. They understand the importance of demonstrating that a team of educators is working with individual students.

Take turns leading the class to the next activity with transitions. They both walk students to schoolwide events or to other classes.

Share any teacher space, including the classroom, desks, or tables. They both have access to all classroom supplies and both are invested in the organization of the classroom.

Check the language they use unknowingly. They use the phrases *our classroom, we created,* and *ours* instead of *my classroom, my class,* and *that is mine.* There is a sense of shared ownership, responsibility, and accountability. They are truly a team and communicate this through the language used in conversations, conferences, and in their daily teaching.

Make sure the behind-the-scenes work is done together. Everyone does all the tasks. Tasks are split up to maintain equity. Both teachers plan, design, and work on lesson plans. They work together to universally design lesson plans from the beginning. They both create accommodations, modifications, and differentiate the content, process, and materials.

Rotate and share in implementing assessments and conferencing with students. Assessment data are easy to talk about because both educators teach, work with, and assess each learner.

Collaborate to the fullest extent.

Problem-solve, critically reflect, and make changes to their classroom on an ongoing basis as a way to continually improve their skills, meet students' needs, and provide the best inclusive education they can create for their students!

Teams often use the Program Planning Matrix in order to determine where the IEP goals can be seamlessly integrated throughout the school day. This helps teams brainstorm ways to creatively integrate IEP goals into the general education context with a specific focus on meeting individualized goals and objectives. See Figure 5.6 for a reproducible Program Planning Matrix that you can use.

INCLUDING THE FAMILY

Collaborating with families and including and implementing their ideas when planning for their child's education is just as important as working with other professionals. Research has found that family involvement and engagement are critical factors in creating and maintaining strategies for supporting higher achievement for students

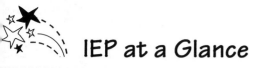

IEP at a Glance

Student: _____ Grade: _____ Age: _____

Date completed: _____

Goal: _____	Goal: _____
Objectives:	Objectives:
•	•
•	•
•	•
•	•
•	•
•	•
•	•
•	•
•	•
Goal: _____	**Goal:** _____
Objectives:	Objectives:
•	•
•	•
•	•
•	•
•	•
•	•
•	•
•	•

Figure 5.2.   Individualized Education Program (IEP) at a Glance.

(continued)

From Causton-Theoharis, J. (2009). *The paraprofessional's handbook for effective support in inclusive classrooms* (p. 35). Baltimore, MD: Paul H. Brookes Publishing Co., Inc.; adapted by permission.

In *The Educator's Handbook for Inclusive School Practices*
by Julie Causton and Chelsea P. Tracy-Bronson (2015, Paul H. Brookes Publishing Co., Inc.)

Figure 5.2. *(continued)*

(page 2 of 2)

Goal: _____	Important student information
Objectives: • • • • • • • • •	• • • • • • • • •

From Causton-Theoharis, J. (2009). *The paraprofessional's handbook for effective support in inclusive classrooms* (p. 35). Baltimore, MD: Paul H. Brookes Publishing Co., Inc.; adapted by permission.

In *The Educator's Handbook for Inclusive School Practices*
by Julie Causton and Chelsea P. Tracy-Bronson (2015, Paul H. Brookes Publishing Co., Inc.)

Dear Educational Team,

_____ is working on the following occupational therapy skills (see the left-hand side). It would be beneficial to provide her/him with as many opportunities as possible to engage in these activities (see the right-hand side).

Skills	Activities
Fine motor skills	Drawing, writing, typing, zipping, pinching, grasping, opening packages
Tripod grasp	Painting, writing, tracing, coloring
Bilateral coordination (using two hands doing the same or different things)	Cutting, clapping, writing (while stabilizing paper), jumping, catching and throwing, stepping stones

I use the following materials and prompts to help support these skills within your classroom. Let's try to reinforce these new skills throughout the day.

Skills	Materials with activity	Prompts
Tripod grasp	The writing claw The grip sharp	"Three fingers do the work." "Your pinky and ring finger can take a rest."
Bilateral coordination	Using a ruler during math Tying shoe laces Jumping	"Use one hand to write, one hand to support." "Make sure both hands are dancing." "Make sure you alternate your feet on the stepping stones."

Additional tips and tricks:

Make pencil grips available for all students in the class during writing. I will drop off extras for you to use.

We are also working on bilateral hand use. Two ways you could support this development during the day are having students 1) use a Slinky as a fidget during read-aloud and 2) use the whip-around strategy to review content. Encourage students to use the Slinky by shifting their hands just enough to get the Slinky to move back and forth. To use the whip-around strategy, students toss the ball to classmates as each reviews one important content concept. This allows students to practice moving their hands to throw and catch.

Please contact me. I am always available for problem solving.

Sue Endwell

Phone number
E-mail

Figure 5.3. Occupational Therapy Plan at a Glance example.

Dear Educational Team,

<u>Chloe</u> is working on the following speech and language therapy skills (see the left-hand side). It would be beneficial to provide her/him with as many opportunities with these activities as possible (see the right-hand side).

Skills	Activities
Swallowing	Drinking, sucking on a straw, chewing gum, small snack eating (i.e., Cheerios)
Producing the /l/ sound	Songs, chants, rhymes with the repeated /l/ sound
Voice volume	Walk-and-talks, presenting to peers, partner work, opportunities to socialize

I use the following materials and prompts to help support these skills within your classroom. Let's try to reinforce these new skills throughout the day.

Skill	Materials with activity	Prompts
Swallowing	Feeding aids (adapted spoon) Modified cup	Present her with the modified cup and spoon when needed.
Producing the /l/ sound	Picture support with the ABC chart	"Tongue on top teeth." "Open your mouth."
Voice volume (for student who whispers when talking)	Megaphone Audio recorder	"Can they hear you in the back of the room?" "Can you hear yourself?" "Volume level 5."

Additional tips and tricks:

I will drop off the audio recorders. Chloe likes to play it back when she reads. This could be a center for all during practice for Readers Theater. I will also drop off the feeding aids (cup and spoon).

For the /l/ sound production, please provide as many practice trials during the day that naturally occur. She becomes embarrassed if it seems like someone is correcting her speech, so just provide opportunities for practice, and help with data collection (on the sheets provided). Also, be sure to clearly model /l/ sound production during phonics instruction. It is most helpful if these skills are seamlessly built in and not made obvious to her or to her peers.

Please allow Chloe to have water throughout the day, as this helps with both swallowing and drooling. Additionally, she needs permission to chew gum during the day. I have a story that explains gum chewing to the students; I am happy to come and read it if you would like. This helps students understand Chloe's swallowing and drooling issues and helps students know how to best support her. I asked Chloe and her parents, and she would like the book read to her classmates.

Please contact me. I am always available for problem solving.

Mia Black

Phone number
E-mail

Figure 5.4. Speech and Language Therapy Plan at a Glance example.

Dear Educational Team,

Lilly is working on the following physical therapy skills (see the left-hand side of the table below). It would be beneficial to provide her/him with as many opportunities with these activities as possible (see the right-hand side).

Skills	Activities
Strength and endurance	Standing, passing out materials, sitting without additional trunk support for extended periods of time
Gross motor	Whole-body learning activities; throwing and catching
Positioning wheelchair in the environment	Navigating between desks and other classroom furniture, circulating between tables, navigating crowded school hallways with friends

I use the following materials and prompts to help support these skills within your classroom. Let's try to reinforce these new skills throughout the day.

Skill	Materials with activity	Prompts
Strength and endurance	Sitting in chair for teamwork Timer	"Let's work hard for 15 minutes, then you can choose a break with a friend." "Turn on your core muscles." "Let us know if you feel shaky."
Gross motor	Koosh ball whip around	"After you answer the question, toss the Koosh ball across the circle."
Positioning wheelchair in the environment and advocating for self	Independently moving to another group Independently moving throughout the school building	"Do you have enough room to move?" "Who can you ask to move that?"

Additional tips and tricks:

Encourage Lilly to navigate through the school hallways and her classroom as independently as possible. With her new electric wheelchair, she often bumps into furniture. Our goal is to encourage independence with her mobility and advocacy skills if something needs to be moved.

Throughout the day, please add in gross motor movement activities with the classroom learning. It will help strengthen Lilly's muscles. It also supports her to be alert and active.

Please contact me. I am always available for problem solving.

Ella Decker

Phone number
E-mail

Figure 5.5. Physical Therapy Plan at a Glance example.

Program Planning Matrix

Student: _____ Teachers: _____ Date: _____

Individualized education program goals (in a few words)	Class schedule								

Key: X, instruction provided; O, classroom participation plans with general adaptations required; S, specific adaptations to class activities and materials may be needed; TA, task analytic instructional plan.

Figure 5.6. Program Planning Matrix.

From Janney, R., & Snell, M.E. (2013). *Modifying schoolwork* (3rd ed., p. 190). Baltimore, MD: Paul H. Brookes Publishing Co.; adapted by permission.

In *The Educator's Handbook for Inclusive School Practices*
by Julie Causton and Chelsea P. Tracy-Bronson (2015, Paul H. Brookes Publishing Co., Inc.)

with disabilities (Bouffard & Weiss, 2008; Epstein, 2001; Pushor & Murphy, 2004). Often, however, collaboration with the family is the first to be shelved due to the many pressures and time constraints of an educator's busy day. Although we know you cannot conjure up a 25th hour for your day, there are many ways that teams can more effectively include families in the collaboration process.

Consistent Communication

Families should have the ability to advocate for their child and have ongoing access to information about their child's education. This means educators should regularly share information about the child and fully include families in team discussions and meetings. This consistent sharing of information can take many forms, including phone calls, e-mails, a Google Document or DropBox folder that all team members have access to, or even an educator–family notebook that can be carried from school to home each day by the student. Whatever form this communication takes, it is important that families and team members have the opportunity to engage in daily or weekly discussion about a variety of information about the student, such as progress on IEP goals, homework and assignments, strategies or ideas to try (e.g., "Ian mastered VoiceThread last night, so maybe he could incorporate that into his oral history project next week."), trigger warnings or a "heads-up" (e.g., "Danny woke up late this morning, so he's feeling a bit frustrated."), and notes related to praise and concern (e.g., "Kate rocked the science experiment!").

See the Whole Child

Families of students with disabilities have often experienced interactions with school teams that are negative (Beratan, 2006; Engel, 1993; Ferguson & Ferguson, 2006) or reflect the dominant narratives of disability as something to be "fixed" within their child (Fried & Sarason, 2002; Sauer & Kasa, 2012). In order to most effectively collaborate with parents, then, it is important that educators help to shift this negative paradigm and begin to focus on seeing the whole child and not just the disability, challenges, or perceived deficits. This means that, when discussing educational plans and support strategies with families, educators should focus on the student's strengths and abilities and always come to the table with ideas and solutions for challenges. When educators are positive and solution oriented, families can see that the team is focused on accommodating and supporting their child. This allows for more effective brainstorming about what might work in (and out) of the classroom and helps educators and families collaborate together to develop creative and engaging ways to increase the student's learning in the general education classroom.

Build Trusting Relationships

Families are the ones who know their child best, so taking the time to build trusting relationships with them is an important factor in the success of a collaborative school-to-home relationship. Educators who approach families with a positive attitude and who are willing to learn from and with the family to meet the needs of the child are often the most successful. As an educator, this means you should make the effort to value and respect the voices of the family and provide frequent opportunities for families to feel that they are truly part of the team. Some educators we know use the following suggestions to help build trusting relationships with families:

- Ask families for information about their children.
- Ask about accommodations and adaptations they may make for their child at home or in the community.
- Ask about any supports the family may need at home and put them in touch with helpful resources.
- Provide families with ample opportunity to make choices about their child's education.
- Provide family training and education workshops at the school.
- Invite families into the classroom for whole-class debates, performances, unit culmination presentations, gallery walks, and other special activities.
- Attend a community event or activity the family is involved in.
- Hold an IEP meeting or informal parent–teacher meeting in a neighborhood coffee shop or diner.

WHAT IF CONFLICT ARISES AMONG TEAM MEMBERS?

Ideal team functioning is like a well-oiled machine in which each cog runs continually and smoothly, each harmoniously performing an individual function for the good of the entire machine. However, team functioning does not always feel this smooth. Conflicts among adults do arise.

The Bonner Foundation, a nonprofit education organization, has suggested eight steps for conflict resolution. *Conflict* is defined as "a mental or physical disagreement in which people's values or needs are in opposition to each other or they think that they are opposed" (Bonner Foundation, 2008). The Bonner Foundation's suggestions for handling conflicts are listed here, along with our related suggestions:

1. "Identify positions ('what are they saying') of each side of the people in conflict." Write down your perspective and the other person's perspective.
2. "Learn more about true needs and desires behind each side." Write down your beliefs about the other person's needs and desires. Write down your own needs and desires.
3. "Ask clarifying questions for more information." Ask the other person, "Why do you feel the way you do?" "What do you think you need in this situation?" Reframe the problem into a question.
4. "Brainstorm possible solutions." Without judging the ideas, write down as many ideas as you can.
5. "Discuss how each solution would affect each side, and figure out possible compromises." Talk through each of the potential solutions. Discuss which ones

would work and which ones would not work, from your perspective and from the other person's perspective. Generate more ideas, if necessary.

6. "Agree on a solution." Determine which solution would work the best for both of you. Write out a plan for carrying out the solution and determine how long you plan to implement the solution.

7. "Implement solutions." Give your idea a try for the determined amount of time.

8. "Reevaluate solutions, if necessary." Come back together to discuss the solution and what is working or not working about this solution. Continue the process as necessary.

MAKING THE TIME TO COMMUNICATE

One of the most common problems educators mention involves not having enough time to communicate or collaborate with the other professionals with whom they work. When special educators are collaborating in inclusive environments, they should be observing, discussing, and problem-solving with the general education teachers, related service providers, and paraprofessionals to find the most practical strategies to support a student's participation.

However, even when educators can find the time to collaborate, they often find that the meetings are not efficient or well-planned. Many teams utilize team meeting minutes (see Figure 5.7 for a reproducible form) as a way to make meetings more effective. For teams that struggle to find meeting times, different school teams have solved this problem by using strategies described in the following list. Examine each strategy and see whether it will help your team to communicate more regularly and more effectively. The following strategies have been successfully used to carve out more meeting time:

- *Video or independent work time*—Create a weekly meeting time during which students are expected to watch instructional videos or to work independently for 15 minutes. Allow them to watch or work independently while the team meets.

- *Use a parent volunteer*—As a parent volunteer reads a book to the students or leads a review game, meet together for 15 minutes.

- *Use another teacher team*—Put two classrooms together for a half hour each week for a certain portion of the curriculum or community-building activities. One teaching team supervises the students while the other team meets. The teams then switch.

- *Meet during specials time*—Ask the specials teachers whether their schedule has an extra 15 minutes during any one day. Use that time to meet together.

- *Use a paraprofessional*—Figure out when a paraprofessional from another team is not being utilized and ask him or her to read aloud or monitor independent student work for 15 minutes.

- *Meet before or after school*—Take 15 minutes before or after school to have a "sacred" meeting time for teaching teams.

Team Meeting Minutes

Date: _____

Team members present and assigned roles: _____   Team members absent: _____

Facilitator: _____

Recorder: _____

Timekeeper: _____

Consensus builder: _____

Observer: _____

Today's agenda items	I – Information D – Discussion R – Requires decision	Presenter	Time guidelines
1.			
2.			
3.			
4.			
5.			
6.			

Items discussed:

Figure 5.7. Team Meeting Minutes form.

(continue

From Causton, J., & Theoharis, G. (2014). *The principal's handbook for leading inclusive schools* (pp. 70–71). Baltimore, MD: Paul H. Brookes Publishing Co., Inc.; reprinted by permission.

In *The Educator's Handbook for Inclusive School Practices* by Julie Causton and Chelsea P. Tracy-Bronson (2015, Paul H. Brookes Publishing Co., Inc.)

Figure 5.7. *(continued)* (page 2 of 2)

Task delegated, time lines, follow-up:

Activity	Person responsible	Time line

Agenda items for next meeting:

.

.

.

.

.

.

Next meeting date: _____

From Causton, J., & Theoharis, G. (2014). *The principal's handbook for leading inclusive schools* (pp. 70–71). Baltimore, MD: Paul H. Brookes Publishing Co., Inc.; reprinted by permission.

In *The Educator's Handbook for Inclusive School Practices*
by Julie Causton and Chelsea P. Tracy-Bronson (2015, Paul H. Brookes Publishing Co., Inc.)

- *Schedule a "mystery reader"*—Each week, invite a community member to read aloud to the class for 30 minutes. Use these 30 minutes for planning.

If you simply cannot use any of these strategies to elicit more face-to-face meeting times, some teams have come up with alternatives to meeting face-to-face:

- *Communication notebook*—Establish a notebook that all members of the team read and respond to each day. Team members can write questions in the notebook and obtain responses. Notebooks also can be used to discuss schedules or student-specific information.
- *E-mail*—E-mail can be substituted for the communication notebook; team members can contact each other with questions, comments, or schedule changes.
- *Mailbox*—Use a mailbox in the classroom for each staff member. Direct all notes or general information to that place.
- *Proofread*—As notes are written that go home to the students' parents, have the teaching team proofread each of the notes. This way, not only are the notes proofread, but everyone receives all of the necessary information.
- *Lesson-plan sharing*—Keep lesson plans out and accessible to all members of the team. Use the notes to communicate about upcoming content. Ask the person who writes the plans to delineate each team member's role for each lesson. The educational team might also keep lesson plans electronically on a shared space for ease of collaboration.

COMMONLY ASKED QUESTIONS ABOUT COLLABORATION

Q. I am not sure what I am supposed to be doing when I provide push-in services. We (the other educator and I) have never co-designed or collaborated to plan lessons, so mostly I just sit and support two students who receive specialized instruction as part of their IEP. What should I do?

A. Set up a time to meet with the other teacher. Ask questions such as, "How can we both have useful roles during science while meeting Zack's and Priscilla's IEP goals?" "When you are giving whole-class instructions, how can I support you?" "How can you integrate Zack's IEP goals during the rest of the day?" These conversations that merge academic learning experiences with specially designed instruction are crucial in ensuring that IEP goals are generalized throughout the day.

Q. I have read about common co-teaching arrangements, but we do not use any of them at my school; instead, I just sit and support or walk around and support. How can I suggest that we use these strategies?

A. Show your teaching partner the different arrangements. Begin a conversation, asking whether the arrangements might be useful to your team. Sketch a diagram that shows what each of the co-teaching arrangements look like; this helps

	Monday	Tuesday	Wednesday	Thursday	Friday
Parallel teaching					
Station teaching					
Team teaching					
One teach, one observe					
Alternative teaching					
One teach, one assist					

Figure 5.8. Co-teaching matrix.

others envision teaching arrangement possibilities. Let the teachers know that you are willing to have a meaningful co-supporting role in their inclusive classroom. One special educator used Figure 5.8 to brainstorm arrangements and appropriate lessons for her inclusive writing class. She collaborated with the general educator to determine when it might be beneficial to use each of the co-teaching arrangements.

Q. What if I feel uncomfortable with a role I have been assigned?

A. Communicate your concerns to your teaching team. The role might not have to be changed; it could be shared. If you believe you are being asked to do something outside the scope of your job, talk to the teaching team first and then to your principal or director of special education.

Q. Can a paraprofessional co-teach?

A. Paraprofessionals certainly can lead stations and small groups, lead portions of a lesson, and take on complementary roles while another educator is teaching. Educators should design the sequence of the lesson, the appropriate differentiation strategies, and any needed modifications and adaptations. Clearly communicate expectations to ensure that the paraprofessional knows exactly what to do.

CONCLUSION

Working as a team member and within a school setting can be challenging, but it also can be rewarding. Understanding each team member's roles, including your own, can bring clarity to your work. Learning more information about each of your teammates is essential to building trust within your team. Further, using common co-teaching and co-supporting arrangements can clarify specific roles and responsibilities within the classroom. Communication is key: The more effectively you communicate and solve conflicts as you work together, the better your team will function, enabling you to deliver more seamless support to students. The next chapter focuses on providing academic supports to allow students to reach their full academic potential.

6

Providing Academic Supports

CLEARING A PATH
FOR PEOPLE WITH SPECIAL NEEDS
CLEARS THE PATH FOR EVERYONE!

"Teachers must be willing to not just give me a desk and then leave me to fill the chair. I need to be asked questions, and given time for my thoughtful answers. Teachers need to become conductors, and guide me through the many places I may get lost."

—Jamie (Syracuse University student who has autism)

"Everyone is a genius. But if you judge a fish on its ability to climb a tree, it will live its whole life believing that it is stupid."

—Albert Einstein (as cited in Kelly, 2004, p. 80)

If a child can't learn the way we teach, maybe we should teach the way that they learn.

—Ignacio Estrada (as cited in Card & Card, 2013, p. 40)

Inclusive lesson design involves planning lessons with the needs of certain students in mind, allowing for lessons that are more accessible, effective, and fun for everyone.

INCLUSIVE, DIFFERENTIATED, AND COLLABORATIVE PLANNING TEMPLATE

Inclusive educators proactively design curriculum units and lessons to be accessible and useable for all learners from the onset. Many teams of educators collaborate to develop thoughtful and differentiated instruction. Figure 6.1 offers an example of a planning template that inclusive educational teams might use. The following considerations guide educators in designing purposeful instruction that meets the needs of all learners in the classroom: 1) students, 2) content, 3) thinking divergently, 4) the learning plan, 5) assessment, and 6) debriefing. In the following subsections, we explore each of these considerations.

Students

The first step in designing inclusive lessons is to think about the learners in your class. Identify three students who represent an academic, behavior, and social range of the learners in your class. Be sure to think about students with a disability and/or English language learners. Write a positive student profile for each of these students that includes likes, dislikes, intelligences, strengths, and information about their communication, behavior, and academic and subject-specific performance. The purpose of this step is to proactively think about the range of learners in your class and design with their strengths and needs in mind.

Content

The second step is to know the content standards and concepts you intend to teach. Examine the Common Core standards. Design your plans around these standards.

This planning template is designed to help teams develop thoughtful and differentiated instruction.

Step 1: The Students

A. Identify target students

Select specific students to keep in mind during this lesson-designing process (at least three). These students should represent an academic, behavioral, and/or social range of learners in your class (e.g., struggling, average, high-performing). Specifically consider students who have a disability and English language learners.

Write a short, *positive* student profile for each of the students; at minimum, you must include the following information: 1) likes/dislikes, 2) intelligences/strengths, 3) communication, 4) behavior, 5) academic and subject-specific performance, 6) other pertinent information.

Step 2: The Content

A. Subject/theme, concept, problem, or topic for unit

What grade-level specific national and state standard(s) is/are being addressed?
What are the important ideas and concepts?

B. What do you want students to know and be able to do?

Step 3: Think Divergently!

A. Concept maps/webs/brainstorms

☐ **What aspects of this subject could we teach?**

☐ **How could we teach it?**
- o *How will you share information? How will the students engage in the learning?*
- o Consider: *Demonstration, modeling, minilecture, draw and tell story, student research, inquiry project, games, simulations, centers, video, or other options.*

☐ **What are the various products students can create to demonstrate their new knowledge?**
These should tie specifically to the lesson objectives.
- o Consider: *Work samples, song, play, photo essay, mural, article, demonstration of a skill, booklet, individual or group presentation, videotape, CD, teaching another person, exhibit, or other options.*
- o Consider: *Will these products vary by student? Will students have a choice? Will different levels of mastery be accepted?*

☐ **How can we assess it?**
- o *How will these products be assessed? What criteria will be used?*

☐ **How will we address the strengths of the target students?**

☐ **How will we address an array of Gardner's multiple intelligences?**

☐ **How will we address student culture? How is this culturally relevant?**

☐ **How will we differentiate? Extend? Modify? How will we challenge *all* students? How will we give students choice?**

B. Topic research/resources

Are resources or research needed in order to plan? _____

(continued)

Figure 6.1. Inclusive, differentiated, and collaborative planning template. (From Theoharis, G., & Causton-Theoharis, J. [2011]. Preparing pre-service teachers for inclusive classrooms: revising lesson-planning expectations. *International Journal of Inclusive Education* [15]7, 743–761; adapted by permission of the publisher [Taylor & Francis Ltd., http://www.tandfonline.com].)

Figure 6.1. *(continued)*

Step 4: The Learning Plan

A. Goals/objectives

What do you want students to know and be able to do?

☐ Whole-class objectives/emphases
- o Essential: What every student will learn and do.
- o Expected: What most students will learn and do.
- o Enrichment: What a few students will learn and do.

☐ Student-specific objectives

B. Pre-assessment

Gather information on each student *before* you teach. How will you gather this information? What do students know about this topic?

C. Prerequisite skills

What other skills do students need to have in order to participate in this lesson (e.g., cooperative skills, language, writing, technology)? For students who may not have these skills, how will you teach the skills or modify the lesson (e.g., preteach, peer support, communication device)?

D. Definitions of targeted terms

List the targeted terms or content-specific words and definitions.
(formal or content-related definition/grade-level-appropriate definition)

E. Impact on planning

How will the information from the pre-assessment and prerequisite skills affect your planning?

F. Duration/times of lesson/unit

G. Learning sequence (check one)

☐ The learning cycle: *engage, explore, explain, apply*

☐ Hunter's sequence: *input, modeling and checking for understanding, guided practice, and independent practice*

☐ Math (and others): *the launch, the exploration/investigation, and the discussion/congress*

☐ Inquiry sequence: *define problem/question, speculate on answers, plan investigation, gather information, analyze information, reach conclusion*

☐ Other: *describe*

H. The nitty gritty

☐ How will you facilitate learning of the goals/objectives?

☐ Who needs individual accommodations? Who needs modifications? What specific supports or aids do specific students need?

☐ Use your divergent concept maps.

Think about the following: How will students be grouped during this lesson? What physical spaces will be used? How will the physical arrangement of the room(s) be configured for the lesson to ensure student success? What teaching strategies will be used to help the students learn? Preteaching?

I. Engaging hook and closure

J. Each lesson

☐ Agenda
☐ Student-friendly objectives
☐ Behavioral considerations

K. Co-teaching and collaboration (What adults will be taking part in this? What are their specific roles?)

Circle the types of co-teaching arrangements to be used:

Parallel teaching; station teaching; team teaching; one teach, one observe; alternative teaching; one teach, one assist

What does each adult do before, during, or after the lesson?

Adults' names:

Specific tasks before lesson/unit:

Specific tasks during lesson/unit:

Specific tasks after lesson/unit:

Step 5: Assessment

A. Evaluation of students' learning

1. Formative assessment
   a. What information will you collect throughout or in an ongoing manner?
2. Summative assessment (should be connected to the goals and objectives)
   a. What are you assessing? How you are assessing it? What criteria are you using?
   b. Are you using a rubric or tool to assess the work?

Step 6: Debriefing Individual/Team

A. When, where, and how will adults debrief and evaluate the outcomes of the lesson/unit?

B. Analyzing/thinking about student learning

What did your students learn from your lesson? Whole class and target students?

C. Thinking about teaching (student participation, planning, preparation, collaboration, and teaching)

1. Thinking about teaching the specific content from this unit
   a. Where did students/you have difficulty with the content?
   b. Where did students/you have success with the content?
   c. What would you do differently? What were you proud of?
2. Thinking about collaboration/teaming from this unit
   a. What would you do differently? What were you proud of?

Think specifically about what you want students to know and be able to do as a result of the lesson.

Thinking Divergently

The third step requires you to think divergently about the structures and strategies you might use to deliver the lesson and collect assessment data. Think about how you will teach content and engage students in the lesson. Brainstorm what products students might create to demonstrate their understanding. Incorporate elements of multiple intelligences into the lesson so students can approach the content and demonstrate understanding from multiple entry points. Recall your target students. Reflect on which types of products will allow the range of learners to demonstrate their newly learned knowledge. Be sure that all students will be challenged. You might create a list of ideas or a concept web. The purpose is to think divergently about how the lesson might be structured and brainstorm in a way that makes sense to your educational team.

The Learning Plan

The fourth step is to develop a learning plan. Create whole-class objectives. Think about the essential standards that every student will learn and be able to do. Next, think about what most students will learn and be expected to be able to do. Last, think about enrichment learning experiences that a few students will learn and be able to do. Also, create any student-specific objectives to incorporate IEP goals. This ensures the lesson is designed with a range of learners in mind.

You must also create a plan to collect preassessment data prior to your teaching. Use this to inform your planning. Design the learning sequence for the lesson, based on your district's curriculum resources, the subject area, and the previous background of your team members. Fit this section to your needs. The important part is to think about individual accommodations, modifications, and supplemental aids and supports that specific students need to be successful. Build these into the lesson from the onset. Every learner needs access to the lesson content. Think about creating an agenda and how you will explain the objectives to students. Design purposefully engaging and fun lesson hooks and closures.

Lesson Hooks   When designing lessons, educators often think about how to proactively pique student interest and excitement around a curriculum topic in order to motivate them to learn. The goal of lesson hooks is to gain students' attention, get them prepared for the topic of study, and capture their interest in a very brief amount of time. Figure 6.2 lists great lesson hooks that we have seen educators use in their classrooms.

One eighth-grade teacher created footprints that included context clues and information from the previous chapter of a fiction book they were reading together. She affixed the footprints to the floor, starting in the hallway and continuing around

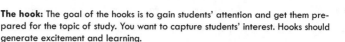

The hook: The goal of the hooks is to gain students' attention and get them prepared for the topic of study. You want to capture students' interest. Hooks should generate excitement and learning.

☐ Dress like a character.

☐ Provide a mystery box.

☐ Unveil a secret message.

☐ Create a letter to be delivered by the principal, the president of the United States, or a stuffed animal.

☐ Wrap up a book and open it.

☐ Hide clues about the topic around the room.

☐ Provide stepping stone clues or footprints with lesson information on the floor for students to follow.

☐ Create a simulation or physical change to the environment.

☐ Use a ticket in the door (an index card that prompts students to respond to a specific learning target) that allows students to respond or reflect on one aspect of learning from the previous day and serves as a link to an upcoming lesson.

☐ Create a photo gallery or exhibit.

☐ Put something in a brown paper bag, and have students guess what they will be studying.

☐ Have students stand back to back while one student reads the question from a previously prepared index card and the second student responds. The pair then turns to face each other, feedback is provided, and the pair does a celebratory high five. The partnership has an interactive discussion around the content.

☐ Play a song/music/audio clip related to the unit of study.

☐ Bring in real life "things" (e.g., insects, souvenirs) related to the unit of study.

☐ Play a YouTube/media clip featuring an inspiring story or event around the content.

☐ Organize a scavenger hunt (e.g., have students collect materials and "tools" needed for a science lab kit, such as a magnifying glass, special notebook/pen, and other needed items).

☐ Provide props (e.g., for a mystery reading unit, provide detective hats and badges).

☐ Dress up as something applicable to the topic.

☐ Demonstrate an experiment.

☐ Put on a skit (maybe have other teachers or older students help).

☐ Create and have students open a "time capsule" that contains items directly related to the unit of study.

☐ Create or locate a 30-second television commercial to prompt student interest.

☐ Create or locate a 30-second radio announcement.

☐ Use Voki to create a video related to the lesson.

☐ In order to increase anticipation and student interest, read mystery clues (from another teacher or principal) throughout the day that will eventually lead to students guessing what the upcoming lesson will be focusing on.

Figure 6.2.   Lesson hooks.

the perimeter of the classroom. As students entered the classroom, each had the opportunity to use the footprints to review the events of the previous chapter. The last footprint prompted students to make a prediction about what might happen next in the chapter and to use three points of supporting evidence. There was a footprint for students to jot down their ideas. With this engaging and easy-to-execute lesson hook, students began class by reviewing information and thinking about book content, and best of all, they were excited to read further in order to discover whether their predictions were accurate.

Lesson Closures   When designing lessons, inclusive educators often design a closure of a lesson that provides a culminating experience for students and allows them to gain a sense of student learning. The goal of a closure is to wrap up the lesson in a way that is exciting and helps students to review the content or make it more concrete. Figure 6.3 lists lesson closures that we've seen educators implement purposefully and successfully.

One tenth-grade English teacher affixed a tape line horizontally across the classroom. After recapping the lesson about how to provide text-based evidence in argumentative texts, the teacher posed three opinion questions. Students had to determine their opinions and where they stood in relation to the topic. Once on their "side" of the line, they were then asked to pair with a peer on the opposite side of the opinion line. Each student had to prepare and present his or her argument to the partner of the opposing opinion by thinking of three pieces of evidence to support his or her claim. As we watched this lesson closure, we realized that using the opinion line was an effective strategy for the teacher to close the lesson in an upbeat, bodily kinesthetic, interpersonal way while simultaneously solidifying the content of the lesson.

Co-Teaching and Collaboration   Inclusive educational teams intentionally brainstorm co-teaching and instructional arrangements. Ask, "What adults will be taking part in this lesson? What are their specific roles? What types of co-teaching are we using? Do task cards need to be created for paraprofessionals? How are related service providers purposefully engaging in instruction that best utilizes their expertise of their specific disciplines?" This part of lesson design is so imperative that we have devoted an entire chapter to it. Review Chapter 5 for practical strategies to increase collaboration and co-teaching with other educational professionals.

Assessment

It is crucial to monitor students' learning progress toward their goals and objectives. Collect multimodal formative assessments to gain a clear idea of student understanding at various points across the lesson or curriculum unit. Gather evidence of student learning. Ask, "What information will I collect throughout or on an ongoing basis?" Analyze this evidence to determine what instructional supports, accommodations,

Closures: The goal of a closure is to wrap up the lesson in a way that is exciting and helps students to review the content or make it more concrete.

☐ Turn and talk

Students turn to a peer and tell him or her something. They could share something they learned, a question they have, anything.

☐ Ticket out the door

Students jot down the major points they learned during the lesson and hand it in as they leave the classroom.

☐ 3-2-1 blast off

Students tell three things they learned, two new vocabulary words they learned, and one question they considered during the lesson.

☐ Tie it to the introduction

Tie your closure to your introduction.

☐ In a word

Students share one word that indicates how they are feeling about the topic of study (e.g., inspired, passionate, saddened).

☐ Whip around

Each student quickly shares one specific point he or she has learned, then tosses a Koosh ball to the next person, until each person has shared and touched the Koosh ball.

☐ Silent brainstorm

One student writes a fact learned on the class whiteboard, then passes the marker off to another student. Students watch as classmates add to the silent brainstorm and purposefully try not to replicate responses. The end result is a class brainstorm.

☐ Sticky note collage

Each person independently writes something he or she has learned and sticks it on a class chart.

☐ Popcorn share

Each student thinks of one learning point to share. The teacher selects one student to share. That student "pops" by standing up, sharing his or her learning point, then sitting back down and calling on the next person. Students try not to repeat ideas. This strategy encourages diverse student responses, fosters student accountability, encourages active listening, and serves as a rapid class formative assessment.

☐ Back to back

Students stand back to back and quiz each other about the content. If they get a question right, they turn around, jump in the air, and give a high five.

☐ Response cards

Ask a question and have students write their answers on whiteboards or index cards. Then hold them up so their responses are visible to peers and the teacher.

☐ Graffiti

Students work in cooperative groups. Each student in the group has a different-colored marker. Students simultaneously respond to a question by writing and sketching visual representations on chart paper. The result is a large chart paper that represents students' ideas related to a specific learning objective shown in a visual and written manner.

☐ Where do you stand? (e.g., opinion line)

The teacher marks on the wall a continuum of agree to disagree, and students have to decide where they stand on an issue (i.e., "We should have gone to war in this case.").

☐ Top 10 list

Groups of students work together to create a top 10 list that incorporates humor and the lesson content. Students read their top 10 lists out loud.

(continued)

Figure 6.3. Lesson closures.

Figure 6.3. *(continued)*

☐ Sticky note flowchart
Have students indicate each step of a process involved in solving problems to show their conceptual understanding in a visual way.

☐ Bumper sticker
Each student writes a slogan or statement and draws a visual representation of one part learned during the lesson.

☐ Stepping stones
As a formative assessment, each student steps on a "stone" that has a question on it, saying the answer out loud on the way out the door.

☐ Video clip
Students summarize their learning in under 30 seconds by talking into the video camera. These are replayed at the beginning of the next day's lesson.

☐ Voki
In groups, students create a Voki video that summarizes the main points of the lesson. At the beginning of the next day's lesson, the groups view a different group's Voki.

☐ Self-assessment
Students indicate their level of perceived understanding with a 3-2-1 or green-yellow-red system. The numbers and colors mean the following: three or green (competent), two or yellow (proficient), or one or red (needs more support).

☐ Inside/outside circles
Students are split into two groups: ones and twos. Ones stand to form a circle and will be the outside of the circle. Twos stand on the inside and face a partner (who is a one). The teacher poses a question. The number one and two partners who are standing across from one another share their answers. Then all of the twos on the inside of the circle rotate clockwise once and stand in front of a new partner. The teacher poses a question. Each partnership shares. This formative assessment strategy increases student accountability because each partnership is reviewing the content learned and shares its lesson understanding.

☐ Museum exhibition
Students walk around the "museum" to look at other students' products and take keyword "notes" of two positive elements they saw on a sticky note.

☐ Pictionary
Use this game to review key concepts and understandings.

☐ Greeting card
Students write a greeting card, letter, or postcard to another teacher or family member about key learning of the lesson (put these in real envelopes).

☐ Time line on the ground
Students create a time line as a review for chronological events, steps, or procedures.

☐ Obstacle course
Have students go around the room with a buddy and stop to review concepts or pictures, read sticky notes, and answer questions.

☐ Bodily kinesthetic chant
Students create a chant with movements to remember key information.

☐ Create a mural
Have students show learning in pictorial form on the wall.

and modifications you need to provide. Meet students' needs by designing additional learning experiences based on this data. Continue to collect and analyze evidence. Then make changes to your instructional plans.

It is also imperative to plan the summative assessment. Ask, "What am I assessing? How am I assessing it? What criteria am I using? Am I using a rubric or tool to assess the work?" Analyze this summative assessment data alongside the preassessment and formative assessment and determine learning outcomes in relation to the Common Core standards.

Debriefing

Inclusive educational professionals engage in ongoing critical reflection about the natural teaching and learning cycle. This reflection aids in enhancing student learning outcomes. Think about student participation and learning, as well as your planning, preparation, and teaching.

Consider thinking about when, where, and how adults will debrief and evaluate the outcomes of the lesson and unit. You might ask the following questions related to teaching specific content of the lesson:

- What did students learn from this?
- What did the class as a whole learn?
- What did individual students learn?
- What did students have success with?
- What did students have difficulty with?
- What would we do differently next time?

You might ask the following questions about teaching:

- What did we learn about co-teaching together?
- What would I change?
- What am I proud of?
- What might I adjust for the next lesson?
- Was the lesson fun, and how engaged were students?

Analyze the instructional strategies, materials, and planned supplemental supports. You might ask the following questions:

- Were the accommodations, modifications, or supplemental aids and services appropriate for the target students?
- What might I adjust to better meet students' needs?
- What strategies did I use to encourage independence and investment in the learning process?

Consider the learning environment. You might ask the following questions:

- Was the learning environment conducive to learning?
- Did it meet individual students' needs? What needs to be changed?

- How did the learning environment promote students' sense of belonging and community?
- How did learners apply their new knowledge?
- How did students engage in metacognitive thinking, self-evaluation, or self-correction to improve and develop deep understanding?

Directly include the students in the debriefing process. You might ask students the following questions:

- What did you have success with?
- What did you have difficulty with?
- What did you like the most?
- What would you suggest for next time?
- How might you use this new knowledge elsewhere in your life?

BASIC DIFFERENTIATION

Once you've reviewed the steps in the previous section, which were designed to support you and your team in developing thoughtful and purposeful differentiated instruction, we encourage you to try one or all of the following differentiation tools. Often we find that these tools help to immediately and easily support educators to accommodate the diversity of learners in an inclusive classroom.

Product Grid

After figuring out a student's learning style, design instruction to match his or her strengths and intelligences. One strategy that inclusive educators use is to create learning experiences that align with the student's preferences. See Table 6.1 for a multiple intelligences product grid. For example, if Anne prefers bodily kinesthetic activities, create learning experiences that allow her to display her content area learning using this modality. She may create a puppet show, conduct a hands-on demonstration, or act out a skit that incorporates the content.

Multiple Intelligences Think-Tac-Toe

When developing a curriculum unit, some educators build choice into the projects that students create. The Multiple Intelligences Think-Tac-Toe in Figure 6.4 provides a reproducible template for this. In each of the boxes, write an intelligence (e.g., musical, logical mathematical, interpersonal). Brainstorm various ways that students might demonstrate their knowledge of the content you are studying using each of the intelligences, and list those in the boxes. Throughout the course of the unit, students select one project from three boxes to create a straight line. For example, Joe selects musical, interpersonal, and linguistic intelligences and creates one project from each of those boxes. In the musical box, he creates a song that infuses the content. From

Table 6.1. Multiple intelligences product grid

Linguistic	Logical/Mathematical	Spatial	Bodily/Kinesthetic	Musical	Interpersonal	Intrapersonal	Naturalist
Advertisement	Advertisement	Animated movie	Calligraphy	Audio-videotape	Advertisement	Bulletin board	Artifact collection
Annotated bib	Annotated bib	Art gallery	Charades	Choral reading	Animated movie	Chart	Diorama
Bulletin board	Chart	Bulletin board	Collage	Fairy tale	Bulletin board	Collage	Field study
Code	Code	Bumper sticker	Costumes	Film	Chart	Collection	Field trip
Comic strip	Collage	Cartoon	Dance	Instrumental	Choral reading	Comic strip	Fossil collecting
Debate	Collection	Chart	Demonstration	Juke box	Comic strip	Diary	Insect collecting
Demonstration	Computer program	Clay sculpture	Diorama	Musical	Debate	Editorial essay	Leaf collecting
Diary	Crossword puzzle	Collage	Etching	Poem	Demonstration	Fairy tale	Original song
Editorial essay	Data base	Costumes	Experiment	Rap song	Editorial essay	Family tree	Photo essay
Fairy tale	Debate	Demonstration	Film	Riddle	Fairy tale	Journal	Rock collecting
Family tree	Demonstration	Diorama	Flipbook	Role playing	Film game	Learning center	Scientific drawing
Fiction story	Detailed illustration	Display	Food	Song	Interview	Maze	Spelunking trip
Interview	Edibles	Etching	Hidden picture	Sound	Journal	Poem	Time line
Jingle	Experiment	Film	Mosaic		Lesson	Riddle	

(continued)

109

Table 6.1. *(continued)*

Linguistic	Logical/Mathematical	Spatial	Bodily/Kinesthetic	Musical	Interpersonal	Intrapersonal	Naturalist
Joke book	Fact file	Filmstrip	Mural		Mazes	Time line	
Journal lesson	Family tree	Flipbook	Musical		Museum exhibit		
Letter	Game	Game	Musical instruments		Pamphlet		
Letter to the editor	Graph	Graph	Needlework		Petition		
Newspaper story	Hidden picture	Hidden picture	Painting		Play		
Non-fiction	Labeled diagram	Illustrated story	Pantomime		Press conference		
Oral defense	Large scale drawing	Maze	Paper mache		Role playing		
Oral report	Lesson	Mobile	Plaster of Paris model		TV program		
Pamphlet	Map with legend	Model	Play		Write a new law		
Petition	Mazes	Mosaic	Poem				
Play	Mobile	Mural	Press conference				
Poem	Model	Painting	Puppet				
Press conference	Petition	Paper mache	Puppet show				
Radio program	Play	Photo essay	Radio program				

Linguistic	Logical/Mathematical	Spatial	Bodily/Kinesthetic	Musical	Interpersonal	Intrapersonal	Naturalist
Riddle	Prototype	Picture story	Role play				
Science fiction story	Puzzle	Pictures	Transparencies				
Skit	Recipe	Play	TV program				
Slogan	Riddle	Political cartoon					
Soliloquy	Survey	Pop-up book					
Storytelling	Time line	Prototype					
TV program	Transparencies	Rebus story					
Write a new law	Venn diagram	Slide show					
	Working hypothesis	Story cube					
	Write a new law	Travel brochure					
		TV program					
		Web home page					

Reprinted by permission from Taylor, T. Roger. (2015). *Multiple intelligences product grid*. Oak Brook, IL: Curriculum Design for Excellence, Inc.; retrieved from https://www.rogertaylor.com/clientuploads/documents/references/Product-Grid.pdf and Taylor, T. Roger. (2007). *Differentiating the curriculum: Using an integrated, interdisciplinary, thematic approach* (pp. 59–60). Oak Brook, IL: Curriculum Design for Excellence, Inc.

Multiple Intelligences Think-Tac-Toe

Topic: _____

How can I bring in numbers, calculations, logic, classifications, or critical thinking skills? **Logical mathematical**	How can I use visualization, visual aids, color, art, or metaphor? **Visual spatial**	How can I bring in music, environmental sounds, or set key points in rhythmic or melodic frameworks? **Musical**
How can I incorporate living things, natural phenomena, or ecological awareness? **Naturalist**		How can I involve the whole body, incorporate movement, or use hands-on experiences? **Bodily kinesthetic**
How can I evoke personal feelings or memories or give students choices? **Intrapersonal**	How can I use the written or spoken word? **Verbal/linguistic**	How can I engage students in peer sharing, cooperative learning, or large-group simulation? **Interpersonal**

Topic: _____

Figure 6.4. Multiple Intelligences Think-Tac-Toe.

From Tomlinson, C.A. (2003). *Fulfilling the promise of the differentiated classroom: Strategies and tools for responsive teaching.* Alexandria, VA: Association for Supervision and Curriculum Development; adapted by permission.

In *The Educator's Handbook for Inclusive School Practices* by Julie Causton and Chelsea P. Tracy-Bronson (2015, Paul H. Brookes Publishing Co., Inc.)

the interpersonal selections, he works with a partner to create a board game that they play and then teach classmates to play. From the linguistic options, he writes a newspaper story. In the end, Joe has three different projects that display portions of his content knowledge.

Independent Learning Contracts

Some teachers work with students to create independent learning contracts. These allow students to make individual decisions around which topics they would like to study in depth. Figure 6.5 shows a reproducible example of an independent learning contract. For example, Kara first writes the question or topic of study before noting what she will read, write, draw, look at, or listen to and what she will need to complete her study. She creates a date to finish by and determines suitable ways to disseminate her learning. Kara then meets individually with the teacher to ensure that the plan connects distinctly with content. Inclusive educators often use independent learning contracts because they inherently support learners to use materials and investigate topics in ways that make sense to individual learning needs.

"For many teachers, the thought of having a student with a disability in their class seems like a completely unrealistic proposition if not a terrifying nightmare. Yet these same teachers are often unaware of the possible minor adaptations which could be made in the classroom to accommodate such students."

—Kunc (1984, p. 2)

WHAT MODIFICATIONS AND ACCOMMODATIONS DO YOU USE THROUGHOUT THE DAY?

We both use several modifications and accommodations throughout the day to be successful. For example, Julie sets her alarm to wake up at 5:00 a.m. She goes to the gym for a 1-hour workout before the demands of the day begin; this improves her ability to sit for long periods of time at work and to teach for long periods of time. Chelsea wakes up early to allow herself an hour of uninterrupted time to write before anyone else in the house wakes up, before the phone rings, and before checking e-mail. Both Chelsea and Julie use an electronic calendar to keep daily appointments. Chelsea has a binder with colorful sections she uses as a daily to-do list. There is a section for each of the big projects she is working on. She crosses each item off as she completes it. Julie typically writes her daily to-do list on her laptop. She prioritizes each item by writing numbers in the left-hand margin of the list. We both use systems to help us to organize our lives in efficient ways. When Julie cleans her house, she sets an alarm for 15 minutes and races around the house to see how much she can get done before setting the alarm again for the next room.

Our point is that we know what we want or need to get done and then rely on these personalized strategies and supports to ensure that we can achieve those

Independent Learning Contract

Name: _____

I want to know

My question or topic is _____

_____

To find out about it,

I will look at and listen to:

I will write:

I will need:

I will draw:

I will read:

I will finish by _____

I will share what I learned through _____

_____

Figure 6.5. Independent Learning Contract.

From Tomlinson, C.A. (1999). *The differentiated classroom: Responding to the needs of all learners.*
Alexandria, VA: Association for Supervision and Curriculum Development; adapted by permission.

In *The Educator's Handbook for Inclusive School Practices*
by Julie Causton and Chelsea P. Tracy-Bronson (2015, Paul H. Brookes Publishing Co., Inc.)

desired outcomes. Although you personally may not need the same specific adaptations, tailored supports are necessary in everyone's lives. That is, all individuals need their environments, time schedules, and behavior modified or adapted to allow them to be successful members of society.

Educators regularly design accommodations to provide needed environment, time, behavior, social, and academic supports that allow students to be successful in academics. The rest of this chapter does just that; that is, we discuss accommodations, modifications, and adaptations that enable students with disabilities to benefit from general education. We describe general, content-specific, and environmental strategies and discuss the topic of assistive technology.

As an educator, your expertise is intended to design learning experiences that allow students to participate in and benefit from special education, perform educational activities, and participate in school. You provide strategies, modifications, adaptations, consultation, and skill development that allow students to succeed in the school environment and help them navigate the academic terrain of schooling.

IDEA 2004 recognizes that education for students with disabilities is effective when it is based on high expectations, participation, and progress in the general education curriculum alongside peers without disabilities to the maximum extent possible. Under IDEA 2004, special education means "specially designed instruction . . . to meet the unique needs of a child with a disability" (§ 300.39). This specially designed instruction "means adapting, as appropriate to the needs of an eligible child . . . the content, methodology, or delivery of instruction," in order 1) "to address the unique needs of the child that result from the child's disability" and 2) "to ensure access of the child to the general curriculum, so that the child can meet the educational standards within the jurisdiction of the public agency that apply to all children" (IDEA 2004, § 300.39 [b][3]). The educational team is responsible for ensuring a student has purposeful access to the general education curriculum and "specially designed" special education.

The following sections in this chapter focus on several modifications and specific ways to adapt learning experiences to meet the academic needs of your students. First, we describe general strategies that will enable you to support students, and then we discuss content-specific ideas and environmental strategies. Finally, we suggest strategies that can help you work across all content areas.

ADAPTATIONS, ACCOMMODATIONS, AND MODIFICATIONS

The following information about the differences between modifications and accommodations comes from the PEAK Parent Center (n.d.) in Colorado Springs, Colorado. Accommodations and modifications are adaptations made to the environment, curriculum, instruction, or assessment practices that enable students with disabilities to be successful learners and to participate actively with other students in the general education classroom and in schoolwide activities.

Accommodations are changes in how a student gains access to information and demonstrates learning. Accommodations do not substantially change the instructional level, content, or performance criteria. The changes are made to provide a student with equal access to learning and equal opportunity to show what he or she knows and can do. Accommodations can include changes in presentation, response format and procedures, instructional strategies, time and scheduling, environment, equipment, and architecture.

Modifications are changes in what a student is expected to learn. The changes are made to provide a student with opportunities to participate meaningfully and productively along with other students in classroom and school learning experiences. Modifications include changes in instructional level, content, and performance criteria. Modifications are necessary for some students for some content, but inappropriate modifications can be detrimental to a student's education. For example, Table 6.2 lists what we have sadly witnessed as the top 10 worst classroom modifications.

The following lists contain examples of accommodations and modifications that can be provided in general education classrooms. IEP teams determine accommodations and modifications that meet the unique and individual needs of their students.

Table 6.2.　Top 10 worst classroom modifications

Number	Modification
10.	The seventh-grade class is doing math, but one student is using *Sesame Street* blocks to work on counting.
9.	The class is watching a video, but one student who is blind is sent out of the room because she cannot see.
8.	The classroom is arranged with desks in groups of five, but one student is seated in a group with only two desks, one for him and one for his assistant.
7.	While the rest of the high school class is doing reports on nutrition, one student is given a tub of dry beans and rice to "explore."
6.	Fourth-grade students are adding adjectives to sentences, but because the speech-language pathologist has not yet put adjectives on one student's communication board, the student does not participate in this lesson.
5.	During silent reading, the special educator takes one student to the back of the classroom to work on buttoning.
4.	Because one student has dressing goals on her individualized education program, she puts on and takes off her shoes two times when she gets ready for gym class.
3.	Because one student does not yet read, she listens to a music tape while the teacher reads aloud to the class.
2.	A student who uses facilitated communication is provided with a facilitator *only* during language arts class.
1.	A 12-year-old student goes with the second-grade class to physical education because his gross motor skills are "at that level."

Accommodations

- Test taken orally
- Large-print textbooks
- Additional time to take test
- A locker with an adapted lock
- Weekly home–school communication tool, such as a notebook or daily log book
- Peer support for notetaking
- Lab sheets with highlighted instructions
- Graph paper to assist in organizing and lining up math problems
- Tape-recorded lectures
- Use of a computer for writing

Modifications

- An outline in place of an essay for a major project
- Picture communication symbol choices on tests
- Alternative books or materials on the same theme or topic
- Spelling support from a computerized spell-check program
- Word bank of choices for answers to test questions
- Use of a calculator on a math test
- Film or video supplements in place of text
- Questions reworded using simplified language
- Projects substituted for written reports
- Important words and phrases highlighted

Deciding which accommodations and/or modifications to use is a process that depends on the assignment and needs of each individual student. Figure 6.6 provides you and your educational team with a four-step process to help you design appropriate adaptations and supports that will promote each student's active participation and skill development in the general education classroom. The process includes guiding questions to promote conversation and problem solving among you and the rest of the student's educational team.

As a teacher, you are expected to design the accommodations and/or modifications throughout a student's school experience. However, you may not necessarily be the primary person who implements those accommodations or modifications, and therefore the team conversation about the student's skills, strengths, needs, and necessary supports is a critical part of this work. For example, you may plan out all of the modifications for a lesson, and then both the paraprofessional and the OT who work with the student may implement the plan. Both general and special educators can be responsible for designing and carrying out adaptations, as well as for evaluating whether the adaptations are working (i.e., evaluating whether the student has increased access to skills, independence, and peer interaction). When the appropriate adaptations are made, *all* students can have meaningful access to the general education curriculum (PEAK Parent Center, n.d.).

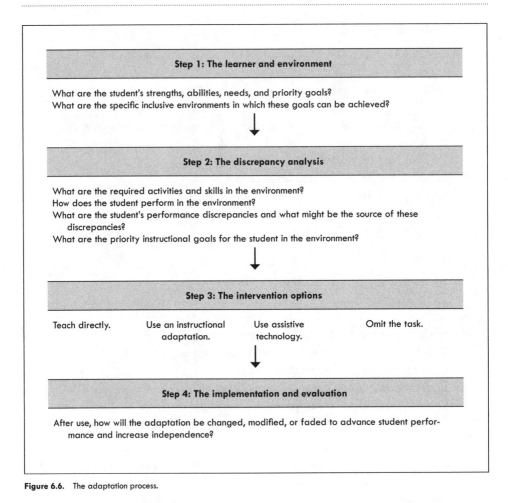

Figure 6.6. The adaptation process.

GENERAL STRATEGIES

Some strategies for providing academic support include keeping expectations high, focusing on strengths, asking the student, breaking tasks into smaller steps, and providing extended time.

Keep Expectations High

If a student has a disability, it does not mean that the student cannot complete assignments and projects in the same way as anyone else. Before attempting to modify or alter a student's assignment, ask yourself whether the assignment actually needs any changes. Too often, education professionals overmodify for students or decide to make the same modification for every student with the same disability. Sometimes, the best thing to do for a student is not to change your expectations for him or her but, instead, to change the type or level of support.

Focus on Strengths

When planning lessons for students, it is easy for educators to become overwhelmed by what a student cannot do. For example, when providing support to Steven, a third-grader with Down syndrome, it was easy to think, "Steven does not read; how am I to help him understand the science content in this chapter?" It helps to reframe your thinking and ask yourself what the student *can* do. Focus instead on the student's strengths; with Steven, you might think, "Steven is a very social guy. He can easily comprehend big ideas. He is masterful at drawing what he knows and labeling parts. He also can answer questions."

When his teachers focused on Steven's strengths of listening, social interaction, and understanding main ideas, the lesson design process became much easier. When other students were required to quietly read the chapter from the science book, Steven's partner read the chapter aloud. At the end of each section in the text, Steven and his partner were required to say something about the section, and Steven, as he listened, worked on a drawing depicting the big ideas from that section. Steven and his partner then asked each other questions about the section and the drawing. This worked so well for Steven and his partner that the teacher decided to have the entire class read the science text that way for the rest of the year.

Ask the Student

If you are unsure of how to best reach, teach, or provide support, you do not need to make that decision alone. If you are unsure about what will work best, ask the student. For example, you could ask, "During this lesson, would you rather bullet the five big themes or dictate them to someone else?" and "During this lesson on factors, would you like to use the study sheet or try it without?"

Break Tasks into Smaller Steps

For some students, it might be useful to break tasks into smaller parts. For example, one student preferred having a to-do list posted on her desk for any independent work time. A special educator would write down the big tasks that needed to be completed, and the student would complete them independently and cross out each task. If you have a student who does not read, you could create a picture list and have the student cross out each picture as he or she completes each task.

Extend Time on Tasks

Many students can complete the same work as anyone else if they have extra time. In these cases, it may be helpful to slowly increase the time allotted for certain tasks. Also, if the other students have an hour to complete a test, you could allow the student to take the test in parts—one part on the first day, the second part on the next.

INSTRUCTIONAL ADAPTATIONS

In order for students to be successful, small changes in instruction can prove to be necessary. Through changing materials or instructional methods, many students can get the support they need.

Change the Materials

Sometimes, all a student needs for success is a different type of material. A change in writing utensil, size or type of paper, or seating can make a substantial difference for a student. For example, every time Brett was expected to write, he would put his head down on the desk or angrily break pencils. The team of teachers, therapists, and paraprofessionals who supported the classroom met and discussed the potential reasons for Brett's behavior and how the team might make writing more pleasant for him. As a result of this conversation, the OT recommended letting all students choose their writing instruments and paper size. When this choice was offered, Brett chose a black, felt-tip marker and a half-sheet of paper. For some reason, the change of materials proved much better for him, and he wrote for longer periods of time. He later explained that he would get nervous if he saw "a whole blank piece of paper" and that he hated "the feel of the pencil on the paper."

Present a Limited Amount of Information on a Page

Some students prefer to see less information at once. The layout of information should be clean and free of distraction. Adequate white space, for example, can make an assignment appear less confusing. This modification can easily be made by copying different segments of an assignment onto different pages. In addition, Wite-Out tape helps limit certain distracting information or pictures. Then, when the item is photocopied, the student has less information to wade through. An index card or a word window (i.e., a piece of cardboard with a small rectangular window covered with cellophane that allows students to see one line of text or one word at a time) can also help students limit information as they read by themselves.

Make Things Concrete

Many students need concrete examples, such as pictures or videos, that support the concepts taught in class. Having someone on the team search the school library and Internet for pictures and videos to support learning is helpful. The teacher can then incorporate these teaching aids into minilectures and teaching centers. Use of visual supports benefits not only the students with disabilities but also everyone in the class.

Preteach

Preteaching big ideas such as vocabulary or major concepts can be useful for many students. Preteaching should be done before a concept is "officially" taught to the rest of the class. You may introduce a concept, term, or idea to a student before the rest of the students learn it. For example, as the students were preparing for a magnet lab, the special education teacher taught some of the key science vocabulary to Brett. He was then able to enter the magnet lab understanding the terms *attract* and *repel*. This allowed Brett to come into the class prepared and more confident.

Teach Organizational Skills to Everyone

It is common for students with and without disabilities to struggle with organization. In a seventh-grade classroom, performing binder checks at the end of each class to make sure the notes are in the correct color-coded spot as students leave the room is helpful. In one example we observed, this organization check supported not only Adam, who chronically struggled with keeping things organized, but also countless others who needed similar support. Another team we know made a checklist of all the items students needed to take home each day. These lists were made available for any student to use.

ENVIRONMENTAL ADAPTATIONS

Changes can be made to the classroom environment that may help students to be successful with academic tasks.

Use Movement

Most students need to move their bodies often. When asking students to memorize discrete concepts or pieces of information, use visual cues, signs, or movements. Many students who have trouble memorizing can be helped by using movements or visual cues. Challenge students to come up with their own movements that match the concepts of specific words. For example, one sixth-grade teacher had her class do "spelling aerobics." When spelling words, if the letters were "tall letters" (e.g., *t, l, b*), the students would stand up tall and put their arms up; if letters were "short" (e.g., *o, e, a*), the students would put their hands on their hips; and, if letters hung below the line (e.g., *p, g, q*), the students would touch their toes. For instance, to spell the word *stop,* the students would touch their hips, reach up, touch their hips, and then touch their toes. What makes this particular example so powerful is that the movement is purposeful and connected to the content.

Use a Timer

Timers can be useful for students who like to know how long tasks will take or who need help organizing their time. For some students, visual timers, or timers on which the student can see how much time is left, can be particularly useful.

Use Engaging Transitions

All students are more engaged when they enjoy classroom life, laugh, and connect with peers. With the demands of the Common Core, it can be difficult to infuse play into the life of the classroom. We suggest thinking purposefully about the transitions you utilize. Transition times are opportune moments to infuse movement, music, interactions, and chants into the classroom. Table 6.3 offers engaging transition ideas to help you get started. Brainstorm fun and interactive transition strategies with your inclusive team at your next meeting.

"Izzy is a kindergarten student. Whenever transitions in the classroom occur, he has loud tantrums. Because of Izzy's difficulty with transitions, his teacher recommends to use a timer to alert him when the transitions are coming. I handed him an old track timer and told him that he is in charge of letting the other students know when it is cleanup time. After first practicing with the timer, Izzy took his responsibility very seriously. He walked around from group to group, reminding the kindergartners that there are only '5 minutes until cleanup time . . . 4 minutes . . . 3. . . .' He continues to remind his friends until the timer goes off. He then shouts, 'Clean up, everyone!' What a difference!"

—Sharon (general education teacher)

Use Anchor Activities

In inclusive and well-differentiated classrooms, students often complete assignments at different rates. Anchor activities are tasks that students know to do when they complete their assigned work or when there is time before an activity or lesson begins. Anchor activities can also be utilized to help teachers build in class time for individual or group conferences with students. However, anchor activities are not time-fillers or busywork; they must be meaningful and connected to essential student learning and be structured and explained well enough for students to work on independently. In Figure 6.7, we offer a list of engaging anchor activity ideas to help you get started, but we encourage you to brainstorm with both your students and your team to design even more exciting anchor activities for your inclusive classroom.

PROVIDE SUPPORT

How support is provided is a key factor in student success. The type and level of support given can influence how likely a student is to be independent or interdependent with peers.

Offer Support, Do Not Just Give It

Do not assume that a student needs help. If a student is struggling, encourage him or her to ask a peer first. Several teachers that we know use the rule "Ask three before me,"

Table 6.3. Engaging transitions

Movement

Start a class or an activity with an interesting or humorous way to enter the space (try the crab walk or backward walk).

Take 45 seconds to have a dance party.

Use snaps (over and over—signal an all-at-once stop with a conductor-like finish).

Use claps (start slow and have class build up to a fast pace—signal a stop all at once with a conductor-like finish).

Call out a "45-second challenge," such as jumping jacks, yoga tree pose, or another physical activity.

Lead a firework cheer (rub hands together, make a sizzle sound, then clap hands and say, "Oooh, ahhhh").

Raise the roof! (Say, "Raise the roof" and have students pump their arms up with palms up three times in a row.)

Act out a karate chop (said aloud along with the motion for extra fun!).

Take 5 minutes to do whole-body stretches.

Organize a walk-and-talk activity (give the class a question related to the content, set a timer, and tell them to discuss the answer while walking around outside for 4 minutes).

Music

Play a short part from a song, such as the chorus of "Get Up, Stand Up" by Bob Marley, to cue the students to a new task or activity.

Use musical instruments to signal transitions—a clap of the tambourine can signal *freeze*, a light shake can mean *start moving*, and a repetitive tap can mean *get stepping!*

Preteach a particular rhythm. When you're ready for a transition, begin to clap it out and have students complete the rhythm.

Collaborate with the music teachers. Learn the songs students are singing in chorus or music. Sing as you are cleaning up and making the transition to the next activity.

Timers

Project a visual timer on the SMART Board to signal when students should be ready to work. We recommend the one called Time Timer.

Use an egg timer.

Call and response (remember, these can be led by the teacher or a designated student)

Call: "Tootsie Roll!"
Response: "Lollipop!"

Call: "We've been talkin'."
Response: "Now we stop!"

Call: "What do we want?"
Response: (math, reading, AP government, recess . . . you pick!)

Call: "When do we want it?"
Response: "Now!"

(continued)

Table 6.3. *(continued)*

Call and response (remember, these can be led by the teacher or a designated student)

Call: "Ready to rock?"
Response: "Ready to roll."

Call: "Class!"
Response: "Yes!"

Call: "Class, class, class!"
Response: "Yes, yes, yes!"

Call: "May I have your attention, puuh-lease!"
Response: "Yes you may!"

Call: "Gaga, and Bieber, and Drake" (adjust artists for student age and preferences)
Response: "Oh my!"

Call: "Got me looking so . . ."
Response: "Crazy right now!" (freeze in a silly way)

Call: "Ba da ba da ba"
Response: "I'm lovin' _____" (insert subject or task in the bank)

Call: "All set?"
Response: "You bet!"

Call: "A, B, C!"
Response: "Easy as 1, 2, 3!"

Call: "Holy moly!"
Response: "Guacamole!"

Call: "Yackity yack!"
Response: "Don't talk back!"

Chants

The disco chant: "That's the way, uh huh, uh huh, I like it, uh huh, uh huh!"

The na na na chant: "Na na naaa na, heyy heyyy hey, goo-ood job!"

The coaster cheer: "Click, click. Yeeeehaw!"

"Hocus pocus, everybody focus!"

"Macaroni and cheese, everybody freeze!"

"Peanut butter, jelly time

Peanut butter, jelly time

Peanut butter jelly, peanut butter jelly, peanut butter jelly . . ." (faster and faster)

"Chicka chicka, boom boom!"

which encourages peer support and peer interaction. Another teacher we know designates particular "ask me" students. These students always have the written directions for any assignments, and if one is struggling, he or she first goes to the assigned students. Another strategy to try includes monitoring whether a student is struggling and asking, "Can I help you get started?" before offering support. If the student says, "No," respect his or her wishes.

Anchor activities: The goal of an anchor activity is to provide students with engaging and meaningful ways to expand upon essential learning related to a current unit of content in self-directed ways.

- Create graphic organizers.
- Provide computer activities (related to lesson).
- Create a digital story.
- Use content-related silent reading.
- Use activity boxes.
- Work on ongoing projects (e.g., create ads, blogs, brochures, videos).
- Use learning/interest centers.
- Write a story.
- Create a play or skit.
- Do vocabulary work.
- Illustrate a lesson.
- Use listening stations.
- Draw or create a digital comic (related to a lesson).
- Write or solve riddles.
- Create math problems for assignments or tests.
- Create a folder of review activities for the unit.
- Write songs or jingles to help recall content.
- Use mini-lab science centers.
- Create a mini-experiment.
- Create brain teasers.
- Create a mind map/mind web to explain a complicated concept.
- Plan a minilesson for the class.
- Journal.
- Write a letter to an author/historical figure/scientist/mathematician.
- Research a historical figure/politician/author or other relevant person and create a short digital presentation for the class or class web site.

Figure 6.7. Anchor activities.

Silent Support

Receiving support is not always a comfortable thing. It also can be distracting to class-mates. Therefore, when students are working, aim to use a soft voice. Or consider a silent support. For example, write a note or point to the directions. Or make a larger announcement not aimed specifically at anyone; this strategy not only benefits the student you have identified but may also provide a needed support for other learners in the class.

Peer Support

Peer support is one of the best ways to support students. To set a supportive classroom tone, you can explain to all students that their job is to help each other. However, more specific uses of peer support might be the use of collaborative learning in which students work in teams or partnerships, the rotation of peer tutors based on expertise in subject areas or skills, or the implementation of cross-age peer tutors in which older students tutor or collaborate with younger students. Peers can also provide support by reviewing class content, directions, or assignments together; reading material aloud to another student; providing physical support; or helping with organization. There are unlimited ways to use peers in the classroom; however, some caution is necessary regarding peer support. Do not set up "helping relationships"—for example, Sonja always helps Jose. Instead, encourage students to help each other. Figure out times when Jose can help Sonja and others in the classroom.

ACROSS-CONTENT STRATEGIES

Tables 6.4 and 6.5 detail modifications and accommodations for different types of content and activities that are commonly used across content areas.

Remember, you will be responsible for designing accommodations and modifications and should know many different types of modifications and how best to use them with students who may need them. If you see an idea in Table 6.4 or Table 6.5 that you would like to try with a student, talk to the team to decide whether it would be an effective strategy. Discuss how to use it, when to use it, and when you might fade the strategy or idea.

Commonly Occurring Activities Across Content Areas

Support can look very different for students in different content areas. Sometimes, a different teacher is responsible for each content area, and this can result in different expectations. Some students prefer certain subjects and perform better in them. For example, Ricky enjoyed music, so he needed almost no support in that class. He would enter the music room, gather his folder and instrument, and be ready to go. In science, he did not seem fond of the teacher or the subject, and he therefore needed more support to get started with tasks. Although a student's support might look different from class to class, teachers use similar activities across different subject areas.

Table 6.5 highlights activities that are used commonly across subjects. Teachers may require students to do any number of these things throughout the day. Nonetheless, different students may have difficulty with each of these activities for different reasons. The considerations listed on the right side of Table 6.5 have proved helpful for many students of all abilities.

ASSISTIVE TECHNOLOGY

Assistive technology is any type of technology that helps people with disabilities perform functions that might otherwise be difficult or impossible.

> Assistive technology in special education refers to any devices or services that are necessary for a child to benefit from special education or related services or to enable the child to be educated in the least restrictive environment. (IDEA 2004, 34 C.F.R. § 300.308)

Table 6.4. Content-specific modifications

In this subject	Consider these modifications, adaptations, and accommodations
Reading/language arts	Listen to books on tape/CD. Read with a peer. Follow along with a word window. Read from a computer with headphones. Work with a peer and have him or her summarize. Read enlarged print. Use CCTV (closed-circuit TV)—a video magnifier that enlarges the font. Rewrite stories in more simple language. Use books with repetitive texts.
Mathematics	Calculators TouchMath (each number has the correct number of dots on the actual number) Hundreds charts Number lines Flash cards Count stickers Manipulatives (e.g., Unifix cubes, counting chips) Worksheet modified with easier-to-read numbers Pictures or visuals Larger cubes Chart paper to keep track of columns Talking calculator Numbered dice instead of dotted dice Real-world problems—problems with students' names in them
Physical education	Different-sized sporting equipment Silent activities (for those who are sensitive to noise) Choice stations Change the size of the court.
Art	Choice of materials Bigger/smaller materials Slant board Precut materials Stencils Smocks and aprons with pockets Gloves for kids who do not like to get messy Wikki Stix Posted steps about the process Modified scissors
Science	Hands-on experiences Teacher demonstration A role play Guest speaker Posted steps indicating the process
Social studies	Highlighters or highlighting tape A way to connect the content to self DVDs Visuals Maps A written task card (a card with a step-by-step process written on it)

(continued)

Table 6.4. *(continued)*

In this subject	Consider these modifications, adaptations, and accommodations
Music	Songs in the student's native language Instruments Signs while singing Rhythms to clap out Tapes/CDs of music to practice at home Music videos to watch

The term *assistive technology device* as outlined in IDEA 2004 means "any item, piece of equipment, or product system, whether acquired commercially off the shelf, modified, or customized, that is used to increase, maintain, or improve functional capabilities of children with disabilities" (20 U.S.C. § 1401 [a][25]).

> The term *assistive technology service* means any service that directly assists a child with disabilities in the selection, acquisition, or use of an assistive technology device. The term includes the following provisions:
>
> • The evaluation of the needs of a child with a disability, including a functional evaluation of the child in the child's customary environment;
>
> • Purchasing, leasing, or otherwise providing for the acquisition of assistive technology devices by children with disabilities;
>
> • Selecting, designing, fitting, customizing, adapting, applying, maintaining, repairing, or replacing of assistive technology devices;
>
> • Coordinating and using other therapies, interventions, or services with assistive technology devices, such as those associated with existing education and rehabilitation plans and programs;
>
> • Training or technical assistance for a child with disabilities or, where appropriate, the family of a child with disabilities;
>
> • Training or technical assistance for professionals (including individuals providing education or rehabilitation services), employers, or other individuals who provide services to, employ, or are otherwise substantially involved in the major life functions of individuals with disabilities. (IDEA 2004, 20 U.S.C. § 1401 [a][26])

Assistive technology includes mobility devices (e.g., walkers or wheelchairs), software, keyboards with large keys, software enabling students who are blind to use computers, or text telephones that enable students who are deaf to talk on telephones. A student who struggles with the fine motor skills involved with writing might use an AlphaSmart device. A student who struggles to communicate might type his or her ideas into a computer, which then speaks the ideas aloud, or use an iPad with the application Proloquo2Go.

If a student uses a type of assistive technology, you and your team should learn as much as you can about it. If possible, ask for specific training on the technology so that you can assist the student in using the device, programming it, or fixing it if necessary. See the Chapter 6 Appendix for a list of useful web sites and resources for assistive technology.

Table 6.5. Common activities and supports

When the students are asked to	Consider providing students with
Sit and listen	Visuals to look at Movement breaks An FM system (that amplifies the teacher's voice) A rug or mat to help determine where to be An object to signify who is speaking (e.g., a talking stick) A ball to sit on Choice about where to sit A focus object for students to hold or manipulate A signal to start listening The book that is being read A topic bag—filled with objects that relate to the content A job to do (e.g., help another student, write ideas on the board)
Present orally	Choice about the supports necessary Note cards Visuals A handout A voice recorder A videotape/DVD A microphone PowerPoint A preprogrammed communication device
Take a test	A review of test strategies A review of the information A practice test A double-spaced test Easy questions first A reader for the test A reduced number of choices by eliminating one or two choices In matching, a long column divided into smaller sections A computer As much time as needed An oral exam A performance-based test The option of drawing or labeling Simplified language
Complete worksheets	A word bank Clear directions File folder labels for students to stick answers onto Highlighted directions Fewer problems or questions Choice about type of writing instrument
Discuss	A talking object Note cards with students' ideas written on them Peer support A preprogrammed communication device with a question on it A piece of paper to draw ideas or concepts Choice about how to participate in the discussion The text the students are discussing A highlighted section of the text—have the student read and others discuss

(continued)

Table 6.5.   *(continued)*

When the students are asked to	Consider providing students with
Take notes	A lecture outline to complete during the lecture A chart A graphic organizer The teacher's notes from the day before An AlphaSmart keyboard Choice about how to take notes A copy of the teacher's notes with key words eliminated Lecture notes with pictures Photocopies or carbon copies from another student A laptop computer
Use a computer	A task card for how to start up the program A modified keyboard Enlarged font IntelliKeys An adjusted delay on the mouse An alphabetical keyboard A large keyboard Choice about what to work on
Read a text	A book on tape Larger-print font A highlighter Choral reading Background information about the text Bullets of the main ideas Sticky notes to write questions on "Just-right books" Puppets A reading light Choice about what to read
Be organized	Color-coded folders A planner An agenda written on the board Assignments written on the board in the same place Assignments that are already three-hole punched A picture schedule A sticky note, on the desk, of things to do A homework folder A desk check A clock or timer on desk A verbal rehearsal of the schedule A consistent routine
Write	An option to tell a friend his or her story before writing it A whole-group discussion Graphic organizers The use of bullet writing Pencil grips An option for the student to dictate the story to an adult or a peer Words on a piece of paper that the student rewrites Stickers to fill in blanks An option to draw instead of write Raised-line paper—so students can feel lines

Table 6.6.   Twenty-one ways to use a sticky note

As an individual agenda

As a to-do list

For a positive note in a pocket

To mark page numbers

As a reading guide

To highlight sections of text

To place under the directions

To write questions to the students in their reading books

As a written reminder about behavior

As a way to monitor hand raising (every time students raise their hand and answer, they mark the note)

To cover up sections of a worksheet

As a word bank (so students don't have to write but can, instead, place word in blank)

For students who have a lot to say and blurt out a lot—have them write their questions on sticky notes and select one or two to ask

To add ideas to a brainstormed list

For students to give feedback to each other on projects or papers

To label parts of a diagram

To create a matching game

To put students into groups

For students to write questions or comments and then to give to their teacher as a ticket out the door

To ask a question to a peer, such as "Do you want to sit with me at lunch?"

To summarize the main idea of a lesson, story, or activity

TWENTY-ONE WAYS TO USE A STICKY NOTE

One educator wrote a student a positive comment on a sticky note every day. The student brought that note home and read it with his parents. The purpose of the notes was to provide only positive comments to the student. These notes really helped the student feel good about his performance at school. Sticky notes are amazingly versatile, especially when used to support students academically. Table 6.6 shows 21 great ideas for using sticky notes.

COMMONLY ASKED QUESTIONS ABOUT ACADEMIC SUPPORTS

Q.   One student asks me to "go away" when I work with him. I cannot just let him sit there and fail. What should I do?

A.   Listen to the student. If a student requests that you not work with him or her, do not support the student at that time. Instead, figure out how you might provide support without being physically next to the student. The lists in this chapter should be helpful to you.

Q.   When a direction is given, a student calls my name and asks me to come and help. I am trying to fade my support, but the student will not do anything without me by her side. What should I do?

A.   This student has become very dependent on adult support. Try talking to the student about the need to try things by herself or about asking peers for help. Encourage all students in the class to use and provide help to one another. Involve your team in determining ways to increase the student's independence. Make sure the solutions will make the student feel empowered to become more independent—not punished for her dependence.

CONCLUSION

As an educator, you construct ideas and design and implement the adaptations, assistive technology, or data collection procedures that are used. It is essential that you provide your teams with recommendations about accommodations and modifications that will support students during the academic and social portions of the day. The time that a teaching team spends discussing the types of academic support necessary to enable students to learn certain subjects or perform certain activities, how to fade support, and how to best adapt material and instruction across curricular areas is time well spent. It is interesting to note that when teams make these changes for specific students, they often end up making improvements to teaching for all students. This chapter has focused on the many strategies you can use to support academics. The next chapter highlights behavioral support strategies.

6
Appendix

USEFUL WEB SITES AND
RESOURCES FOR ASSISTIVE TECHNOLOGY

AbleData
http://www.abledata.com

AccessIT (The National Center on Accessible Information Technology in Education)
http://www.washington.edu/accessit/index.html

Alliance for Technology Access
http://www.ataccess.org

CAST (Transforming Education Through Universal Design for Learning)
http://www.cast.org

CATEA (Center for Assistive Technology and Environmental Access)
http://www.assistivetech.net

National Center to Improve Practice in Special Education Through Technology, Media
   and Materials
http://www2.edc.org/NCIP

NATRI: National Assistive Technology Research Institute
http://natri.uky.edu

RehabTool
http://www.rehabtool.com/at.html

University of Connecticut Center for Students with Disabilities
http://www.csd.uconn.edu

READING AND WRITING RESOURCES

Kurzweil 3000: *http://www.kurzweiledu.com*
Kurzweil is software that enables learners who struggle with text to use curriculum materials, allowing them to independently read, develop study skills, and complete writing projects.

CAST e-Reader: *http://www.cast.org*
CAST provides text-to-speech software for students who find reading challenging.

Screenreader: *http://www.screenreader.net*
This software enables the computer to read words that are in applications on the computer.

Co:Writer Universal: *http://donjohnston.com/cowriter/#.VBsd3vldXmc*
This software supports students' writing by enabling word prediction, grammar, and vocabulary in word processing programs.

Write:OutLoud: *http://donjohnston.com/writeoutloud/#.VBse0fldXmc*
This software provides auditory support to learners as they type words, sentences, and paragraphs. After listening to word usage, grammar, and misspellings, students can make the changes in their work independently, through hearing and seeing what they wrote.

7

Providing Behavioral Supports

CONSIDERING HER STUDENTS WITHOUT
DISABILITIES, MRS. BAKER
REALIZES DAVID'S UNUSUAL
BEHAVIORS AREN'T THAT UNUSUAL.

"As a classroom teacher, my biggest frustration is behavior. Today, for example, I am try-ing to teach the quadratic formula, and I am most worried if Nathan will stay seated. It can be very challenging. . . . Teaching in general is hard work . . . but managing behavior while staying focused on the content . . . that is what exhausts me."

—Maria (general education teacher)

Like Maria, many who teach find behavior to be one of the biggest issues that a teacher faces. Julie once was giving a presentation to a large group of teachers. She asked them to list the most challenging behaviors they had seen among their students. The teachers thought about it for a while and then shared their lists with her as she wrote their ideas on chart paper. The lists included swearing, fighting, yelling, shutting down, becoming silent, running out of the room, hitting, and injuring oneself (e.g., biting one's own arm).

This same group of teachers was asked whether they had ever engaged in those behaviors themselves. She told them to raise their hands if they ever had sworn, fought, yelled, shut down, become silent, run out of a room, hit someone, or done anything to hurt themselves. The sound of nervous laughter filled the room as almost everyone raised their hands. This is no reflection on that particular group of teachers. Most people, on occasion, behave in ways that would be considered challenging or concern-ing. The group was asked to distinguish the students' challenging behaviors from their own behavior, and one teacher responded, in a half-joking manner, "When I have bad behavior, I have a darn good reason!" Guess what? So do students.

Next, the group members thought about what they needed when they had engaged in this type of behavior. They brainstormed this list: a hug, time away, some-one to listen, a glass of wine, a nap, a cool-off period, changing the subject, and talk-ing to someone. That is a good list that would calm down many individuals who were engaged in challenging behavior. Notice, however, not only what was suggested, but also what was *not* suggested. No teacher reported needing a sticker chart. No one said they needed to be lectured to or be removed from the room. Instead, like most people, these adults needed support, comfort, and calm, gentle understanding. One of the easiest ways to rethink behavior is to remember that students need that, too.

In your job, you likely will work with students who have challenging behaviors. These may range from relatively nonconfrontational behaviors such as skipping class or shutting down to more significant or externalizing behaviors such as fighting with other classmates, running out of the school, or hurting oneself. This chapter begins with a discussion of typical responses to challenging behaviors and an overview of PBS. Then we present a series of recommendations of what to do before, during, and after students demonstrate these types of challenging behaviors. At the end of the chapter, we answer some commonly asked questions.

THE TYPICAL RESPONSE TO CHALLENGING BEHAVIOR

Herb Lovett, a researcher who was at the Institute on Disability at the University of New Hampshire, described the typical response to challenging behavior:

Our initial response to an unwanted behavior is to react, to correct what we perceive to be unacceptable, inappropriate behavior. The thinking behind this perception is that the person exhibiting the behavior has lost control and that those who are in charge—in control—are responsible for regaining it through the application of methods and technologies specifically designed for this purpose. (1996, p. 136)

The major problem with this type of response is that, when the chosen method of control does not work, the teacher tends to become frustrated and, consequently, to use more punitive methods for control. The intentions backfire, and, through a need to control and correct, teachers often create formidable barriers that further alienate them from those they are supposed to support and teach (Lovett, 1996). This way of thinking involves a negative connotation of behavior: "What is wrong with this student?" as opposed to "How can I connect or support more effectively?" In Table 7.1, you will see a listing of new suggestions for supporting students who present challenging behaviors.

Educators who utilize a humanistic behavioral support mindset do not blame the student. Instead, their critical reflection about the curriculum, environment, and

Table 7.1.   Give them what they need

For students who	Give them	For example
Talk a lot	More opportunities to talk	Walk-and-talks, think pair share, debate, turn and talk
Move a lot	More opportunities to move	Stand and write, do graffiti-style work, write Michelangelo style, dance party, back to back
Want to lead	More opportunities to lead	Line leader, paper passer, helper, pointer
Appear shy	More support with social interactions	Write ideas before joining the group, clock partners
Are resistant	More choices	Choice of writing utensil, type or color of paper, types of manipulatives
Have tantrums	Time to calm down and then provide a plan when finished	"When you are ready, let's write down your first step."
Bully others	More opportunities to strengthen friendships	Tables at lunch based on interest, supported conversations with peers
Shut down	More ways to express frustration	"I need a break" card, a whiteboard to write feelings down
Make noise	Opportunities to make noise	A mouse pad to drum on, repetitive lines in read-aloud
Interrupt	Opportunities to share during lessons	Turn and talk, say something, social break, cooperative learning groups
Have issues with assigned seating	Opportunities to select the best way to work	Use a clipboard on the floor, use a music stand, write Michelangelo style, do graffiti-style work

social space provides a deeper understanding of the challenging behavior. In this chapter are ideas and suggestions to move away from these typical responses to behavior toward a much more humanistic method of supporting students.

POSITIVE BEHAVIOR SUPPORT

PBS has been developed "as a movement away from the traditional mechanistic, and even aversive behavior management practices that were being applied to individuals with disabilities" (Bambara, Janney, & Snell, 2015, p. 4). This approach "emphasizes using collaborative teaming and problem-solving processes to create supports, programs, and other interventions that stress prevention and remediation of problem behaviors by providing effective educational programming and creating a supportive environment" (Bambara, Janney, & Snell, 2015, p. 5). Behavior is a form of communication, and educators should approach situations with a problem-solving mindset. The basic tenets of PBS as a framework are as follows:

1. Behavior is learned and can change.
2. Intervention is based on studying the behavior.
3. The intervention emphasizes prevention and teaching new behaviors.
4. Outcomes are personally and socially valued.
5. Intervention requires comprehensive, integrated supports. (Carr et al., 2002; Janney & Snell, 2013)

Note that approaching behavior with a PBS framework requires a team approach. You should not be expected to design and implement PBS yourself. Nevertheless, understanding the basic tenets is important, because you likely will be responsible for helping to carry out this framework and other behavior plans for some students.

PROACTIVE BEHAVIOR MANAGEMENT

Most challenging behavior can be avoided or managed by thinking ahead. Thinking ahead involves determining what works for the student.

· · · · · · ·

Gabe, a student with autism, has a very difficult time with changes in his schedule. He needs to know when transitions will occur. If he is surprised by a change in the schedule, he hides in his locker, paces, or runs around the room. One way to avoid this issue is to prepare Gabe for each day's schedule. The teaching team does this by having a peer greet Gabe at the bus in the morning. Gabe and his peer then walk to the room together, and when they reach the classroom, they review the agenda for the day. Gabe also has an individual copy of the schedule in his planner. This strategy represents one of the most successful ways to prepare Gabe for the day ahead and to reduce his anxiety about the schedule.

· · · · · · ·

Building a Relationship

Lovett highlighted the importance of relationships and connections as more central than anything else related to supporting students' behavior:

> A positive approach [to behavior] invites people to enter into the same sort of relationship that most of us have and treasure: ongoing, with mutual affection and regard. In such relationships, we all make mistakes, are all in some ways inadequate and yet it is not the level of success that is the ongoing commitment. In the context of relationships, the success and failure of our work becomes harder to assess because the key elements no longer involve simply quantity but the more complex issues of quality. We professionals have routinely overlooked the significance of relationships. (1996, p. 137)

Getting to know your students and learning what they enjoy can be a truly helpful way to address challenging behaviors. Knoster stressed, "Creating a suitable level of rapport with students is an absolutely essential prerequisite for helping students behave" (2014, p. 25).

• • • • • • •

Margee, an eighth-grade teacher, shared with us that she had a student she really did not like. She said, "I want to like him. But I don't. His behavior in class drives me nuts." We discussed several ideas for getting to know and getting to like this student. We decided on spending just 2 minutes each day during which she talks to him about anything other than his behavior or his academic performance. So she thought of a list of questions to ask him. She would sit next to him and just chat with him about skateboarding, his dog, his brothers, movies he enjoys, and other details of his life. She would just open the conversation and give him the opportunity for loving and kind communication. She reported that it was the best thing she ever did. "Not only did I enjoy our conversations, but I realize I really like this kid now! And, he likes me, and confides in me . . . and his behavior in my class is much better. After school, he stops sometimes and asks if he can help me. We have come a long way. And it was all from just stopping and listening."

• • • • • • •

The example of Margee and her student demonstrates that the act of listening can create a closer connection between teacher and student. The seemingly small intervention of listening created an opportunity for the student to open up more to the teacher and for both of the parties to begin to see each other in a more positive light. There are many different ways to form relationships and to let students know that you trust them and that they can trust you. Some different methods include generally being there for the student if he or she needs you, having fun with the student, learning about the student's home life, making a home visit, seeing the same movies that the student enjoys, participating in the same activities the student likes, and talking to the student about his or her friends and hobbies. The next subsection discusses additional ways to build rapport each day with students.

How Do I Build Rapport with Students?

Latham (1999) provided steps for parents to build rapport with their children. These steps have been modified for educators to use with students and are included here:

1. Demonstrate age-appropriate touch (high five, hand shake), facial expressions (reflect the nature of the situation), tone of voice (e.g., your voice also should match the situation), and body language (e.g., appear relaxed, keep your arms open, be attentive, look at the student).
2. Ask open-ended questions (e.g., "What are you doing after school?" "Tell me about that movie.").
3. Listen while the student is speaking. Ideally, talk less than the student (do not interrupt or change the subject).
4. Demonstrate the use of empathetic statements. Act like a mirror and reflect the child's feelings by expressing your understanding and caring.
5. Ignore nuisance behavior and let the smaller issues go.

Matching Instructional Practices to Student Strengths

One of the simplest ways to support students' positive behavior is to match instructional techniques to student strengths. For example, when a student who is a successful artist is allowed to draw his or her ideas during the social studies lecture, the student is more likely to be engaged and have positive behavior.

· · · · · · ·

Mike teaches a student, named Alex, who needs to move often. Mike, the general education teacher, decided to put chart paper on the wall and have all students stand and use markers to do a brainstorming activity instead of doing it at their desks. Alex is more successful, and the other students seem to really enjoy this approach.

Before this, Alex often misbehaved because he struggled to sit still. He was consistently out of his seat, wiggling, and moving. What Mike sensed was that Alex's misbehavior indicated a learning preference (a bodily kinesthetic learning preference). So he used a strength-based approach to support him.

· · · · · · ·

Knowing and understanding how students misbehave can help you identify what they need. Research has demonstrated that taking advantage of students' strengths can decrease negative behavior and increase on-task behaviors (Kornhaber, Fierros, & Veenema, 2004). See the following examples:

*   If students are constantly moving or are bodily kinesthetic learners, they need more movement during instruction. For example, EunYoung needs to move during instruction. So, when the teacher reads aloud to the class, EunYoung is allowed to sit in a rocking chair. The teachers in EunYoung's class let the students sit however they like during certain class activities.
*   If students are continually talking or are interpersonal learners, they need more interaction during learning. For example, Gwen works best when she is able to

talk with peers. So, before writing a journal entry, she is given a few minutes to talk to a friend about what she plans to write.

- If students are constantly singing or are musically gifted, they need more music in school. Lucy enjoys music, so the teacher uses music during writing workshops. The music helps Lucy stay focused, and other students also enjoy it. The teacher also discovered that music with a Latin beat helped with speedier transitions.
- If students enjoy making connections to their own lives or are intrapersonal learners, they need more time during school to make personal connections to the content. For example, Jerry enjoys making personal connections. So, during the *Little House on the Prairie* unit, Jerry's assignment is to determine how each of the settlers is like him and different from him.
- If students draw or doodle or are spatial learners, you can make art part of the learning process. For example, Rubin likes to draw. So, while he listens to a mini-lecture about cellular division, Rubin has the option of drawing and labeling the concepts.
- If a student enjoys mathematical calculations or is highly logical, you can use math and logic to strengthen the student's learning in other subjects. For example, Jorge loves math and struggles during English. So, the team has Jorge make Venn diagrams, time lines, and graphs about the characters in *Romeo and Juliet*. This helps him keep track of all of the characters, and, during discussion, he shares his charts with other students to help them remember the details of the book.

Set Up the Environment in a Way that Promotes Positive Behavior

It is your job to create an accessible learning environment. Have you ever walked into a classroom that felt controlled and stiff? Have you been in an environment that felt warm and welcoming? Have you ever been in a learning environment that you wanted to escape from? What type of learning environment promotes learning? The following list offers ideas to help promote a more comfortable classroom environment:

- Arrange desks in a way that allows for easy student interaction. A circle of desks grouped into tables is more likely to promote interaction.
- Seat students with disabilities in different locations in the room. Do not group students with disabilities together.
- Create a calm, relaxed place in which students feel comfortable moving around and engaging with others.
- Create structure by posting the agenda or daily schedule.
- Add soft lighting to a corner area, so students can adjust lighting options.
- Add different types of seating (e.g., sit discs, arm chairs, rocking chairs).
- Do not isolate any student by seating him or her in a separate location.
- Make the classroom feel like a space for students by adorning the walls with student work.
- Have music playing softly in the background at key times.

- If students are expected to sit on the floor, a soft, carpeted place will make them feel more comfortable.
- If a student struggles with personal space, have all students sit on carpet squares.
- If a student does not like to be called on in class without warning, set up a system to let the student know when the teacher will call on him or her.

Meet Students' Needs

All human beings require certain things to be happy and, therefore, well behaved. These things have been called *universal desires* (Lovett, 1996). Autonomy, relationships, interdependence, safety, trust, self-esteem, belonging, self-regulation, accomplishment, communication, pleasure, and joy are needs for all human beings. Helping students meet these needs is essential to creating learning environments in which students feel comfortable and safe; such feelings, in turn, help resolve behavior issues.

Autonomy　Autonomy means the right or power to govern oneself or to be self-determined. To help students feel autonomous, provide choices and allow them to make as many decisions as possible. Examples include choice in seat location, whom to sit by, the materials to use for a project, the topic of a project, the type of writing instrument, whether to have something modified, and what to eat. Allowing students more choices enhances their ability to make decisions and become independent people.

Relationships and Interdependence　An entire chapter of this book (Chapter 8) has been dedicated to relationships. This is because relationships are deeply important in the lives of students. Students need to be allowed to have relationships and connections with their peers. Opportunities should be created for students to help one another. Chapter 8 suggests several strategies for facilitating relationships and building connections among students. When these needs are not met, students will invariably try to gain each other's attention. This bid for attention occurs in a variety of ways: It may be through hitting, tapping, or pestering. Students might also seem lonely and choose to sit by themselves. They may seem angry and try to get removed from certain settings through challenging behaviors.

Safety and Trust　Creating a safe, trusting relationship requires you to follow through when you say you are going to do something. Demonstrate that you can be trusted and that you are not there to punish or hurt any students. Keep your promises to students; it has been shown that "many people who engage in difficult behaviors have too much experience with broken promises" (Pitonyak, 2007, p. 18). Continually send the message that you are there to be trusted to help and support, not to punish and manage. Do not remove students from the learning environment. Every time a student is removed for a time-out or a brief stint in the hall, a clear message is sent to that student. The message is, "You are not welcome here. Your membership in this community is contingent on your behavior." This tends to create a vicious cycle:

Students think that they do not belong, and they act in ways to demonstrate such thoughts; if they are removed, their suspicions are reinforced.

Pleasure and Joy   All students need pleasure and joy in their learning environments. When supporting a student, ask yourself, "How often does this student experience pleasure or joy in the classroom?" "How often does this student laugh or have fun with others?" "How can more time be devoted to pleasure and joy in the environment?" Identifying and designing meaningful ways to answer these questions in order to create more joy in the classroom can be an overlooked piece of the busy day-to-day responsibilities of an inclusive educator. Yet it is essential! The experience of pleasure and joy can help to spark student curiosity, build and sustain friendships, increase confidence, and inspire students to take on greater challenges. When supporting your students, remember that celebrating success, encouraging joy, and allowing space for laughter and fun are critical for their learning.

Communication   All students deserve the right to communicate their needs and wants. In one classroom, the teacher asked about the weather and date. One student using a communication device pushed a button to make the device say, "I know the answer." He pushed the button again and pushed it three more times during the morning meeting. He was never called on to answer. It seemed that the teacher was beginning to feel frustrated by the noise of the device, and eventually she walked over and took the device away from him. He later found the device and pushed the button to make the device say, "I feel sad." This story illustrates an important point. Communication is not something to be earned and taken away. Any attempt to communicate should be honored, because all people need and deserve to be heard.

If students do not believe they are being heard, they will attempt to communicate their thoughts, feelings, and needs through their behavior. Students will assert their own independence, behave in certain ways to receive pleasure and joy, act out when they do not feel safe or need to communicate something, and act out when they do not feel safe or need to communicate something. Purposefully creating opportunities for communication is essential to helping students avoid negative behavior. Students might be communicating something such as "I am lonely," "I do not feel safe," or "I do not know how to tell you what I need." The behavior they exhibit might not be easy to identify as communication, but it is important to remember that all behavior is communication. Part of the job of educators is trying to figure out what students are attempting to communicate in their behavior.

ASK YOURSELF: WHAT DOES THIS PERSON NEED?

"I wish my teacher would listen to my ideas. How do you know if you don't try it?"

—Olivia (sixth-grade student)

For each student, make a plan to help him or her receive more of the things that will fulfill his or her needs. For example, if you believe a student needs more choice, you should provide the student with more choice. If you think a student needs more movement, add movement to the lesson plans.

We are aware that this recommendation contradicts most behavior systems and plans. Many people believe that if you give others what they need, they will just act out more. The opposite, however, is true. If you help meet students' needs, they will not need to misbehave to get what they want (Kluth, 2010; Lovett, 1996; Pitonyak, 2007). See Table 7.2 for more ideas for thinking about behavior.

Here are some great questions to ask yourself:

- What might this person need?
- Does this person need more pleasure and joy in his or her school day?
- Does this person need more choice or control over what happens to him or her?
- Does this person need to feel more as if he or she belongs?
- Does this person need more relationships and interdependence?
- Does this person need more autonomy?
- Does this person need more access to communication?

First, determine each student's needs, and then work with your team to determine avenues to meet those needs.

Provide Choice in Format and Body Positioning

Allow students choices for how they complete the academic task. For one student who moves a lot when learning, we found that providing her and her classmates with window markers proved to be an excellent strategy for writing lists, brainstorming, or planning out writing assignments. Using Crayola washable markers on nonporous desks also benefited students who liked to stand while working. Providing a vinyl shower curtain and whiteboard markers or chalk for writing on the sidewalk instantly engages students as they practice math facts or brainstorm writing topics for their next books.

Providing choice in body positioning is another strategy. Students can be given the choice of doing some assignments "graffiti style," which allows them to tape paper onto the walls and complete work while standing up. Some students prefer to lie on the ground to do work, and having clipboards available allows these students to write comfortably. Another strategy we refer to as "Michelangelo style" involves affixing a worksheet underneath the desk, allowing a student to work lying on his or her back while writing. Another option is to adjust the height of some desks, allowing students to stand at a desk to complete their work. Having music stands gives students the option of a moveable and height-adjustable workspace that easily adapts to a student's preferences. Students might also be given the option to use a sit disc at their seat or a therapy ball instead of a chair. A comfortable couch or cozy reading chairs allow students to engage in tasks for longer amounts of time. When teachers provide choice in body positioning, students can focus and be successful in their work. See Table 7.3 for examples of things that you might provide choices about.

Table 7.2. Asking new questions about behavior

Challenging behavior	Deficit thinking questions	New questions
Constantly moving	Why won't Zoey sit crisscross during read-aloud time?	How can I restructure the read-aloud experience so Zoey can move and learn simultaneously?
Talking	Why is Liam interrupting during math when I am trying to teach a lesson?	How can I create interactive discussions during lessons, sending the message that meaningful participation is valued?
Singing	Why does Mia continue to hum during reading workshop when I've told her that this is an independent work time?	What sensory supports can I make available to Mia so that she is productive during reading workshop but also does not distract others in our learning community?
All about me	Why does James continue to talk about activities and things he has done outside of school when we're exploring new science topics?	How can James share his background knowledge about science to motivate those around him? How can being a "science expert" support James's reading of nonfiction texts?
Shutting down	Why does Jazz hide her face when unfamiliar adults speak to her?	How can we support Jazz to develop relationships and interact effectively with new adults?
Asking why	Why does Ashley constantly challenge me by asking "why"?	What research opportunities can be built into learning experiences that allow Ashley to develop intricate knowledge about the "why" of concepts being studied?
Challenging or arguing	Why does Isaiah frequently bicker with classmates during playground time?	What social skills could be taught to allow Isaiah to play and engage in cooperative learning groups effectively?
Running out	Why does Aiden scream and run out of the class?	Does Aiden have an effective communication system? What does this behavior communicate? Are the academic tasks differentiated to meet Aiden's needs?
Engaging in self-injurious behavior	Why does Chloe pick her fingers until they bleed and do other things that just hurt herself?	What is the function of this behavior? Did I ask Chloe why she does this?
Being rough with support staff	Why does Jack swat the paraprofessional when she is just trying to re-explain the directions?	Is the paraprofessional providing too much academic and social support in close proximity? How can we fade support? How can we teach Jack to ask for support when he needs it?

Table 7.3.   Suggestions for providing choice

PIG grouping: work in a partnership, as an individual, or in a group

Marker or pencil

Window marker on table or window

Computer or laptop

Small paper or chart paper

Standing or sitting

On floor with a clipboard or on grass outside

Listening or reading

Draw it or write it

Use sidewalk chalk or pencil and paper

Keep going or take a 5-minute break

Use a music stand or an easel

"Graffiti style" or "Michelangelo style"

Use a chair or therapy ball

Utilize Students as Problem Solvers

When a student becomes out of control, educators often try to implement a behavior management program that helps students comply with classroom rules, in order to do something to rectify the situation. Kohn argued, "Our responses to things we find disturbing, might be described as reflecting a philosophy of either doing things to students or working with them" (2006, p. 23). By working with students, teachers can transform their orientation to position students as expert problem solvers. This involves asking students what they need to be successful in a certain situation. Allow students to brainstorm solutions to problems and implement their ideas.

WEATHERING THE STORM

When confronting challenging behavior, school personnel often react by imposing consequences, threatening to impose consequences, removing rewards, or ignoring the behavior; in some instances, school personnel might force students to behave. Forcing a student to behave might involve physically moving a student or providing hand-over-hand assistance.

We once watched a power struggle occurring in a seventh-grade classroom. The teacher had asked the student to sit up and follow along. The student kept his head down on the desk. She repeated the direction, "Hunter, pick your head up and follow along." He did not pick up his head. She gave him a warning: "If you don't start to follow along, I am going to assume you would rather be in the office." The student did not move. She called the office and had someone come to get him and remove him from the classroom. He spent the rest of the day in in-school suspension, where he slept.

These types of situations are very difficult; you may have witnessed similar situations. There might not be easy solutions in these cases, but educators too often jump to threats and isolation as their first line of defense. Researchers have determined that, although negative reinforcement may stop a behavior in the short term, it is not an effective or humane way to stop the behavior for the long term (Kohn, 2006).

We admit that it is easy for us to suggest alternatives; we were not the ones becoming increasingly frustrated as a student would not listen to us. Nonetheless, consider some different reactions the teacher might have had. How do you think the interaction between the teacher and the student with his head on the desk might have changed had the teacher done any of the following?

- Walked over to the student and quietly asked, "What do you need right now?"
- Given the student a piece of paper and said, "Draw for me what is wrong."
- Calmly asked the student whether he needed a break or a drink of water
- Asked the student to help her with a classroom job
- Given the student a responsibility: "Could you run this book to the other English teacher for me?"
- Changed the activity entirely and asked the student to help her get ready for the next activity
- Interpreted the student's behavior and said, "Are you finished?" or "Something seems wrong; can you help me understand what it is?"

Had the teacher responded with any of these reactions, we doubt that the student would have ended up spending the day in in-school suspension with instructional time lost and at a major personal cost to the student and the teacher.

Alfie Kohn, a thoughtful researcher on rewards and punishments, suggested that rewards and punishments work in the short term. However, all educators need to ask themselves, "Work to do what?" and "At what cost?" When educators think big about what they want for their students in life, they might think they want all their students to be self-reliant, responsible, socially skilled, caring people. Rewards and punishments produce only temporary compliance. They buy obedience (Kohn, 2006). They do not help anybody develop an intrinsic sense of responsibility. In your own life, think of a task that you do not enjoy doing. For example, suppose, like us, you personally dislike taking out the garbage. Now, think for a moment: What if every time you took out the garbage, someone said to you, "Good job taking out the garbage"? Would that be more motivating? It is doubtful. Sometimes, things people think are rewarding are actually not. It is also important to rethink providing rewards such as gum, candy, or stickers for "working hard." This reinforces the notion that what the student is doing is undesirable and needs a reward.

All Behavior Communicates Something

It is important to understand that all behavior communicates something. If a student is engaging in challenging behavior, ask yourself, "What might this student be communicating?" Once you have made your best guess at what the student needs, try to meet that student's needs. One educator did this beautifully. A student, Hayden, was continually tapping a classmate, Sarah, on the back; the tapping seemed to bother Sarah. Instead of assuming that Hayden was trying to be obnoxious or to get attention, the educator interpreted Hayden's behavior as an attempt to interact with a friend. The teacher whispered to Hayden, "Do you want to move closer and talk with Sarah? One way to start the conversation is to just say, 'Hi.'" Hayden moved closer and said, "Hi," and the conversation went on from there.

Some useful ways to interpret what a student is communicating include the following:

- *Ask him or her.* Say, "I see you are doing X; what do you want me to know?" or "It must mean something when you bang your head. What does it mean?"
- *Watch and learn.* Record everything the student does before and after a behavior. Meet with the team and try to determine what the student is attempting to gain from behaving this way.
- *Attribute positive motives.* One of the most important things is to consider what you believe about a particular student. Attribute the best possible motive consistent with the facts (Kohn, 2006). Assume that the student does not have malicious intent; the student probably is trying to get his or her needs met or to communicate something.

Every situation can be filtered through two different lenses. When you attribute the best possible motive consistent with the facts, you often see things in a positive and, possibly, more accurate light. This positive spin opens the door for more humanistic approaches to behavior. On the other hand, when behavior is interpreted as malicious or mean spirited, it is all too easy to respond in a similar way.

Have you ever been out of control? What do you need when you are out of control? Do you need someone to listen, someone to talk to, someone to not give you advice, a nap, or some time away? When students are in the heat of the moment, they often need the most caring, from a calm person. They need an adult who is safe, calm, and cool and who will gently, calmly provide support.

What students do not need in the heat of the moment (or ever, for that matter) is to be ignored; to be yelled at; to be treated with hostility, sarcasm, or public humiliation; or to be forcefully removed from the situation.

Paula Kluth, an expert on behavior management (particularly with students who have autism), offered this advice:

> When a student is kicking, biting, banging her head, or screaming, she is most likely miserable, confused, scared or uncomfortable. The most effective and the most human response at this point is to offer support; to act in a comforting manner, and to help the person relax and feel safe. Teaching can come later. In a crisis, the educator must listen, support and simply be there. (2005, p. 2)

How Are the Other Students Behaving?

When students are supported by adults in the classroom, they invariably are under extra scrutiny. This sometimes leads to behavior expectations that are more stringent for students with disabilities than for other students. In one case, we heard a teacher tell a student to sit up tall while working, although two other students in the room were sleeping and one other student was crawling on the floor. Observe how the other students are expected to behave; the student being supported should not be expected to perform at a higher behavior standard.

Nothing Personal

As a special educator, Julie dealt with her fair share of challenging behaviors. The hardest thing was not to take anything personally. She had a student who was particularly good at figuring out her buttons and pushing them (or so she thought). The best advice she ever heard was to remember that the offensive behavior was "nothing personal." The students she supported invariably had challenging behavior. Whether she was working with them or not, they all were learning how to manage their own behavior. Sometimes she would tell herself, "It is not personal. Even though this student has just called me a name, it is not about me right now."

The challenging behaviors of some students are functions of their disabilities. Just as you would not get angry with a student who was having difficulty walking or reading—because you would assume that this was a function of the student's disability—you should not get angry with students who are struggling to behave. The best, most humane way to respond in these situations is to be helpful and supportive.

Think Like a Parent

Remember that every student is someone's child. When faced with a student's challenging behavior, imagine that you are someone who deeply loves the student. Try to imagine what it would be like if you had watched the child grow and learn from infancy onward; how would you react from that perspective? How might you react if it were your son, daughter, niece, or nephew? If you react from a position of love and acceptance, you are much more likely to respond with kindness and humanity than with punishment and control.

HELPING STUDENTS TO MOVE ON

If a student has just had a significant behavioral outburst, he or she may be embarrassed, tired, or still holding on to negative feelings. It is important to help students move past these experiences. After an outburst, you should let the student know that the crisis is over, validate his or her feelings, and help him or her move on. The phrases listed in Table 7.4 are offered as a guide to help you think about how you can talk to students to get them beyond emotional crises. The most important thing is for you to have a calm, loving tone in your voice as you communicate with the student.

Help the student repair any damage. When an adult makes a mistake or loses his or her temper, he or she first needs to repair the damage. Once, while giving a presentation, Julie made the mistake of using someone in the audience as an example. She did not think it would embarrass that person but subsequently learned that it had.

Table 7.4. How to communicate with a student after a behavior issue occurs

To communicate to a student	You might respond with
That the crisis is over	"You are done with that now."
	"The problem is done."
	Having the student draw the problem and then having him or her cross it out to signify that the situation has ended.
That you validate this student's feelings	"It is okay to feel that way. I understand that was hard for you."
	"Now it is over."
	"I am sorry that was so hard for you."
	"I can tell you were really frustrated, angry, or upset."
	Drawing a picture of the student and then drawing thought bubbles over the student's head. Ask the student to help you identify what he or she was thinking and feeling.
That it is time to move on	"What do you need now?"
	"What can I help you with to get you back to work?"
	"Do you want to take a rest and prepare to get yourself back together?"
	"Would you prefer to get right back to work?"
	"Draw for me what you need right now."

She felt awful; she had to repair the damage. She did so by writing a note of apology. Writing an apology note might not be the best way for a student to repair the damage after a behavioral outburst; the point is that you should help the student identify what might help fix the situation and involve him or her in repairing it.

The solution should match the problem. For example, if a student knocks books off a shelf during a tantrum, the best solution is to have the student pick up the books. If a student rips up his artwork, the solution might be to have him either tape it together or create a new piece. If a student yells at a peer, a solution might be to have him or her write an apology note, draw an apology picture, or simply say, "I am sorry." You do not want to make the repair bigger than the problem. The main goal should be to get students back to work in a timely manner.

COMMONLY ASKED QUESTIONS ABOUT BEHAVIORAL SUPPORTS

Q. If a student is not punished, will he or she not simply repeat the behavior?

A. We do not believe in adding on a punishment. In fact, much research has been done on the use of time-outs and punishments. This research suggests that punishments work in the short-term but have long-term negative effects on students (Kohn, 2006).

Q. One of my students is not aggressive toward peers—only toward adults. What does that indicate?

A. This type of aggression usually indicates a problem with the type or intensity of support being provided. Students often lash out at therapists, paraprofessionals, or teachers who make them feel different or uncomfortable because of the support being given. For example, there was a 12-year-old girl who was being aggressive toward the paraprofessional. The paraprofessional was providing intensive support by sitting next to the girl. The paraprofessional was also using a technique called "spidering" (crawling a hand up the back of the student's hair). The student seemed embarrassed and uncomfortable with that type and level of support. When the paraprofessional moved away from the student, the aggression stopped.

Q. We usually support Nathan by having the paraprofessional sit next to the student. I am wondering if this is the best way to support him.

A. Side-by-side support is rarely the best way to support students academically and can lead to challenging behavior. Modify the work, change the writing utensil, or give written prompts on a sticky note. You should provide the type and level of support that the team deems appropriate. However, if you think it is not helpful to the student, work with your team and discuss when it might be appropriate to fade your support: What would fading look like for this student? What other types of support can be in place to allow for student success?

Q. Should a student leave the room if he or she is distracting other students?

A. Leaving the room should be the absolute last resort. Try many different stay-put supports. Help the student stay in the environment for all of the reasons mentioned in this chapter. If a student is told to leave every time he or she makes a noise, that student learns that membership is contingent on being quiet or good. Of course, you want to think about other students, but when inclusion is done well, all students understand that a certain student may make noise and that the student is working on that, just as other students may be working on other skills. Most students are surprisingly patient when given the chance and some information.

CONCLUSION

The way teams of educators plan for, support, and react to behavior is critical to student success. Remembering that all behavior communicates something and that all people need love and patience will help you to be successful when educating students

who have challenging behavior. We know that educating students who have challenging behavior is not easy; therefore, the last chapter of this book (Chapter 10) focuses
on caring for yourself so that you can have the energy and ability to provide the best
possible education for all students. The next chapter of this book, Chapter 8, discusses
how the ideas of dignity and respect can help facilitate social relationships.

8

Providing Social Supports

Standing Back

MYSTERIES OF FRIENDSHIP.

· · · · · · ·

Seth sits down at the lunch table all by himself. Five minutes later, a few students sit at the same table. The distance between the other students and Seth makes it clear that they are not sitting with him. Seth quietly eats his lunch. Chewing carefully and using his napkin, Seth finishes his lunch and slowly packs up his belongings. He looks over at the other students. They are engaged in a conversation about their soccer team. No one says a word to Seth during lunch, and he does not talk with anyone during the entire lunch period. He puts his head down on his arm and closely examines the threads on his sweatshirt until the bell rings to indicate that lunch is over. Seth stands up and walks over to Judy, the paraprofessional who will walk him to his next class.

· · · · · · ·

There are students like Seth at every school and in many classrooms. Often, when a student has a disability or receives support, the student's social isolation can be significant. Some students who have disabilities can undeniably have rich social lives, friendships, and social relationships. Special education services and supports can serve either to stigmatize and separate or to facilitate social interaction and friendship. This chapter is intended to help you take steps to improve the social lives of students such as Seth and to give ideas and suggestions for making educational experiences social in nature. Specifically, this chapter focuses on the importance of friendships, how to provide subtle and natural supports, and how to support structured and unstructured time. We also discuss teaching the rules of social interaction and commonly asked questions about social supports.

THE IMPORTANCE OF FRIENDSHIPS

Think about your own life. How important are friendships? What do friends add to your life? For us, our own friends are critical to our quality of life. They provide entertainment and support; we have fun together, and they share in the joys and successes of our lives. When thinking about your own schooling experience, were you motivated to get to school to see your friends? Friendships and relationships are a key part of every student's life.

"We humans want to be together. We only isolate ourselves when we are hurt by others, but alone is not our natural state."

—Wheatley (2002, p. 19)

"Every year I tell his team that I want my son with autism to have relationships and friends. I want them to give him the skills and then facilitate and support only when necessary. I do not want anyone hovering over him and blocking peer interaction. He has social stories for the lunch room and playground and is making huge strides. He has friends. . . . Not 'helpers.' And that's what he needs. The academic piece is of course important but will come with time and teaching at home and school, but the social piece is what he needs the most."

—Carly (parent)

This chapter focuses on how educators can facilitate students' relationships with their peers and bring people together instead of hindering the students' social interactions.

Think about how it would feel if, at a certain time of day, someone came over to work with you on one of your major weaknesses (e.g., balancing your checkbook). What if he or she sat down next to you during your workday and publicly worked on that skill with you, whether or not that made sense during your schedule? How would you feel? Would you feel a loss of choice? Loss of privacy? Or of freedom? What do you think your friends and co-workers would think of this addition to your life? Do you think they would avoid you? Do you think people would flock to you? Now, imagine: How do you think the presence of a paraprofessional or special education teacher affects the students you teach?

Sometimes, a new adult in a classroom is a magnet. Other students (particularly those in younger grades) want to connect with the adult and interact. However, the unintended consequence of side-by-side support has been widely documented— specifically, the interference with peer relationships and friendships. Giangreco, Edelman, Luiselli, and MacFarland (1997) have identified several ways in which side-by-side support (or the physical closeness of an educator to the student) can hinder students with disabilities. These ways include interference with the ownership and responsibility of general educators (i.e., teachers see the student as "yours," not theirs), separation from classmates, dependence on adults, impact on peer interactions, limitations on receiving competent instruction, loss of personal control, loss of gender identity, and interference with the instruction of other students.

Unfortunately, many who engage in push-in special education services come in to the classroom and do the same thing they would have done in a separate room designated as the special education classroom. In other words, they may pay no attention to the general education content or activities and instead pull a student to a back table to work on a specific skill. This is not what is meant by *in-class support*. However, it is often seen. Working so closely one-to-one could be very embarrassing and stigmatizing to the student and is not what is intended by push-in services. The placement of one student directly next to a special educator (nearly attached) can be described as the *Velcro phenomenon*. As an educator, it is important to avoid being "Velcroed" to a student. Velcroing might include holding hands, walking next to a student, sitting next to a student, having a student on your lap, pulling a student to the side for one-to-one intervention in the classroom, and so forth. There are many different alternatives to such intensive close proximity; we provide some suggestions in this chapter (see the sections Five Ways to Naturally Support Students and Six Ways to Facilitate Relationships).

What Does Research Say About Velcro?

In a research study, a second-grade student named Gary was observed as he worked in his classroom and played with his friends. Gary was supported by a paraprofessional throughout his day. During a 4-week period, Gary participated in only 32 interactions with his peers. Twenty-nine of those interactions occurred on the day when the paraprofessional was absent. Only three interactions occurred when the paraprofessional was with him, and the paraprofessional ended two of those three interactions by asking him to get back to work. The presence of the paraprofessional had a significant impact on Gary's ability or willingness to connect with other students (Malmgren & Causton-Theoharis, 2006). Although this study was conducted with paraprofessionals, it was not the job title but the support strategies that interfered with social interactions.

SERVICES INSTEAD OF RELATIONSHIPS: WHAT IS QUALITY OF LIFE REALLY?

In an interview, Norman Kunc, a scholar who has cerebral palsy, was asked about the effect of pull-out therapy services on his life. He stated,

> Now there may be some therapists who say, "I want to help [students] function better so that they can do more things." Although that seems to be an enlightened perspective, I still have serious concerns about it because professionals mistakenly equate functioning level with quality of life and that may not be what's going on for some folks. Professionals say, "If I can help you function better, then your quality of life will improve." (Giangreco, 1996b/2004)

Michael Giangreco, who was interviewing Kunc, asked, "What are your concerns with that way of thinking?" Kunc responded,

> If you think about it, nondisabled people often don't equate the quality of their own lives with their ability to function in a certain way, so why apply it differently to people with disabilities? Rather than functioning level, I think most people would agree that the quality of life has to do with important personal experiences, feelings, and events, like relationships, having fun, and making contributions to the lives of other people. If you think about the most meaningful moments in life, they probably don't have to do with your functioning level. I'd bet they have more to do with other things like getting married, the birth of your first child, your friendships, or maybe going on a spiritual retreat; they probably don't have to do with your functioning level. Ironically, developing relationships, the opportunity to make contributions to your community, even fun itself is taken away from people with disabilities in the name of trying to get them to function better to presumably improve the quality of their lives. So I didn't get to go to regular school and then I missed the opportunity to make friends. Why? Because professionals were trying to improve my quality of life by putting me in a special school where I am supposed to learn to function better. So they take away the opportunity for me to have friends and subsequently they actually interfere with the quality of my life. (Giangreco, 1996b/2004)

This interchange raises important questions about balancing the purpose of specialized services with the human cost. It also should make educators think about ways to teach that create more opportunities for meaningful moments in life and rich social opportunities. At the least, it should cause educators to think more carefully about how services are carried out.

HIDING IN FULL VIEW: SUBTLE, GENTLE, AND RESPECTFUL SUPPORT

"Please remember, talk to kids AFTER CLASS."

—Jesse (middle school student with Asperger syndrome)

At this point in the book, we move toward the "art" of providing inclusive services. Believe it or not, there is a great deal of finesse, subtlety, and elegance that goes into excellent inclusive support. This part of the job requires the most nuance, careful action, and, at times, inaction. When Jamie Burke, a college student with autism, spoke about adult support and its impact on his social interactions, he emphasized that the support he received should be subtle so that it would not interfere with his desire for a social life. He stated, "We are willing and ready to connect with other kids, and adults must quietly step into the background, camouflaging their help as a tiger who may hide in full view" (Tashie, Shapiro-Barnard, & Rossetti, 2006, p. 185). As you think about the services provided to students, find ways to camouflage your support. As you work with paraprofessionals, be sure to discuss and come up with support plans that keep the paraprofessional in the background so that a student is able to socialize naturally and work with peers.

FIVE WAYS TO NATURALLY SUPPORT STUDENTS

Students need to move toward independence as they grow. Providing support in natural ways is one way to help reduce dependence on support personnel. The following suggestions from Causton-Theoharis and Malmgren (2005) can help you maximize student independence and interdependence with peers and minimize student dependence on adults.

1. *Do not sit or place a chair meant for adult support next to a student.* Where you position yourself during instruction is very important. There is rarely a reason to sit directly next to a student. Even if a student needs close support because of behavior or physical support, that student probably does not need you next to him or her 100% of the time. Never have a space permanently reserved for an adult next to a student. Remove the empty chair next to the student. Do not have any students sit on your lap or hold your hand unless that is commonly done for all students (e.g., in a preschool setting). If you think that the expectation in a particular school or classroom is for you to sit next to a student, ask your team the following questions:
   - When is it absolutely necessary to sit next to a student to provide one-to-one support? (Examples of this type of necessary support are when providing medical assistance or lifting/transferring a student.)
   - Are there times during the day when I could provide the student with less support? If so, when?
   - When and how can we help this student increase independence?
   - When should I move away from this student?
   - Could a peer provide key supports to this student?

2. *Do not remove the student.* Friendships and relationships occur because of common experiences over long periods of time. Every time a student is removed from an inclusive classroom for special education or therapy services, that student loses potential time to interact, socialize, and learn with and from other students. If a student leaves for a sensory break, consider putting the sensory materials in the classroom; if a student is leaving because of challenging behavior, try to determine

strategies that will help the student stay in the classroom (for strategies for working with students who have challenging behavior, see Chapter 7).

3. *Encourage peer support.* If a student asks for your help with something, have the student ask a peer instead. Make this the norm for all students. One useful way to set this up is to have all students follow the rule "Ask three before me." Set up partnerships during instructional time. Have students work together. Set up play partners, transition partners (partners for walking to and from classes), choice time partners, lunchtime partners, math partners, and so forth. Make sure the student you are purposefully designing social experiences for has a choice about whom he or she selects as a partner. Giving students the skills to seek peer support promotes a valid and important lifelong skill.

4. *Encourage independence and interdependence.* If a student is able to complete a task in your presence without adult support, have him or her complete the task without supervision the next time. For example, a team was having difficulty with Steven completing his dismissal routine. They came up with a 10-point checklist. At first, all the students in the class used the checklist. Next, Steven had a smaller magnetic version inside his locker. Finally, Steven memorized the checklist and occasionally asked a peer for help with zipping his coat. Continually ask yourself what the next step is that will enable a student to become more independent and less dependent on adult support. If a student will still need assistance, consider having interdependence (or successfully completing the task with other students) be the goal.

5. *Fade your cues.* One of the simplest yet most effective ways to increase interaction for students is to fade assistance. Fading assistance means actually reducing the type and level of support given to a student in a systematic way. Reducing support promotes independence, interdependence, and interaction with peers. Take a look at the cuing structure list shown in Table 8.1. The goal with this structure is always to move away from the most obtrusive supports (those on top) to the least obtrusive supports (those on the bottom) for students whenever possible (Doyle, 2008).

Providing natural or unobtrusive supports is a very important first step toward helping students feel like everyone else. The next step in helping students connect with one another is to facilitate relationships and assist students with positive social interactions by becoming a bridge linking students and their peers.

YOUR ROLE AS A BRIDGE BETWEEN STUDENTS WITH DISABILITIES AND THEIR PEERS

You can become a bridge connecting students; you can blend in, provide more natural supports, and facilitate relationships among students. The following subsection offers six ways to help students relate to one another to form lasting friendships.

Six Ways to Facilitate Relationships

These ideas have been modified from Causton-Theoharis and Malmgren (2005):

Table 8.1. Types of support

Type of support (listed from most intrusive to least)	Definition	Example
Full physical	Direct and physical assistance used to support a student	Hand-over-hand assistance while a student writes his or her name
Partial physical	Physical assistance provided for some of the total movement required for the activity	Putting a zipper into the bottom portion and beginning to pull up; the student then pulls the zipper up the rest of the way
Modeling	A demonstration of what the student is to do	The adult does an art project; the student uses the art project as a model.
Direct verbal	Verbal information provided directly to the student	"Josh, stand up now."
Indirect verbal	A verbal reminder that prompts the student to attend to or think about what is expected	"Josh, what should happen next?"
Gestural	A physical movement to communicate or accentuate a cue (e.g., head nod, thumbs up, pointing)	Adult points to the agenda written on the board.
Natural	Providing no cue; allowing the ordinary cues that exist in the environment to help the student know what to do	The bell rings for class. The teacher asks students to move to the rug. A message on the chalkboard reads, "Turn to page 74."

Source: Doyle (2008).

1. *Highlight similarities among students.* In a general education classroom, students are continually talking and sharing stories about things not related to the curriculum (e.g., hobbies, extracurricular activities). Become conscious of conversations going on around the student and point out similarities. For example, as students are talking about T-ball, you might say, "Oh, Josh's sister plays T-ball." Or, as students are settling down with their library books, you might point out similarities among their books: "The two of you both selected books about computers. You can sit together and compare your books."

2. *Help students invite each other to socialize.* Some students are very eager to socialize but do not know how to approach other students. It can be helpful for an educator to be proactive about all of the potential social situations that occur throughout the school day. Think ahead about social possibilities and ask the student, "Who do you want to play with at recess today?" "How can you ask him?" "Who do you want to sit next to in study hall?" If you have a student who is nonverbal, provide a picture list of the students in the class and help the student program his

or her device to ask a friend. An index card that says, "Do you want to play with me?" or "Will you be my partner?" can be very useful in such situations.

3. *Provide behavioral supports that are social in nature.* When a student is rewarded for doing a good job, make the reward something social. This way, the reward can be more fun for all involved, and it will have the added benefit of allowing students to learn and practice social interaction. Some examples of these types of interactive behavioral supports follow:

- Shoot baskets with a friend.
- Eat lunch with a friend.
- Make bead necklaces with a friend during study hall.
- Play a computer game with a friend.
- Go to the library and read with a friend.
- Make an art project before school with a friend.

4. *Provide your student responsibilities that are interactive and collaborative.* Students are commonly assigned responsibilities within the classroom and school environments. This is done to help students contribute to the classroom community and to build a sense of belonging. Educators are key participants in helping create partners for these tasks. For example, change the job chart in the classroom so that all jobs are done with buddies. When jobs arise in the classroom, ask students to do the jobs together: "Sue and Joryann, can you please pass out these papers?"

5. *Help other students understand.* Peers are much more likely to interact with students if they understand necessary information about each other. Provide honest answers to students' questions. Chelsea once heard a little girl ask, in reference to another student's FM audio device, "Why does he wear that thing on his head?" The educator said that it was private and that she should get back to work. The student got back to work, but an important question had been left unanswered. In the mind of the little girl, the subject was not to be talked about. As an unintended result, the student using the FM system might seem taboo. Your job is not to share confidential information about students with their peers. However, there are times when providing basic information about a student or the type of support they are receiving may be helpful to the student. If you are unsure about whether to share information, ask the student, the special education service coordinator, and the team of educators with whom you work. As a more proactive way of addressing such subjects, some teaching teams have decided to bring their classes together to talk about what makes everyone special. For example, the students in one middle school classroom all listed things that made them unique. Then they posted this information on a bulletin board. Some students listed, "I live with my grandmother" or "I speak two languages." One student in this class wrote, "I know sign language." This type of conversation can be used to describe specific behaviors or the accommodations that a student receives. Information can be shared about how and when to assist a particular student (e.g., do not talk in a baby voice, do ask whether he or she needs help). Before initiating a discussion of this type, make sure the student is comfortable with the plan, and involve all parties in deciding what information the student wants to share.

6. *Get out of the way!* When a conversation among students has begun, give the students space so that a natural conversation can occur; eventually, a relationship may evolve. Think about where you should stand; try to be as unobtrusive to the student as possible. If you remain close, it will be clear to everyone around that you are there, creating an invisible barrier between other students and the one you are supporting. Instead, while fading, move away and focus your attention on something else.

SUPPORT DURING UNSTRUCTURED TIME

Social interaction occurs at all times during the school day. Unstructured times are some of the most important times to provide support that will help students connect to one another. Examples of key times are listed in the following subsections, with some suggestions that should be useful.

Before and After School

Students spend a lot of time traveling to and from school. This is a perfect time to facilitate social interaction. For before and after school, help the family find a travel partner or someone in the neighborhood to walk to school or ride the bus with the student.

In the Hallway

Have walking partners in the hallway between classes. Chelsea observed one educator who had the class engage in partner Simon Says. During this 5-minute transition, students did mirrored activities with their partners as they walked down the hall. For example, the teacher had them raise one hand, then the other, stick out their tongues, hop on one foot, and, when they arrived, balance on one foot. Many of these skills used during the Simon Says game were skills directly related to two specific students' IEP goals. Not only was this a creative way to infuse therapy skills, but all of the students loved and requested this transition game. Another team had a student push an eighth-grade student named Samantha in her wheelchair while another student walked alongside her. This allowed Samantha to have some space from an adult and a chance to converse. If a student does not communicate verbally, program the device that the student uses to have common, chatty phrases, such as "How's it going?" As the student moves through the hallway, he or she can initiate interactions.

At Lunchtime

Lunchtime is an important socialization period that must be proactively designed. Be thoughtful about how direct services at lunchtime affect natural interactions. Where students sit at lunch is very important. Do not have students with disabilities sit together at one table. Instead, help students to select lunch places at which they will feel the most comfortable and, at the same time, have increased likelihood of interacting with peers.

Some schools create interest tables at which students' interests (e.g., chess, fashion, soccer) are printed on table tent cards. Students sit at tables that interest them and can freely converse about their preferred topic. Other schools have "lunch bunches." Organizing a lunch bunch is a useful way to help a student who struggles with social interaction during the lunch period and is perfect for providing some types of services. A lunch bunch involves gathering a group of students during the lunch period for a particular purpose (e.g., planning the end-of-year picnic, creating a class yearbook). This heterogeneous group of students can meet weekly to complete the task. It is imperative that this mixed group is not composed only of students with disabilities. At the end of the year, the lunch bunch might celebrate its accomplishments with a pizza party. The objective is to bring students together in a more intimate setting, to foster social interaction, and help form friendships.

Music can be provided at lunchtime to create a calming atmosphere. A team in one school employed this strategy because Jonah, a student with autism whom they supported, had found the lunchroom to be overwhelming to his senses. After asking him what kind of music he would like to have on, the team piped Beatles music into the lunchroom, providing a calming atmosphere for all students. Best of all, Jonah was able to stay in the lunchroom and connect with other students several days a week.

At Free or Choice Time

Help students choose the activities they want to do and which peers they want to participate with them. In high school, where a student sits is crucial. Have each student select his or her peers and location in a room by asking the student where he or she would prefer to sit, and respect that choice. During recess time, or during any other downtime outside of class, bring an activity that is particularly interesting to the student. For example, one student with Down syndrome, Casey, loved to make beaded necklaces at home. The OT was previously working on dexterity strength and fine motor skills in a pull-out fashion using a number of craft activities. Instead, the teacher brought a beading kit to class and told the students that they could use the kit as long as they shared it. She put it on Casey's desk and asked her to be responsible for it. When we walked out to recess to see how it was going, four girls and two boys had formed a semicircle around the bead kit and all of them were making necklaces. Casey was working on fine motor skills, but more important, she was surrounded by peers and engaged in relaxed conversation.

To Select Partners

The words some students least like to hear in classrooms are "find a partner." Inevitably, as students clamor to work with their friends, someone will be left out and need a partner. If that happens, an adult should not become the student's partner. Instead, help the student find a friend. It can be far more helpful to determine partners ahead of time.

One very thoughtful team, tired of seeing the same scenario occur with Kristin, a student who repeatedly finds it difficult to connect with peers, during math class, came up with a new solution. They used purposeful partnering to ensure that each student, including Kristin, had 12 different planned partners. This solution created partners who would remain constant so that students did not have to feel left out. Using the Clock Buddies sheet found online (Jones, 2012; see Figure 8.1), they purposefully set up partners for the rest of the year by having students sign up for hourly partners. From that point on, when the teacher would say, "Find your 2:00 partner," Kristin knew exactly who her partner would be, and she was able to participate successfully in the math center.

SUPPORT DURING INSTRUCTIONAL TIME

During instructional time, walk around the room, supporting all students and answering everyone's questions. It can be very stigmatizing to be the only one receiving help. The best scenario is one in which you provide support to the entire class, with none of the students thinking that you are there to help a specific student. If you are a special educator, avoid calling yourself "the special education teacher." Instead, refer to yourself as just another teacher and someone who teaches everyone. As soon as a student has gotten started, do not hover. Give the student space to work and make mistakes, just like everyone else. Have the student request help in the same way that everyone

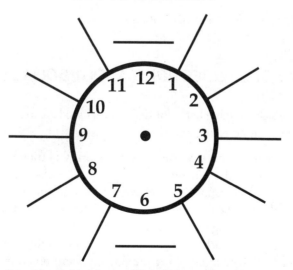

CLOCK BUDDIES

Figure 8.1. Clock buddies sign-up sheet. (From Jones, R.C. [2012]. *Strategies for reading comprehension: Clock buddies*. Retrieved from http://www.readingquest.org/strat/clock_buddies.html)

else does. If you must redirect a student, do so quietly. Also praise quietly and be careful not to oversupport. Each of these aspects is important, and your support should be as unobtrusive and gentle as possible.

To ensure that all students come into contact with a student with disabilities, you can move instructional materials to the student instead of asking the other students to go to a certain station or object. We witnessed a team do this beautifully with Alex, a student in kindergarten who used a wheelchair. All of the students were moving over to a globe to gather information. The team decided to move the globe over to Alex's desk and, as the students came over to look at it, many of them interacted with Alex.

TEACH STUDENTS THE RULES OF SOCIAL INTERACTION

Many students struggle with how to interact with others. It is as if they are playing a game for which they do not know the rules. If you are working with an individual who feels this way, teach him or her the rules explicitly. However, do not teach the rules in isolation or in a separate room with only students who have disabilities. Instead, use everyday moments in the classroom and on the playground to artfully teach students how to interact with one another. There are many resources available to help you. Carol Gray has written several books on writing social stories for students with autism and on drawing social situations in cartoon form to help students understand social rules (see Gray, 2010). For other ideas, ask your team of teachers or do some research online. Educators should not assume loneliness is part of the schooling experience; they can intervene and help students make and maintain friendships.

"Your job as a teacher is not to fix or cure a child; it's to facilitate their active participation, respect and acceptance among peers and to support them in reaching their individual potential."

—*Jordan (parent of a student with disabilities who is educated in an inclusive classroom)*

COMMONLY ASKED QUESTIONS ABOUT SOCIAL SUPPORTS

Q.   This student's challenging behavior makes other students not want to be around him or her. What do I do about that?

A.   First, you have to assume that the student is worthy of friendships and relationships. Help support the student in a way that will both minimize the behavior and help others understand the behavior. One student, Kenny, used to rock back and forth when he felt anxious, and this behavior looked strange to Kenny's peers. Simply explaining to the other students what the behavior meant allowed one bright student to ask Kenny, "What can I do to help you stop rocking?" Kenny typed out a response: "Let me put my hand on your shoulder." From that moment on, Kenny's peers helped him to manage his rocking behavior by asking, "Do you want to lean on me?"

Q.   You suggest that I should not remove the learner, but one student has sensory issues that do not allow her to be in the lunchroom. What do I do about that?

A.   Consider some of the lunchroom ideas discussed in this chapter. Make the lunchroom fit the student. Consider music, lunch partners, interest centers, a comforting item, or a quieter lunch space.

Q.   I understand why I should fade my support, but I worry that will not count as student contact minutes. What can I do while I am fading my support?

A.   This is a common concern. "Direct contact minutes" does not mean you are in direct contact with students (e.g., touching students, providing hand-over-hand support, sitting at their table). Instead, it means they are engaged in learning experiences that you have helped to construct with your expertise. When they are practicing a skill (e.g., handwriting), you can get students started and walk around the room helping others. When you return, you can help reposition the paper and continue moving. When moving away from a student, you can support other students, prepare for an upcoming class by creating modifications, or collect data. Furthermore, you can consult with other teachers and paraprofessionals.

CONCLUSION

You learned about Seth at the beginning of this chapter. Seth is a student who struggles with social interactions. The biggest detriment to his social life is that he has an adult supporting him all school day long and he is pulled out continually for special education services. Friendships and relationships are critical to Seth's development and quality of life. This is true for all students; for those who receive services, care needs to be taken to ensure maximum inclusion and opportunities for social interaction. As educators, you can make new decisions about therapy or pull-out services and decide to conduct them inclusively. The suggestions mentioned in this chapter are meant to support your efforts to include students in the social aspects of school. The next chapter focuses on providing both academic and social supports through the utilization of paraprofessionals.

9

Supporting and Supervising Paraprofessionals

WHAT CAN HAPPEN WHEN
PARAPROFESSIONALS ARE LEFT TO LEARN
THE ROPES WITHOUT APPROPRIATE
TRAINING AND SUPERVISION.

© 1999 MICHAEL GIANGRECO. ILLUSTRATIONS KEVIN RUELLE
PEYTRAL PUBLICATIONS, INC. 952-949-8707 www.peytral.com

Across the country, paraprofessionals are employed by school districts to provide essential support, access, and an inclusive education for students with disabilities. There are different types, roles, and names of paraprofessionals. Some paraprofessionals provide one-to-one student support, and others are hired to be instructional assistants for classrooms. Districts use terminology such as *teaching assistants* or *instructional assistants, teaching aides,* or just *aides.* We use the term *paraprofessional* as an umbrella term to describe educational assistants, who are typically utilized in classrooms to support students during instruction.

Paraprofessionals can be assigned to support specific grade levels, classrooms, or students. It is best to consult with your administrators about the roles and duties of paraprofessionals who are assigned to work within your classroom. Providing direction and support to paraprofessionals is the job of educators. Inclusive educators often state that planning for and directing instructional use of paraprofessionals are roles for which they feel ill prepared. Paraprofessionals are significant members of the educational team, and the strategies and tools shared in this chapter are intended to increase your collaboration with, support for, and supervision of all paraprofessionals.

Remember, like students, paraprofessionals come with a variety of skills and knowledge. Some may be skilled, certified teachers and others may be new to education entirely. One of the first tasks is get to know the paraprofessionals working with you. They may or may not come with the skill set that you would like them to, but it is your job to help get them ready to support students effectively. Determine skills and strengths and figure out how to play to those strengths.

WELCOMING PARAPROFESSIONALS

Developing solid rapport with the paraprofessionals who work with you is vital to cultivating a successful relationship. It is important to create a welcoming environment that is supportive to paraprofessionals. This will foster a collaborative approach when supporting students. It is also important that the paraprofessional is part of the classroom community and knows about key events that will be happening. Table 9.1 suggests ways to welcome paraprofessionals into your classroom.

It is imperative that inclusive educators recognize that paraprofessionals must have common knowledge of the academic, social, communication, and behavioral goals of students. In other words, it is advantageous for paraprofessionals to understand your pedagogy, larger goals of teaching and learning, and approach to management and behavior. The next subsections provide ideas about communicating expectations, training, sharing relevant information, and modeling classroom practices to support the paraprofessionals you work with.

Communicate Expectations

Inclusive educators who communicate their expectations about how to include students can then support paraprofessionals to fully understand their roles and responsibilities within that classroom. We have seen skilled inclusive educators not only directly

Table 9.1. Ways to welcome paraprofessionals into your classroom

---

Ensure the paraprofessional has a designated space in which to put his or her belongings within the classroom.

Make sure that each adult who provides services within the classroom has his or her name listed on the door. This communicates a collaborative team approach to educating all students.

Refer to paraprofessionals as you would any teacher. If you use titles such as Mrs., Ms., or Mr., do the same when using their names in the classroom. It displays respect.

Convey that the paraprofessional is a supportive educator in the room by ensuring that he or she does not have a student desk and chair with a name tag.

Have the paraprofessional read through any classroom newsletters or notes to families, checking for any editing changes needed. If applicable, sign the closing of the classroom newsletter with names of all adults who work in the classroom to convey a team approach.

Include the paraprofessional in the classroom culture by designating certain daily and weekly roles.

Ask paraprofessionals about their opinions and involve them as part of any problem-solving meetings.

Invite paraprofessionals to parent–teacher conferences and open houses. This family interaction allows for their visibility and belonging in the school community.

Write welcome and thank-you notes to paraprofessionals.

Introduce paraprofessionals as part of the teaching team and make introductions that are similar to yours. For example, if you would introduce yourself to new students by showing photos or a few sentimental artifacts that represent unique hobbies, allow your paraprofessional to do so.

---

communicate these expectations but also create task cards that outline teaching procedures for specific academic times to provide direct support to the paraprofessional. This removes the guesswork and larger decision making, and allows paraprofessionals to focus on facilitating learning and interacting with students. Information for implementing a task card system is discussed in detail in a later section of this chapter.

Training

In order for paraprofessionals to understand the structure of the class, teachers should advocate that paraprofessionals be included in any schoolwide trainings or professional development sessions. This includes topics on curriculum development, social skills, and managing behavior. Participation in such training allows paraprofessionals to learn the educational jargon being used, have an overview of the structure and organization of subject-area classes, and gain a sense of belonging within the professional community of educators. The more that paraprofessionals understand about teaching and learning, the goals of inclusive education, and their role, the more effectively they will be able to support students with disabilities within your classes. Having access to training resources about what inclusive education means and best practices for supporting students to achieve their academic, behavior, and social goals allows paraprofessionals to acquire the knowledge to be effective in inclusive classrooms. We also suggest that teams give each paraprofessional the companion handbook *The Paraprofessional's Handbook for Effective Support in Inclusive Classrooms* (Causton-Theoharis, 2009b) in order to increase his or her knowledge of inclusive educational practices.

Share Relevant Information

Paraprofessionals need explicit training on how to best support individual students. If a paraprofessional supports a student with a behavior intervention plan (BIP), the paraprofessional must have the opportunity to review the BIP with an educator. The paraprofessional needs to explicitly know what to do and what not to do in order to legally follow the BIP. The same is true for the IEP. Paraprofessionals should read the IEPs of the students they are supporting. Many educators create IEPs at a Glance as a way to communicate to the paraprofessional about the important parts of the IEP. See Figure 5.2 for an example of the IEP at a Glance.

Modeling

Modeling classroom practices and supports for students with disabilities provides hands-on opportunities for paraprofessionals to learn. Training around implementing modifications, adaptations, and supplementary aids and supports is important. When implementing a new differentiation technique, initiate a conversation with the paraprofessional to facilitate his or her understanding, and help him or her understand the reasons for trying the new strategies. Ask the paraprofessional to lead a small portion of the classroom lesson, and model how you might support a small group or a student with challenging behavior. This helps communicate to the paraprofessional your expectations that he or she will circulate around to small groups in the classroom rather than constantly standing by the one student that was assigned a one-to-one paraprofessional and that he or she will ask questions to promote discussion. Think critically about how you want the paraprofessional to support your teaching, and find a way to model this.

It is also imperative to think about the use of person-first language, your classroom disposition, and interactions with students. Your emphasis on social interactions and the human, relationship-based element of teaching is critical in creating a classroom where everyone working in the classroom feels valued and important. Paraprofessionals are consistently observing and emulating your interactions. Inclusive education centers around relationships, connection, and belonging—which some suggest is the hidden curriculum in inclusive classrooms. We know inclusive educators who make this hidden curriculum of inclusive classrooms explicit and actually talk about it with the paraprofessionals. They discuss their social interactions, disposition, and techniques used to connect with students. Modeling teaching strategies and social interactions allows paraprofessionals to visualize and feel comfortable with their role in the classroom.

COMMUNICATION WITH PARAPROFESSIONALS

Communication with paraprofessionals is essential to implementing inclusive education. Communication that is ongoing and consistent helps to establish expectations and ensure that everyone is working toward shared goals. We suggest planning both weekly and daily interaction as a way to consistently connect with paraprofessionals.

Weekly Planning Meetings

Communication on a weekly basis is essential to making sure the paraprofessional knows about the current unit of study, is updated on any changes in students' home or school lives, considers expectations, and is prepared to implement academic supports that have been planned. We suggest setting up a weekly meeting with the paraprofessional. Providing a draft of an upcoming newsletter or letter that will be sent home to families allows the paraprofessional to be filled in on the events of the class and school. This helps to bring the paraprofessional in as a member of the educational team and saves meeting time to be used for planning purposes.

We recommend involving the paraprofessional in the planning of learning experiences whenever possible. We have also seen many teams of educators use a weekly e-mail to touch base with paraprofessionals. In addition to weekly communication, it is essential to check in with paraprofessionals on a daily basis. You might use the following list of questions to check in with paraprofessionals:

- How is it going during centers?
- How did the adaptations in social studies work?
- Do you have questions about data collection?
- Did you have any questions about the BIP?
- Do you have any suggestions on what adaptations or modifications need to be changed?
- How are you feeling about your instructional role in our classroom?

Daily Problem-Solving Meetings

When teams communicate on a daily basis, it allows for flexible delivery of instruction that is based on immediate monitoring. Reserving 10 minutes before or after school or during a preparation period for team meeting time allows teams to touch base about current lessons, changes to make, and adaptations or modifications that would be appropriate to implement. Teams that are unable to find common planning time can simply have a notebook for jotting down notes, questions, or updates for one another. This daily communication system allows teams to check in without interrupting joint teaching time and without talking about students when the classroom is filled with students.

Just Listen

Remember to take time to listen to paraprofessionals. They often have exceptional ideas or new ways to approach a situation. Be sure to spend time each week listening to what is happening and asking questions to learn more about their experiences in supporting learners. Validate their perspectives and understanding of students and learning. This listening will lead to greater contributions and a sense of teamwork that leads to increased efficacy of inclusive education.

GIVING PARAPROFESSIONALS ROLES

As a supervisor of a paraprofessional, providing clear roles and responsibilities helps set explicit expectations. In addition to general communication about what is working and what needs to change, including paraprofessionals in meetings with educators who are planning lessons is key. Paraprofessionals who are involved in various aspects of the lesson design process develop a sense of shared ownership for the academic success of all students. You might ask for recommendations for providing different adaptations or request assistance in making modifications for the following week. Simply listening to the ideas paraprofessionals have validates their commitment to a team approach to providing services for students. If there are weekly modifications to instructional materials to be made (e.g., enlarged copies, adapted readability of texts), you might ask the paraprofessional to be responsible for this task. Finding ways to enhance paraprofessionals' sense of responsibility, contribution, and commitment contributes to a stronger team that can better meet students' needs.

It is important to note that, although as educators we want paraprofessionals to be highly involved and engaged in the lesson planning and implementation process, we cannot simply expect paraprofessionals to assume all responsibilities for making modifications or adaptations for specific students. This would be beyond their duty. In conjunction with and supervised by certified educators, paraprofessionals can support the instruction of students with disabilities, including preparing modifications and adaptations. To be clear, teams often work collaboratively to create modifications and adaptations, but these functions certainly cannot be completely delegated to paraprofessionals. Your expertise of the curriculum, knowledge of the student, and training in special education are imperative to creating individualized supports.

Task Cards

We also recognize that scheduling and time constraints restrict many teams of educators and paraprofessionals from meeting to design lessons. A strategy we have witnessed many teams use seamlessly has been writing task cards for paraprofessionals. As educators are planning the weekly lessons, assign one person to jot down sequential steps for lessons that the paraprofessional is responsible for conducting.

Figure 9.1 displays a task card example for a paraprofessional who works in a ninth-grade reading class. Even though the paraprofessional might not be able to attend the weekly planning sessions with the team, one educator can meet with the paraprofessional to provide an overview of the lessons and review the sequential steps on the task cards. Teams have found this strategy to be beneficial because it ensures that during the planning, educators discuss each adult's role during the lesson. It also provides a purposeful role for the paraprofessional. Assigning specific roles diminishes the paraprofessional's tendency to sit next to a student with a disability during the entire lesson. The goal of writing task cards is to intentionally provide roles, spread instructional support, and use adults in meaningful ways during every segment of lessons.

There are many roles to assign paraprofessionals during classroom instruction. These include providing one-to-one instruction, running a small-group instructional

---

Lesson Objective: Students will analyze how an author's claims are developed in an informational text.

Tasks

Minilesson

While I conduct the minilesson, construct visual notes on the SMART Board. Upon hearing student ideas, create a graphic organizer that displays the author's main purpose and the supporting claims. Draw, sketch, and add labels.

Workshop

- While students are reading, locating supporting claims in their informational texts, and writing them on sticky notes, conference with five students. The names of the students you are conferencing with are on your reading clipboard conference sheet.
- Be sure to glance over to Jaden between conferences to see if he needs support in getting back on track. If he does, provide written support (use an index card or sticky note), then begin your next student conference. Recall that we are working on building Jaden's reading stamina and independence; provide the support and fade your physical presence (move away) promptly.
- Be sure that Kim has her reading and communication materials out, that she has selected a peer to work with, and that they have begun.
- Today's teaching point is on identifying the author's claims and the ways that these provide evidence for the author's purpose. For each conference, begin with one strength that you notice each reader displays, then one teaching point, and then the specific skill you want the student to continue working on.

Closing

- While I conclude the lesson, check in with Jaden. Be sure he has written his homework in his agenda.
- Support Jaden to organize reading materials neatly in his folder and ensure he takes all needed homework supplies home.
- Be sure that Kim has her communication device, agenda, and communication notebook. Ask her to check her schedule so she knows where to walk for next period.

Figure 9.1. Task card for paraprofessional to use during ninth-grade reading.

station, or facilitating large-group lessons. In the chapter on collaboration (Chapter 5), we discussed each type of co-teaching arrangement that educators can use in classrooms. Each of these arrangements can be used with a paraprofessional. The difference is that educators would not ask a paraprofessional to design a station or center without close supervision, including support with defining objectives and creating a lesson plan. Educators would assume the primary planning role and ensure that the paraprofessional feels comfortable leading the station or center.

INVOLVING PARAPROFESSIONALS IN THE LIFE OF THE CLASSROOM

There are many other ways that educators authentically involve paraprofessionals in teaching and the life of the classroom. Some ways paraprofessionals have been effectively used within general education classrooms include helping with classroom duties, implementing behavior management plans, and collecting data.

Classroom Tasks

One educator decided to create a general checklist for weekly classroom duties that needed to be completed. Next to the row of tasks, there was a row to check when completed and a small box for any comments. These tasks included general classroom upkeep duties (e.g., wiping the tables, watering the plants, cleaning the supplies area), communication with families (e.g., checking agendas, writing notes back to families, getting field trip permission slips), and organizing the classroom library and math manipulatives storage sections. The idea was to involve everyone in the routines of the classroom. Anytime a paraprofessional or educator had a free moment, he or she checked the list, worked on one of the tasks, and initialed that it was completed. This supported paraprofessional involvement. Paraprofessionals also came to know where supplies for modifications and adaptations were located. It also helped to keep the learning environment organized.

Think Ahead

Kathie, a fourth-grade teacher, had the good fortune of having Jill, a paraprofessional, supporting in her classroom. Jill was assigned to support one student named Samantha, but the team was working on helping Samantha become more independent. Instead of having Jill sit to the side, Kathie thought ahead. She created a list of all the things that might provide future instructional support for Samantha and others. For example, one week, her list included the following: 1) search for video of cell division, 2) find pictures of mitosis, 3) locate a hands-on activity related to the process to support visualization and understanding of mitosis, and 4) add next week's spelling and vocabulary into Samantha's communication device. We encourage inclusive educators to think ahead about how paraprofessionals can add to the teaching and learning process.

Supporting Behavior

Paraprofessionals are also involved in implementing behavior management plans. This might involve collecting some data to use in the functional behavioral assessment (FBA) or to monitor how a BIP is being implemented. We have found that a benefit in ensuring that paraprofessionals are explicitly knowledgeable of BIPs is that they become cognizant of their behavior management, how they proactively support students, and how to respond during moments of challenging behavior. A natural extension of this involvement is to have paraprofessionals note circumstances and collect data around specific students' behavior in order to better understand the issues and contribute thoughtfully to discussions. The more that you can have paraprofessionals be involved in the PBSs you implement and collect data around challenging moments, the better the educational team as a whole will become in purposefully supporting behavior.

Involvement in Assessment

Paraprofessionals can be utilized to collect assessment data. Involve paraprofessionals in gathering formative assessment data to help monitor progression of student learning objectives. There are various strategies for this involvement. Some ideas might involve asking each student two open-ended, thought-provoking questions related to the curriculum. Create a template to have the paraprofessional jot down the students' ideas or have the paraprofessional use a digital recorder to keep track of student responses. Another idea might be to have the paraprofessional conduct a performance-based assessment with each student or groups of students. Provide a rubric and ask the paraprofessional to rate the performance and make notations.

The aforementioned examples are two that involve the use of adult time that you might not otherwise have during a busy school day. This could be a useful strategy for involving paraprofessionals in the classroom teaching and learning environment in a way that contributes to better instructional design and decisions. Other formative assessments that paraprofessionals can implement include reviewing 5-minute free writes, checking ticket-out-the-door or exit slips, reviewing response logs, tallying data from self-assessments, or taking snapshots of individual whiteboards during lessons. Think about the formative assessments you utilize across curriculum units and purposefully ask yourself, "How might a paraprofessional contribute to increased assessment data?" and "How might we gain a better understanding of the progression of student learning and thinking so that this data can inform our instructional decisions?"

Paraprofessionals are often involved in data collection for tracking the progression of IEP goals. At the onset of each month, many educational teams meet to determine what data to collect as a way to measure the progression of IEP goals. Assign one or two portions of this data collection to a paraprofessional. This strategy is advantageous because data is collected from multiple members of the educational team. It also helps the paraprofessional become familiarized with the IEP goals, reinforces his or her role in educating the student, and allows him or her to feel a sense of ownership or investment in the educational outcomes of students he or she works with. Purposeful data collection in relation to the achievement of IEP goals sets the educational team up to make data-based instructional decisions.

We have also seen educational teams that have paraprofessionals make some of the needed modifications for summative assessments. After examining a test that is given to an entire class or grade level, the educational team discusses the types of modifications that need to be made. The paraprofessional might make enlarged copies; rephrase test questions to alter the readability level; break larger tasks into distinct, manageable steps; provide visual clues in the margins; set up recording devices and other technology needed; make notations of appropriate break points; or create written directions for any oral portions.

Teach Them How to Fade Support

One of the most important skills to teach paraprofessionals when they are supporting students one-to-one is to support less, or to fade support. Students can become overly dependent on support unless we think carefully about how to give support judiciously. Well-meaning paraprofessionals and educators often oversupport, which can cause problems such as the Velcro phenomenon (Causton-Theoharis, 2009a; Causton-Theoharis, Giangreco, Doyle, & Vadasy, 2007; Causton-Theoharis & Malmgren, 2005). In other words, one of the worst ways to support a student is to position a support person directly next to the student. Ask your team the following questions:

1. When is it absolutely necessary to be physically next to a student when providing support?
2. What are alternatives to sitting next to or being in the same physical space as a student?

Numerous alternatives to side-by-side support exist. One overall goal when supporting students with disabilities is to implement the necessary supplementary aids and supports that are required in order to increase independence. Figure out alternatives to increase independence, advance progression in the academic curriculum, and meaningfully include students with disabilities. Some alternatives include modifying the work, having the student work with a peer, using technology, providing a to-do list, using an agenda, or using a word window. Other ideas are listed in Table 9.2. We suggest collaboratively constructing a list of alternatives to side-by-side support with the paraprofessionals that you supervise. This communicates the message that sitting next to a student with a disability is not the expectation and that there are more useful strategies for providing meaningful support while promoting the academic and social elements of inclusive education.

Table 9.2. Alternatives to side-by-side support

Modify the work.

Have a student work with a peer.

Use technology.

Provide a to-do list and have the student check off items.

Use an agenda.

Use a word window instead of having someone point to the text.

Take visual notes.

Model the required steps at the front of the room.

Create a graphic organizer.

Provide prompts and cues.

Use cooperative learning with roles for group members.

Make text (e.g., books, assignments) accessible with text-to-speech software.

Engage in task analysis and break the assignment into smaller parts.

Have students check in with a teacher or paraprofessional after each math problem is completed.

Thank Them

Being a paraprofessional can be a difficult job. These individuals often have the least amount of education and training yet work with some of the most challenging students in terms of socialization, communication needs, behavioral needs, and academic needs. Therefore, as a supervisor of paraprofessionals, think about how to ensure that they are properly appreciated for their work and effort. Think of innovative and creative ways to applaud their work. Showcase their contributions to colleagues, students, and families. Letting them know that you sincerely appreciate their dedication, time, and efforts is invaluable to creating a strong educational team.

COMMONLY ASKED QUESTIONS ABOUT PARAPROFESSIONALS

Q. Should a paraprofessional who has been assigned as a one-to-one assistant for a student with autism provide the primary reading and writing instruction?

A. Inclusive educators realize that solid literacy instruction must be planned and implemented by a certified teacher. Paraprofessionals often supplement the content instruction provided by a certified educator. However, the paraprofessional instruction should not supplant the instruction delivered by a knowledgeable educator. Supplemental supports and instruction can be planned by certified educators and delivered by a paraprofessional. All too frequently, students with disabilities are provided their education by paraprofessionals.

Q. Should the paraprofessional sit next to the student whom he or she is intended to support academically and socially?

A. The short answer is no. Research suggests that there are unintended effects of close, constant paraprofessional support that involves sitting next to a child during academic or social activities (Malmgren & Causton-Theoharis, 2006). During academic activities, this means the paraprofessional should be circulating the room, providing support to all students as needed and paying close attention to the students who might need more frequent support. During social times, the paraprofessional's goal is to increase natural social interactions with peers, meaning that he or she might initiate or facilitate initial conversation, then fade support. Paraprofessionals support students with disabilities to have genuine access, achieve full participation, and make progress in academic and social experiences. Sitting next to a student with a disability is not needed and is often detrimental to growth.

Q. What should I do if a paraprofessional has never supported a student with a disability within an inclusive class?

A. If a paraprofessional whom you will be working with has never worked with a student with a disability within an inclusive class, you will need to provide training.

It would be best for the paraprofessional to receive professional development in areas of inclusive education prior to beginning, but this is not always possible. It might be your responsibility to provide the paraprofessional with an understanding of inclusive education; academic, social, communication, and behavior supports; fading supports; promoting independence; and other specific information that pertains to students in your class. Communicate expectations of your inclusive classroom and deliberately explain the essential roles of the adults working in the room.

Q.   Can a paraprofessional really run a small group?

A.   Yes, under the direction of a certified teacher. Provide written instructions for the paraprofessional, and supervise and support him or her.

CONCLUSION

Educators across the country work with paraprofessionals who are assigned to support in their classrooms. Paraprofessionals can be wonderful resources as long as they are properly supported and guided. Providing ongoing communication of expectations, training, and support for paraprofessionals is essential to creating a harmonious team. Through positive relationships and mutual respect, a paraprofessional can be an important player on a team dedicated to providing inclusive education for all students.

10

Supporting You, Supporting Them

Caring for Yourself

AFTER HAVING SUCCESSFULLY TAUGHT
STUDENTS WITH A WIDE RANGE OF
CHARACTERISTICS, MS. MILLER DECIDED
TO ADJUST HER WARDROBE TO MATCH
HER TEACHING CONFIDENCE.

© 1998 MICHAEL GIANGRECO, ILLUSTRATIONS KEVIN RUELLE
PEYTRAL PUBLICATIONS, INC. 952-949-8707 www.peytral.com

"The pressures that teachers face today are much more significant than the pressures of the past. There are times when I feel like it is all test prep, making the cut scores for the district, keeping my job, and oh by the way . . . differentiating and supporting learners with disabilities. I often get home, eat dinner, turn on the TV and fall asleep for the night. Then I have to wake up early to start all over again. Feeling the need for some self-care right about now."

—Sean (general education teacher)

As a professor, author, consultant, and, most important, mother of two children, Julie often is in desperate and continual need of recharging. Consequently, she found this chapter to be the most difficult to write. In one memorable quest for ideas, she helped put her kids to bed and soon found herself standing in the self-help aisle at the local bookstore with a close friend. She read different passages aloud. The books stated she should "become a bonsai tree" or imagine herself "on a glen surrounded by animals while breathing deeply." Her first thoughts were, "What is a glen?" and "What kind of animals?" "Are they dangerous?" "Are they rabid?" She and her friend began to laugh until other customers looked at them askance. Everyone takes care of himself or herself differently; every person needs to find the way that works best for him or her individually. This chapter does not provide you with a recipe for how to care for yourself; instead, it offers ideas or examples that may help you. Educators who are not rested, healthy, and reasonably content will have difficulty educating their students. Whether you deal with stress by running a marathon or by taking a bath, it is important to focus on what you enjoy and on what works to help you relieve stress and feel healthy and balanced.

The job of teacher is not easy. Then again, no job worth doing is really easy. You may find the job quite rewarding or quite stressful, or it may vary from day to day. However, one thing is certain: You need to take care of yourself while taking care of others. In essence, you cannot give as fully to others if you are not meeting your own needs. You cannot help others solve problems if you are struggling with your own problems. You also need to set up your own support system. This chapter suggests strategies for problem solving, networking, and taking care of yourself. The chapter (and book) concludes with a new job description for educators.

BUILDING A NETWORK OF SUPPORT

"If you were all alone in the universe with no one to talk to, no one with which to share the beauty of the stars, to laugh with, to touch, what would be your purpose in life? It is other's life, it is love, which gives your life meaning. This is harmony. We must discover the joy of each other, the joy of challenge, the joy of growth."

—Mitsugi Saotome (1986, p. 1)

To sustain yourself as an educator, you need a network of caring support. Do you feel isolated in your workplace? Do you believe that you could use more support? Think of all the people who love you and care about you. Now, consider others at work who also might feel isolated. In your school, classroom, or grade level, create a small team or even a partnership of support.

Create a Team of Support

One fourth-grade team created a support team by taking turns bringing in breakfast on Friday mornings. They ate together and talked, with no agenda. The conversations were fun and lighthearted, and the team members had time simply to connect with each other. Twice a year, they planned a Saturday morning breakfast to which they invited their families. As they ate together, they got to know more about each other and their loved ones. This helped to create a deeper sense of community for the professionals on the team.

Build a Community

A group of educators in one school district met after school every week to do yoga together. They then began running together. This time together helped them create a network of support, and they also got some exercise and fresh air while they talked.

Another group of professionals met in the library and formed a book group that alternated between reading work-related books and books selected simply for pleasure. At the beginning of the year, they set their reading list. They organized themselves in such a way that they ended up convincing the director of special education to purchase the books through their professional development funds. For a useful set of work-related books and articles, see the lists in the Chapter 10 Appendix.

Celebrate Accomplishments

Celebrating achievements, however big or small, is an important piece to this collaborative work. Be sure to compliment your inclusive team on a job well done! Did the special education teacher knock it out of the park on her minilesson on poetry in hip hop? Tell her after class. Did the general education teacher help Trayvone meet his literacy IEP goal this month? Send him an e-mail to tell him how lucky you are to have him as a co-teacher. Did the OT energize the class before a difficult assignment with content-related spelling aerobics? Leave her a note in the mailbox: "Spelling aerobics!? That was awesome!"

Inclusive education is a wildly collaborative process with many benefits and successes for students, faculty, and the entire school community. Sharing your team's success with other teachers, related service providers, administrators, parents, and students is a great way to celebrate yourselves and your students, as well as a great way to spread your inclusive success throughout the school and district. Ask your administrator to help you create ongoing workshops in which tips and strategies are shared between inclusive school teams, or ask about the best way for your team to share successes with the entire district.

Lunch Bunch

Feeling a sense of community is particularly advantageous when figuring out how to restructure portions of the school day that are not going well. One grade-level team met weekly during the Thursday lunch period with the purpose of problem solving around challenging issues. The team grew comfortable sharing challenging moments. Throughout the week, the inclusive team would check in with each other around these issues. Members asked each other questions such as "Were you able to help James find friends to talk to at lunch?" "Did you figure out how to contact the district assistive technology evaluator?" "What can I do to help?" and "How did that challenging parent conference go?" More important, the working lunch allowed team members to problem-solve and offer supportive suggestions. The sense of community and security this team of teachers created was essential in sustaining their commitment to doing this challenging work. Consider initiating this type of formalized support network in your school.

Examine Your Energetic Contribution

We all have worked with individuals who brighten the day with a positive attitude. These people see a problem as a challenge to be solved, they see the good in every situation, and they can generally boost morale with their sunny disposition. They are people we look forward to working with or just being near; they actually can influence our own moods and outlooks, because being positive is contagious.

We have probably all worked with someone who has the opposite effect on a team. Such individuals might see everything through a lens of negativity and pessimism or remain focused on problems, not solutions. These people can also influence the mood or feel of the group. We want you to carefully consider your own energetic contribution to your team of educators and colleagues. What type of energy do you bring to school with you?

Are you likely to walk into a room and warmly greet everyone? Or are you more likely to walk into a room and get down to business? Or are you likely to begin your conversations with co-workers with a complaint or concern?

When problem solving, are you likely to state the problem in a solvable way and get right down to solutions? Are you likely to stay stuck on the problem? Or do you have a "tried-it-and-it-won't-work" attitude?

Think back to your last interaction with your colleagues. What type of an energetic contribution did you bring? What was your body language like? What was your tone like? What did you say or not say? How would you rate your energetic contribution? Additive? Neutral? Negative? Positive?

Now think about your next meeting or discussion with colleagues or parents. How can you set the tone for a positive and productive conversation? Can you add humor or lightness? Can you take a minute or two to truly listen to your co-worker? Can you be sure that you start the conversation on a positive note and remain so? Returning to these questions frequently can help you remember to remain positive and uplifting. This will result not only in a healthier working atmosphere but also in a healthier attitude and outlook for you.

PROBLEM SOLVING

Although you have read this book and have learned ideas and strategies to handle many different kinds of problems or situations, problems inevitably will arise that you may not feel prepared to handle. Learning to effectively and efficiently solve problems can be a form of self-care. By systematically approaching a problem and studying the potential solutions, you are more in control of those problems and your responses to them. When you come across a problem that you are having difficulty solving, consider the following general ideas or suggestions:

- Talk with other teachers in your school.
- Bring the problem to your co-teacher.
- Talk to a related service provider.
- Sit down with the question: In what ways might I (fill in the problem here)? List all the potential solutions.
- Talk to the student.
- Talk with the principal.
- Talk to a parent.
- Talk with paraprofessionals.
- Draw the problem.
- Go for a walk—think only of solutions during the walk.
- Talk to your best friend or partner. Be sure to keep all information about students confidential.

If meeting with others or brainstorming solutions by yourself does not help you discover a new solution, you may need a step-by-step problem-solving process, such as creative problem-solving (CPS).

CREATIVE PROBLEM-SOLVING PROCESS

The CPS process has a long history as a proven method for approaching and solving problems in innovative ways (Davis, 2004; Parnes, 1985, 1988, 1992, 1997). It is a tool that can help you redefine a problem, come up with creative ways to solve the problem, and then take action to solve it. Teachers use it to solve problems with the students they support. Alex Osborn and Sidney Parnes (Osborn, 1993) conducted extensive research on the steps involved when people solve problems. They determined that people typically use a five-step process. Each step is described in the following list.

Explore the Problem
1. *Fact finding*—Describe what you know or perceive to be true about the challenge. Who? What? When? Where? How? What is true and not true about this problem?

2. *Problem finding*—Clarify the issue. View it in a different way. Finish this sentence: In what ways might we . . . ?

Generate Ideas

3. *Idea finding*—Generate as many ideas as possible; defer judgment and reinforcement (i.e., do not say things such as "good idea" or "that will not work," because then you would be passing judgment on the idea).

Prepare for Action

4. *Solution finding*—Compare the ideas against some criteria that you create. How will you know whether your solution will work? See Table 10.1 for sample criteria for this step.
5. *Acceptance finding*—Create a step-by-step plan of action.

The following example describes how this process actually worked in solving a specific problem in one school.

· · · · · · ·

A team working with Trevor, a first-grade student, was having a difficult time getting Trevor off the playground at the end of recess. Trevor would run around and hide, and they could not reach him or get him to go inside. The end of recess time was becoming a bit like a game of tag, except that the team members definitely did not enjoy chasing Trevor. Trevor would climb to the top of the slide, and if an adult came up the stairs, Trevor would slide down. If the adult went up the slide, Trevor would go down the monkey bars. This was almost humorous to watch unless you were members of the team, who felt frustrated and embarrassed. They considered the communicative intent of the behavior and decided that Trevor was likely trying to communicate that he did not want to come in from recess. Knowing that information, however, did not help the team identify what to do to get Trevor inside. They also knew that Trevor had a difficult time with transitions. The entire team sat together and engaged in a CPS process, which is briefly outlined in Table 10.1.

· · · · · · ·

CARING FOR YOURSELF

Have you ever been on an airplane and heard a flight attendant announce that, if there is an emergency, you should place your oxygen mask on yourself before assisting your children? The idea behind that rule is that if the plane crashes, you want to make sure you are available to help the children. If you do not have oxygen, you will not be able to help them. In essence, that is what we mean by caring for yourself: nurturing yourself outside of work so that you can be fully present, helpful, and nurturing to the students you teach.

Meet Your Own Basic Needs

Maslow (1999) identified the basic physiological needs of every human; these include oxygen, food, water, and regulated body temperature. Like any other human being,

Table 10.1. The creative problem-solving process in action

Stage of problem-solving process	Examples from Trevor's team
1. Fact finding	It does not work to wait him out.
	It takes at least 10 minutes to get him off the playground.
	He does not respond to everyone leaving the playground—he continues to play.
	He enjoys playing tag with his friends.
	He has trouble with transitions.
	No one has ever asked him what he needs.
2. Problem finding	In what ways can we help Trevor return from recess promptly and happily?
3. Idea finding	Give him a time-out.
	Have him lose minutes from his recess time.
	Give him a timer or watch.
	Have a peer help him in.
	See how long he will play outside before coming in.
	Do not allow him to go outside for recess at all.
	Make a sticker chart.
	Give him extra recess.
4. Solution finding	We want this solution to . . . (example criteria)
	1. Enhance the image of the student among peers
	2. Promote independence or interdependence
	3. Appeal to the student
	4. Increase and promote belonging
	5. Increase interaction with peers
	6. Seem logistically feasible
5. Acceptance finding	The team finally decided on a solution for this problem, combining three ideas. They first met with Trevor to ask him what would help (they provided him with a menu of ideas); he decided on a timer with peer support. They gave Trevor a watch timer and asked him to identify a peer whom he was to find when the timer went off. When the timer rang (with 2 minutes remaining in recess), the two boys found each other and went to line up together. Problem solved.

Sources: Giangreco, Cloninger, Dennis, and Edelman (2002); Osborn (1993).

you need to make sure your needs are being met before you can help meet the needs of others. You might have to bring healthy snacks to school to keep yourself fueled for a long day at work. You might bring a water bottle with you so that you can stay hydrated throughout the day. You also might want to have a sweater with you or dress in layers; in many schools, temperatures frequently shift. Maslow's next level of need is safety and love. Surround yourself with loving people so that you feel loved and supported. Last, you need to get enough sleep every night. It is much more difficult to be prepared to teach if you are tired and cranky. These needs are at the very core of every person's physical and mental health.

Stop. Breathe. Meditate.

Some people love to meditate. For others, it makes them break out in a sweat. Here we provide several options for working mindfulness meditation into your busy schedule. The goal of these meditations is to take a few minutes to return your thoughts to your body and your mind, for the purpose of stress reduction and mental health.

Walking Meditation   While walking your dog, taking a hike, walking to the copy machine or to the mailbox, focus your attention on one thing. It could be the sound of the cicadas, the feel of the ground beneath your feet, the artwork on the hallway walls, the sounds of the students, or the color of the flowers or trees. When your mind wanders, lovingly return to your original focus.

Red Light Meditation   When on your way to or from work or if you are out doing errands and you stop at a red light, turn off your radio and focus on deep breaths. When your mind wanders, gently return to the focus on your breath.

Eating or Drinking Meditation   As you eat or drink, focus on the various flavors, textures, and sensations of the particular food or drink. When your mind wanders to something else, calmly return to the focus on your sensations.

Waiting Meditation   While in line, in a waiting room, or waiting for students to return from specials, observe your breath or surroundings. Use the time to do a whole-body scan. Are your muscles tense? Are you hot or cold? What sensations do you feel in your body? Notice any sensations and turn loving, calm energy toward those places.

Task-Related Meditation   You can also incorporate mindfulness meditation into daily activities. For example, washing your hands, folding laundry, driving to work, washing dishes, grading papers, and making lunches can serve as mini-meditations if you focus on the experience and the sensations and stop your mind from wandering.

Find an Outlet

Caring for yourself is critical to staying on the job and feeling balanced while doing it. Find ways to sustain yourself while outside of work. Consider physical outlets such as yoga, running, walking, biking, hiking, or swimming. Consider intellectual outlets such as playing games, reading, or writing. Or try more creative outlets such as painting, sculpting, drawing, baking, cooking, scrapbooking, or generally creating something. Consider self-pampering activities such as taking baths, painting your nails, or getting massages. Or consider spiritual outlets such as meditation, prayer, or yoga to keep yourself spiritually balanced. The following is a simple exercise in meditation. Try this exercise to help calm yourself down after a long day or to prepare yourself before going into work.

An Exercise in Meditation: Try It for 10 Minutes

1. Find a comfortable place where you will not be bothered.
2. Sit with your eyes comfortably closed and turn your attention inward. Empty your mind of chattering thoughts. Relax.
3. If your mind begins to drift, gently return your focus inward.
4. Sit for as long as you feel comfortable; try for 10 minutes.
5. When you are finished, answer these questions: How do you feel now? Are you energized, thoughtful, contemplative, relaxed, or anxious? Gently acknowledge those feelings and consider trying meditation another time.

Employing these types of strategies will help you feel balanced, healthy, and calm. See the Chapter 10 Appendix for a list of books that offer more ideas.

CONCLUSION

As we have mentioned, we consider ourselves continual learners, especially in the area of self-care. When working with students, you need to be constantly learning from them and for them. Our hope is that this book will be an impetus for your own learning. When reading this book, try out the strategies, and when you identify a strategy or idea that works, use it again. At the same time, remember that every context, every student, and every minute brings something new. It is important to reflect on when certain ideas or strategies work and how they work. The process is inevitably fluid. At the end of each day, ask yourself the following questions: 1) What worked today? 2) What did not work? and 3) What do I want to do differently tomorrow?

We conclude this book with a new job description for inclusive educators—a call to do things differently. We thank you for reading, and we wish you luck as you help the students you teach to reach their full academic and social potential.

AN INCLUSIVE EDUCATOR'S JOB DESCRIPTION: WHAT YOUR STUDENTS MIGHT WANT YOU TO KNOW

Listen to me. Learn from me. Hear me. Ask me questions. Support belonging. Be there, but give me space. Expect that I will learn. Facilitate friendships. Plan outrageously fun lessons. Let me fail sometimes. Encourage independence. Always speak kindly. Ask, "What do you need?" Be safe. Handle me with care. Be respectful. Be gentle. Ask, "What supports might help you?" Be trustworthy. Remember, I am a person first. If I am loud, be quiet. Encourage interdependence. If I am sad, wipe my tears. Engage me. Help me connect with other students. Assume friendship is possible. Know I am unsure. Allow us to create together, laugh together, and have fun together. Assume competence always. Attribute the best possible motive consistent with the facts. Spark curiosity. Do not control. When I am happy, rejoice with me. Allow choice. Relax. Be a learner yourself. Ask, "How can I best help you?" Let me learn with other students. Share positive stories with my parents. Set me up to be successful. When I have difficulties, kindly redirect. Breathe. Step back. Fade your support. Speak softly. Encourage softly. Redirect softly. Follow my lead. Lead by loving. Be positive. Give me space. Challenge me. Watch me thrive. Include me.

10
Appendix

GREAT BOOK CLUB BOOKS FOR INCLUSIVE EDUCATORS

Giangreco, M.F., & Doyle, M.B. (Eds.). (2007). *Quick-guides to inclusion: Ideas for educating students with disabilities* (2nd ed.). Baltimore, MD: Paul H. Brookes Publishing Co.

Hehir, T., & Katzman, L. (2012). *Effective inclusive schools: Designing successful school-wide programs.* San Francisco, CA: Jossey-Bass.

Kluth, P. (2010). *"You're going to love this kid!": Teaching students with autism in the inclusive classroom* (2nd ed.). Baltimore, MD: Paul H. Brookes Publishing Co.

Kluth, P., & Schwarz, P. (2008). *"Just give him the whale!": 20 ways to use fascinations, areas of expertise, and strengths to support students with autism.* Baltimore, MD: Paul H. Brookes Publishing Co.

Kohn, A. (2006). *Beyond discipline: From compliance to community* (10th anniversary ed.). Alexandria, VA: Association for Supervision and Curriculum Development.

McLeskey, J., Rosenberg, M.S., & Westling, D.L. (2013). *Inclusion: Effective practices for all students.* Boston, MA: Pearson.

O'Brien, J., Pearpoint, J., & Kahn, L. (2010). *The PATHS & MAPS handbook: Person-centered ways to build community.* Toronto, Canada: Inclusion Press.

Schwarz, P., & Kluth, P. (2008). *You're welcome: 30 innovative ideas for the inclusive classroom.* Portsmouth, NH: Heinemann.

Tashie, C., Shapiro-Barnard, S., & Rossetti, Z. (2006). *Seeing the charade: What people need to do and undo to make friendships happen.* Nottingham, United Kingdom: Inclusive Solutions.

Villa, R.A., Thousand, J.S., & Nevin, A.I. (2008). *A guide to co-teaching: Practical tips for facilitating student learning* (2nd ed.). Thousand Oaks, CA: Corwin Press.

GREAT ARTICLES FOR INCLUSIVE EDUCATORS

Causton-Theoharis, J. (2009). The golden rule of supporting in inclusive classrooms: Support others as you would wish to be supported. *TEACHING Exceptional Children, 42*(2), 36–43.

Causton-Theoharis, J., & Malmgren, K. (2005). Building bridges: Strategies to help para-professionals promote peer interactions. *Teaching Exceptional Children, 37*(6), 18–24.

Giangreco, M.F. (1996). "The stairs didn't go anywhere!": A self-advocate's reflections on specialized services and their impact on people with disabilities. In M. Nind, J. Rix,

K. Sheehy, & K. Simmons (Eds.), *Inclusive education: Diverse perspectives* (pp. 32–42). London, United Kingdom: David Fulton Publishers.

Theoharis, G., Causton, J., & Tracy-Bronson, C.P. (2015). *Inclusive reform as a response to high-stakes pressure?: Leading toward inclusion in the age of accountability.* NSSE (National Society for the Study of Education), an annual yearbook published with *Teachers College Record.*

GREAT BOOKS FOR WORKING WITH PARAPROFESSIONALS

Causton-Theoharis, J. (2009). *The paraprofessional's handbook for effective support in the inclusive classroom.* Baltimore, MD: Paul H. Brookes Publishing Co.

Doyle, M.B. (2008). *The paraprofessional's guide to the inclusive classroom: Working as a team* (3rd ed.). Baltimore, MD: Paul H. Brookes Publishing Co.

Hammeken, P.A. (2008). *The paraprofessional's essential guide to inclusive education.* Thousand Oaks, CA: Corwin Press.

Nevin, A.I., Villa, R.A., & Thousand, J.S. (2009). *A guide to co-teaching with paraeducators: Practical tips for K-12 educators.* Thousand Oaks, CA: Corwin Press.

SELF-CARE BOOKS—GREAT FOR ANYONE

Byrne, R. (2006). *The secret.* New York, NY: Atria Books/Beyond Words.

Carlson, R. (1998). *Don't sweat the small stuff at work: Simple ways to minimize stress and conflict while bringing out the best in yourself and others.* New York, NY: Hyperion.

Covey, S.R. (2004). *The 7 habits of highly effective people: Powerful lessons in personal change* (15th anniversary ed.). New York, NY: Free Press.

Fontana, D. (1999). *Learn to meditate: A practical guide to self-discovery.* London, United Kingdom: Duncan Baird.

Hoff, B. (1983). *The tao of Pooh.* New York, NY: Penguin.

Moran, V. (1999). *Creating a charmed life: Sensible, spiritual secrets every busy woman should know.* New York, NY: HarperOne.

Palmer, P. (1999). *Let your life speak: Listening to the voice of vocation.* San Francisco, CA: Jossey-Bass.

Palmer, P. (2004*). A hidden wholeness: The journey towards the undivided life.* San Francisco, CA: Jossey-Bass.

Reynolds, S. (2005). *Better than chocolate.* Berkeley, CA: Ten Speed Press.

SARK. (1991). *A creative companion: How to free your creative spirit.* New York, NY: Fireside.

SARK. (1994). *Living juicy: Daily morsels for your creative soul.* New York, NY: Fireside.

SARK. (1997). *Succulent wild women.* New York, NY: Fireside.

SARK. (2005). *Make your creative dreams real: A plan for procrastinators, perfectionists, busy people, and people who would really rather sleep all day.* New York, NY: Fireside.

Topchik, G. (2001). *Managing workplace negativity.* New York, NY: AMACOM.

Wheatley, M.J. (2002). *Turning to one another: Simple conversation to restore hope in the future.* San Francisco, CA: Berrett-Koehler Press.

References

American Psychiatric Association. (2013). *Diagnostic and statistical manual of mental disorders* (5th ed.). Washington, DC: Author.

Americans with Disabilities Act (ADA) of 1990, PL 101-336, 42 U.S.C. §§ 12101 *et seq.*

Armstrong, T. (2000a). *In their own way: Discovering and encouraging your child's multiple intelligences.* New York, NY: Penguin Putnam.

Armstrong, T. (2000b). *Multiple intelligences in the classroom.* Alexandria, VA: Association for Supervision and Curriculum Development.

Bambara, L.M., Janney, R., & Snell, M. (2015). *Teachers' guides to inclusive practices: Behavior support* (3rd ed.). Baltimore, MD: Paul H. Brookes Publishing Co.

Banerji, M., & Dailey, R.A. (1995). A study of the effects of an inclusion model on students with specific learning disabilities. *Journal of Learning Disabilities, 28*(8), 511–522.

Beratan, G.D. (2006). Institutionalizing inequity: Ableism, racism, and IDEA 2004. *Disability Studies Quarterly, 26*(2). Available at http://dsq-sds.org/issue/view/33

Biklen, D. (2005). *Autism and the myth of the person alone.* New York, NY: New York University Press.

Biklen, D., & Burke, J. (2006). Presuming competence. *Equity & Excellence in Education, 39,* 166–175.

Blatt, B. (1987). *The conquest of mental retardation.* Austin, TX: PRO-ED.

Bonner Foundation. (2008). Conflict resolution: Steps for handling interpersonal dynamics. In *Bonner civic engagement training modules.* Retrieved from http://bonnernetwork.pbworks.com/w/page/13112080/Bonner%20Training%20Modules%20%28with%20Descriptions%29

Bouffard, S., & Weiss, H. (2008). Thinking big: A new framework for family involvement policy, practice, and research. *The Evaluation Exchange, 14*(1–2), 2–5.

Bullock, J. (1992). Touch Math fourth edition. *Intervention in School and Clinic, 28*(2), 119–122.

Byrne, R. (2006). *The secret.* New York, NY: Atria Books/Beyond Words.

Callahan, C. (2008). *Advice about being an LD student.* Retrieved from http://www.ldonline.org/firstperson/8550

Card, D.R., & Card, H.R. (2013). *The missing piece.* Bloomington, IN: Balboa Press.

Carlson, R. (1998). *Don't sweat the small stuff at work: Simple ways to minimize stress and conflict while bringing out the best in yourself and others.* New York, NY: Hyperion.

Carr, E.G., Dunlap, G., Horner, R.H., Koegel, R.L., Turnbull, A., Sailor, W., . . . Fox, L. (2002). Positive behavior support: Evolution of an applied science. *Journal of Positive Behavior Interventions, 4*(1), 4–16.

Casey, K., & Vanceburg, M. (1996). *A promise of a new day: A book of daily meditations.* Center City, MN: Hazelden.

Causton, J., & Theoharis, G. (2014). *The principal's handbook for leading inclusive schools.* Baltimore, MD: Paul H. Brookes Publishing Co.

Causton, J., Udvari-Solner, A., & MacLeod, K. (in press). Creating educational adaptations, accommodations, and modifications. In F. Orelove, D. Sobsey, & D. Giles (Eds.), *Educating children with severe and multiple disabilities: A collaborative approach* (5th ed.). Baltimore, MD: Paul H. Brookes Publishing Co.

Causton-Theoharis, J.N. (2009a). The golden rule of supporting in inclusive classrooms: Support others as you would wish to be supported. *TEACHING Exceptional Children, 42*(2), 36–43.

Causton-Theoharis, J. (2009b). *The paraprofessional's handbook for effective support in inclusive classrooms.* Baltimore, MD: Paul H. Brookes Publishing Co.

Causton-Theoharis, J., Giangreco, M., Doyle, M.B., & Vadasy, P. (2007). Paraprofessionals: The sous chefs of literacy instruction. *TEACHING Exceptional Children, 40*(1), 56–63.

Causton-Theoharis, J., & Malmgren, K. (2005). Building bridges: Strategies to help paraprofessionals promote peer interactions. *TEACHING Exceptional Children, 37*(6), 18–24.

Causton-Theoharis, J., & Theoharis, G. (2008, September). Creating inclusive schools for all students. *The School Administrator, 65*(8), 24–30.

Causton-Theoharis, J., Theoharis, G., Bull, T., & Cosier, M. (2008, March). *Changing the flow of the river: Inclusive school reform.* Paper presented at the American Educational Research Association Annual Meeting, New York, NY.

Covey, S.R. (2004). *The 7 habits of highly effective people: Powerful lessons in personal change* (15th anniv. ed.). New York, NY: Free Press.

Data Accountability Center (n.d.). Building capacity for high-quality IDEA data. Retrieved from http://www.ideadata.org

Davis, G. (2004). *Creativity is forever* (5th ed.). Dubuque, IA: Kendall Hunt.

Donnellan, A. (1984). The criterion of the least dangerous assumption. *Behavioral Disorders, 9*, 141–150.

Doyle, M.B. (2008). *The paraprofessional's guide to the inclusive classroom: Working as a team* (3rd ed.). Baltimore, MD: Paul H. Brookes Publishing Co.

Education for All Handicapped Children Act of 1975, PL 94-142, 20 U.S.C. §§ 1400 *et seq.*

Engel, D.M. (1993). Origin myths: Narratives of authority, resistance, disability, and law. *Law and Society Review, 27*(4), 785–826.

Epstein, J.L. (2001). Building bridges of home, school, and community: The importance of design. *Journal of Education for Students Placed at Risk, 6*, 161–167.

FAS Community Resource Center. (2008). *Information about fetal alcohol syndrome (FAS) and fetal alcohol spectrum disorders (FASD).* Retrieved from http://www.come-over.to/FASCRC

Ferguson, P., & Ferguson, D.L. (2006). Finding the "proper attitude": The potential of disability studies to reframe family/school linkages. In S. Danforth & S. Gabel (Eds.), *Vital questions facing disability studies in education* (pp. 217–235). New York, NY: Peter Lang.

Fontana, D. (1999). *Learn to meditate: A practical guide to self-discovery.* London, United Kingdom: Duncan Baird.

Fried, R.L., & Sarason, S. (2002). *The skeptical visionary: A Seymour Sarason education reader.* Philadelphia, PA: Temple University Press.

Gabel, A. (2006). Stop asking me if I need help. In E.B. Keefe, V.M. Moore, & F.R. Duff (Eds.), *Listening to the experts: Students with disabilities speak out* (pp. 35–40). Baltimore, MD: Paul H. Brookes Publishing Co.

Gardner, H. (1993). *Frames of mind: A theory of multiple intelligences.* New York, NY: Basic Books.

Giangreco, M.F. (1996a). "The stairs didn't go anywhere!" A self-advocate's reflections on specialized services and their impact on people with disabilities. In M. Nind, J. Rix, K. Sheehy, & K. Simmons (Eds.), *Inclusive education: Diverse perspectives* (pp. 32–42). London, United Kingdom: David Fulton Publishers.

Giangreco, M.F. (1996b). "The stairs didn't go anywhere!" A self-advocate's reflections on specialized services and their impact on people with disabilities. *Physical Disabilities: Education and Related Service, 14*(2), 1–12.

Giangreco, M.F. (2004). "The stairs didn't go anywhere!": A self-advocate's reflections on specialized services and their impact on people with disabilities. In M. Nind, J. Rix, K. Sheehy, & K. Simmons (Eds.), *Inclusive education: diverse perspectives* (p. 37). London, United Kingdom: David Fulton Publishers.

Giangreco, M.F., Cloninger, C.J., Dennis, R., & Edelman, S.W. (2002). Problem-solving methods to facilitate inclusive education. In J.S. Thousand, R.A. Villa, & A.I. Nevin (Eds.), *Creativity and collaborative learning: The practical guide to empowering students, teachers, and families* (2nd ed., pp. 111–134). Baltimore, MD: Paul H. Brookes Publishing Co.

Giangreco, M.F., & Doyle, M.B. (Eds.). (2007). *Quick-guides to inclusion: Ideas for educating students with disabilities* (2nd ed.). Baltimore, MD: Paul H. Brookes Publishing Co.

Giangreco, M.F., Edelman, S.W., Luiselli, E.T., & MacFarland, S.Z. (1997). Helping or hovering: The effects of paraprofessional proximity on students with disabilities. *Exceptional Children, 64*(1), 7–18.

Gray, C. (2010). *The new social story book* (10th ed.). Arlington, TX: Future Horizons.

Hammeken, P.A. (2008). *The paraprofessional's essential guide to inclusive education.* Thousand Oaks, CA: Corwin Press.

Hehir, T. (2002). Eliminating ableism in education. *Harvard Educational Review, 72*(1), 1–32.

Hehir, T., & Katzman, L. (2012). *Effective inclusive schools: Designing successful schoolwide programs.* San Francisco, CA: Jossey-Bass.

Henry Ford Organization. (2004). *The Henry Ford Organization annual report 2004.* Retrieved from https://www.thehenryford.org/images/AnnualReport04.pdf

Hoff, B. (1983). *The tao of Pooh.* New York, NY: Penguin.

Huefner, D.S. (2000). *Getting comfortable with special education law: A framework for working with children with disabilities.* Norwood, MA: Christopher-Gordon.

Individuals with Disabilities Education Improvement Act (IDEA) of 2004, PL 108-446, 20 U.S.C. §§ 1400 *et seq.*

Information on bipolar and other mental health disorders. (n.d.). *Borderline personality disorder.* Retrieved from http://www.angelfire.com/home/bphoenix1/border.html

Institut Pasteur. (n.d.). *Louis Pasteur's biography.* Retrieved from http://www.pasteur.fr/en

Janney, R., & Snell, M.E. (2008). *Teachers' guides to inclusive practices: Behavioral support* (2nd ed.). Baltimore, MD: Paul H. Brookes Publishing Co.

Janney, R., & Snell, M.E. (2013). *Modifying schoolwork* (3rd ed.). Baltimore, MD: Paul H. Brookes Publishing Co.

Jones, R.C. (2012). *Strategies for reading comprehension: Clock buddies.* Retrieved from http://www.reading quest.org/strat/clock_buddies.html

Kasa, C., & Causton-Theoharis, J. (n.d.). *Strategies for success: Creating inclusive classrooms that work* (pp. 16–17). Pittsburgh, PA: The PEAL Center. Retrieved from http://wsm.ezsitedesigner.com/share/scrapbook/47/472535/PEAL-S4Success_20pg_web_version.pdf

Keller, H. (1903). *The story of my life.* New York, NY: Doubleday, Page.

Kelly, M. (2004). *The rhythm of life: Living every day with passion and purpose.* New York, NY: Simon and Schuster.

Kliewer, C. (1998). *Schooling children with Down syndrome: Toward an understanding of possibility.* New York, NY: Teachers College Press.

Kliewer, C., & Biklen, D. (1996). Labeling: Who wants to be called retarded? In W. Stainback & S. Stainback (Eds.), *Controversial issues confronting special education: Divergent perspectives* (2nd ed., pp. 83–111). Boston, MA: Allyn & Bacon.

Kluth, P. (2005). Calm in crisis. Adapted from P. Kluth (2003), *"You're going to love this kid!": Teaching students with autism in the inclusive classroom.* Baltimore, MD: Paul H. Brookes Publishing Co. Retrieved from http://www.paulakluth.com/readings/autism/calm-in-crisis

Kluth, P. (2010). *"You're going to love this kid!": Teaching students with autism in the inclusive classroom* (2nd ed.). Baltimore, MD: Paul H. Brookes Publishing Co.

Kluth, P., & Schwarz, P. (2008). *"Just give him the whale!": 20 ways to use fascinations, areas of expertise, and strengths to support students with autism.* Baltimore, MD: Paul H. Brookes Publishing Co.

Knoster, T.P. (2014). *The teacher's pocket guide for effective classroom management* (2nd ed.). Baltimore, MD: Paul H. Brookes Publishing Co.

Kohn, A. (2006). *Beyond discipline: From compliance to community* (10th anniv. ed.). Alexandria, VA: Association for Supervision and Curriculum Development.

Kornhaber, M., Fierros, E., & Veenema, S. (2004). *Multiple intelligences: Best ideas from research and practice.* Boston, MA: Pearson Education.

Kunc, N. (1984). Integration: Being realistic isn't realistic. *Canadian Journal for Exceptional Children, 1*(1), 2.

Kunc, N. (1992). The need to belong: Rediscovering Maslow's hierarchy of needs. In R. Villa, J. Thousand, W. Stainback, & S. Stainback (Eds.), *Restructuring for caring and effective education* (pp. 21–40). Baltimore, MD: Paul H. Brookes Publishing Co.

Kunc, N., & Van der Klift, E. (1996). *A credo for support.* Vancouver, Canada: The Broadreach Centre.

Latham, G.I. (1999). *Parenting with love: Making a difference in a day.* Logan, UT: P&T Ink.

Lovett, H. (1996). *Learning to listen: Positive approaches and people with difficult behavior.* Baltimore, MD: Paul H. Brookes Publishing Co.

Malmgren, K.W., & Causton-Theoharis, J.N. (2006). Boy in the bubble: Effects of paraprofessional proximity and other pedagogical decisions on the interactions of a student with behavioral disorders. *Journal of Research in Childhood Education, 20*(4), 301–312.

Maslow, A.H. (1999). *Toward a psychology of being*. New York, NY: John Wiley & Sons.

Mavis. (2007, October 7). *Living in the hearing and deaf worlds*. Retrieved from http://archive-org.com/page/3736996/2014-02-17/http://www.raisingdeafkids.org/meet/deaf/mavis/

McLeskey, J., Rosenberg, M.S., & Westling, D.L. (2013). *Inclusion: Effective practices for all students*. Boston, MA: Pearson.

McLeskey, J., & Waldron, N. (2006). Comprehensive school reform and inclusive schools: Improving schools for all students. *Theory into Practice, 45*(3), 269–278.

Molton, K. (2000). *Dispelling some myths about autism*. Retrieved from http://www.autism.org.uk

Mooney, J. (2008). *The short bus: A journey beyond normal*. New York, NY: Holt Paperbacks.

Moran, V. (1999). *Creating a charmed life: Sensible, spiritual secrets every busy woman should know*. New York, NY: HarperOne.

Murawski, W.W., & Dieker, L.A. (2004). Tips and strategies for co-teaching at the secondary level. *TEACHING Exceptional Children, 36*(5), 52–58.

National Association of School Psychologists. (n.d.). *Who are school psychologists?* Retrieved from http://www.nasponline.org/about_sp/who-are-school-psychologists.aspx

Nevin, A.I., Villa, R.A., & Thousand, J.S. (2009). *A guide to co-teaching with paraeducators: Practical tips for K–12 educators*. Thousand Oaks, CA: Corwin Press.

No Child Left Behind Act of 2001, PL 107-110, 115 Stat. 1425, 20 U.S.C. §§ 6301 *et seq.*

O'Brien, J., Pearpoint, J., & Kahn, L. (2010). *The PATHS & MAPS handbook: Person-centered ways to build community*. Toronto, Canada: Inclusion Press.

Orwell, G. (1981). Politics and English language. In *A collection of essays* (pp. 156–170). Orlando, FL: Harvest.

Osborn, A.F. (1993). *Applied imagination: Principles and procedures of creative problem-solving* (3rd rev. ed.). Buffalo, NY: Creative Education Foundation Press. (Original work published 1953)

Palmer, P. (1999). *Let your life speak: Listening to the voice of vocation*. San Francisco, CA: Jossey-Bass.

Palmer, P. (2004). *A hidden wholeness: The journey towards the undivided life*. San Francisco, CA: Jossey-Bass.

Parker, K. (2008). *Meet RhapsodyBlue*. Retrieved from http://www.angelfire.com/country/rhapsodyblue22/page2.html

Parnes, S.J. (1985). *A facilitating style of leadership*. Buffalo, NY: Bearly.

Parnes, S.J. (1988). *Visionizing: State-of-the-art processes for encouraging innovative excellence*. East Aurora, NY: D.O.K.

Parnes, S.J. (Ed.). (1992). *Source book for creative problem solving: A fifty-year digest of proven innovation processes*. Buffalo, NY: Creative Education Foundation Press.

Parnes, S.J. (1997). *Optimize the magic of your mind*. Buffalo, NY: Creative Education Foundation Press.

Paul-Brown, D., & Diggs, M.C. (1993, Winter). Recognizing and treating speech and language disabilities. *American Rehabilitation*.

PEAK Parent Center. (n.d.). *Accommodations and modifications factsheet*. Retrieved from http://www.peatc.org/peakaccom.htm

Peterson, J.M., & Hittie, M.M. (2002). *Inclusive teaching: Creating effective schools for all learners*. Boston, MA: Allyn & Bacon.

Pitonyak, D. (2007). *The importance of belonging*. Retrieved from http://www.dimagine.com/Belonging.pdf and http://www.dimagine.com/TASHbelonging.pdf

Pushor, D., & Murphy, B. (2004). Parent marginalization, marginalized parents: Creating a place for parents on the school landscape. *Alberta Journal of Educational Research, 50*(3), 221–231.

Rehabilitation Act of 1973, PL 93-112, 29 U.S.C. §§ 701 *et seq.*

Remick, Jill. (2006, September). *Warren elementary teacher named 2007 Vermont teacher of the year* [Press release]. Montpelier: Vermont Department of Education.

Reynolds, S. (2005). *Better than chocolate*. Berkeley, CA: Ten Speed Press.

Rosa's Law, 2010, PL 111-256, 20 U.S.C. §§ 1400 et seq.

Rubin, S. (2010, January). *Living and thoroughly enjoying life in spite of autism*. Paper presented at the Annandale Cooperative Preschool, Annandale, VA.

Rubin, S. (2014). *Speaking of autism*. Available at http://www.sue-rubin.org

Saotome, M. (1986). The dojo: Spiritual oasis. In *Aikido and the harmony of nature* (pp. 246–248). Boulogne, France: SEDIREP.

SARK. (1991). *A creative companion: How to free your creative spirit*. New York, NY: Fireside.

SARK. (1994). *Living juicy: Daily morsels for your creative soul*. New York, NY: Fireside.

SARK. (1997). *Succulent wild women*. New York, NY: Fireside.

SARK. (2005). *Make your creative dreams real: A plan for procrastinators, perfectionists, busy people, and people who would really rather sleep all day.* New York, NY: Fireside.

Sauer, J.S., & Kasa, C. (2012). Preservice teachers listen to families of students with disabilities and learn a disability studies stance. *Issues in Teacher Education, 21*(2), 165–183.

Schalock, R.L., & Braddock, D.L. (2002). *Out of the darkness and into the light: Nebraska's experience with mental retardation.* Washington, DC: American Association on Mental Retardation.

Schwarz, P., & Kluth, P. (2008). *You're welcome: 30 innovative ideas for the inclusive classroom.* Portsmouth, NH: Heinemann.

Snow, K. (2008). *To ensure inclusion, freedom, and respect for all, it's time to embrace people first language.* Retrieved from https://www.cibc-ca.org/wp/wp-content/uploads/People_First_Language.pdf

Strully, J.L., & Strully, C. (1996). Friendships as an educational goal: What we have learned and where we are headed. In S. Stainback & W. Stainback (Eds.), *Inclusion: A guide for educators* (pp. 141–154). Baltimore, MD: Paul H. Brookes Publishing Co.

Tashie, C., Shapiro-Barnard, S., & Rossetti, Z. (2006). *Seeing the charade: What people need to do and undo to make friendships happen.* Nottingham, United Kingdom: Inclusive Solutions.

Taylor, R.L., Smiley, L.R., & Richards, S.B. (2009). *Exceptional students: Preparing teaching for the 21st century.* New York, NY: McGraw-Hill.

Taylor, T.R. (2002). Multiple intelligences products grid. Curriculum Design for Excellence. Available at https://www.rogertaylor.com/clientuploads/documents/references/Product-Grid.pdf

Taylor, T. Roger. (2007). *Differentiating the curriculum: Using an integrated, interdisciplinary, thematic approach* (pp. 59–60). Oak Brook, IL: Curriculum Design for Excellence, Inc.

Theoharis, G., Causton, J., & Tracy-Bronson, C.P. (2015). *Inclusive reform as a response to high-stakes pressure?: Leading toward inclusion in the age of accountability.* NSSE (National Society for the Study of Education), an annual yearbook published with *Teachers College Record.*

Theoharis, G., & Causton-Theoharis, J. (2011). Preparing pre-service teachers for inclusive classrooms: revising lesson-planning expectations. *International Journal of Inclusive Education (15)*7, 743–761.

Tomlinson, C.A. (2000). Differentiation of instruction in the elementary grades. *ERIC digest.* Available at http://www.ericdigests.org/2001-2/elementary.html

Tomlinson, C.A. (2003). *Fulfilling the promise of the differentiated classroom.* Alexandria, VA: Association for Supervision and Curriculum Development.

Tomlinson, C.A., & Edison, C. (2003). *Differentiation in practice: A resource guide for differentiated curriculum (grades K–5).* Alexandria, VA: Association for Supervision and Curriculum Development.

Tomlinson, C., & Kalbfleisch, M.L. (1998). Teach me, teach my brain: A call for differentiated classrooms. *Educational Leadership, 56*(3), 52–55.

Tomlinson, C.A., & Strickland, C.A. (2005). *Differentiation in practice: A resource guide for differentiating curriculum, grades 9–12.* Alexandria, VA: ASCD

Topchik, G. (2001). *Managing workplace negativity.* New York, NY: AMACOM.

Turnbull, H.R., Turnbull, A.R., Shank, M., & Smith, S.J. (2004). *Exceptional lives: Special education in today's schools* (4th ed.). Upper Saddle River, NJ: Merrill/Prentice Hall.

Udvari-Solner, A. (1997). Inclusive education. In C.A. Grant & G. Ladson-Billings (Eds.), *Dictionary of multicultural education* (pp. 141–144). Phoenix, AZ: Oryx Press.

Udvari-Solner, A. & Kluth, P. (2008). *Joyful learning: Active and collaborative learning in inclusive classrooms.* Baltimore, MD: Paul H. Brookes Publishing Co.

U.S. Department of Education. (2004). *Twenty-fourth annual report to Congress on the implementation of the Individuals with Disabilities Education Act.* Washington, DC: Author.

U.S. Department of Education. (2007, September). *Twenty-seventh annual report to Congress on the implementation of the Individuals with Disabilities Education Act, 2005* (Vol. 1). Washington, DC: Author.

U.S. Department of Education. (2011). Retrieved from http://www.ed.gov

U.S. Department of Education. (2015). *IDEA data center.* https://ideadata.org

Vaughn, S., Moody, S.W., & Schumm, J.S. (1998). Broken promises: Reading instruction in the resource room. *Exceptional Children, 64,* 211–225.

Villa, R.A., Thousand, J.S., & Nevin, A.I. (2008). *A guide to co-teaching: Practical tips for facilitating student learning* (2nd ed.). Thousand Oaks, CA: Corwin Press.

Waldron, N., & McLeskey, J. (1998). The effects of an inclusive school program on students with mild and severe learning disabilities. *Exceptional Children, 64*(2), 395–405.

Weil, S. (2001). *The need for roots.* London, United Kingdom: Routledge.

Wheatley, M.J. (2002). *Turning to one another: Simple conversation to restore hope in the future.* San Francisco, CA: Berrett-Koehler Press.

Will, M. (1986). *Educating students with learning problems: A shared responsibility.* Washington, DC: U.S. Department of Education, Office of Special Education and Rehabilitative Service.

Williams, R. (Presenter). (2008, August 24). Hearing impairment: A personal story [Radio broadcast]. In B. Seega (Producer), *Ockham's razor.* Transcript retrieved from http://www.abc.net.au/rn/ockhamsrazor/stories/2008/2342555.htm

Index

Tables and figures are indicated by *t* and *f*, respectively.

Get all 4 practical guidebooks—great for your whole school team!

The Paraprofessional's Handbook for Effective Support in Inclusive Classrooms

By Julie Causton-Theoharis, Ph.D.

What does a great paraprofessional need to know and do? Find out in this handy survival guide, equally useful for the brand-new paraprofessional or the 20-year classroom veteran. Packed with friendly guidance, practical tips, and first-person stories, this book reveals the best ways to provide effective, respectful services to students in inclusive classrooms.

Stock #: 68998 | 2009 | 144 pages | ISBN 978-1-55766-899-8

The Principal's Handbook for Leading Inclusive Schools

By Julie Causton, Ph.D., & George Theoharis, Ph.D.

This how-to book is the essential guide to bringing schoolwide inclusion from theory to practice. Covering everything from the basics of special education to the nuts and bolts of making inclusion work, two renowned inclusion experts give readers clear guidance they can use right away to lead a fully inclusive school where every student learns and belongs.

Stock #: 72988 | 2014 | 184 pages | ISBN 978-1-59857-298-8

The Speech-Language Pathologist's Handbook for Inclusive School Practices

By Julie Causton, Ph.D., & Chelsea Tracy-Bronson, M.A.

Every inclusive school team needs a great SLP who supports communication skills where they're needed most—in the classroom, as students with disabilities learn and participate alongside their peers. This is the practical, friendly guide SLPs need to go beyond pull-out services and deliver successful communication and language supports as part of a school team.

Stock #: 73626 | 2014 | 184 pages | ISBN 978-1-59857-362-6

The Occupational Therapist's Handbook for Inclusive School Practices

By Julie Causton, Ph.D., & Chelsea Tracy-Bronson, M.A.

Filled with ready-to-use guidance and tips, examples that relate directly to an OT's daily practice, and first-person insights from seasoned OTs, this guidebook is key to helping students develop new skills in key areas, from motor skills and mobility to academic achievement and friendships.

Stock #: 73619 | 2014 | 184 pages | ISBN 978-1-59857-361-9